Running Prophecy

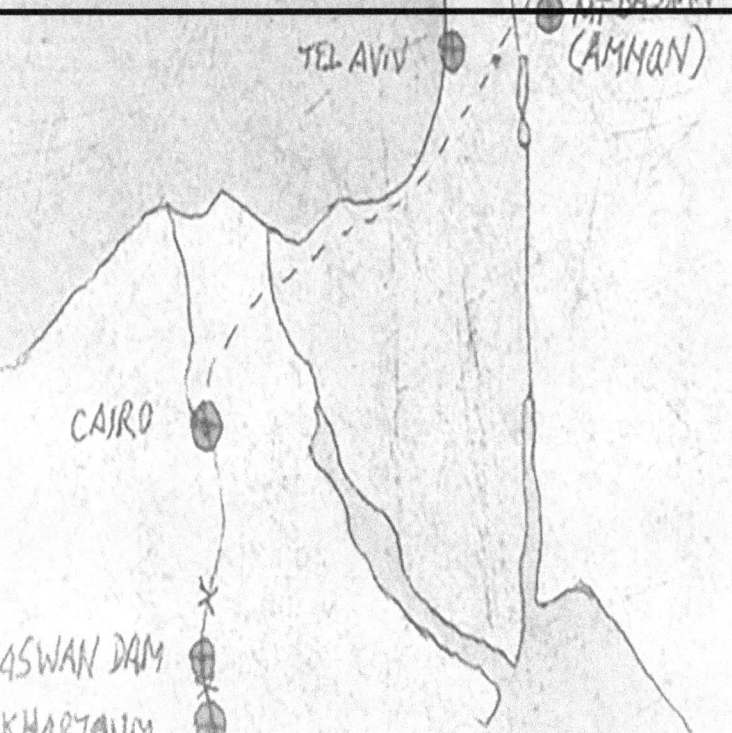

Running Prophecy

Curtis A. Routley

ARPress

ILLUMINATING IDEAS,
EMPOWERING VOICES

ARPress
45 Dan Road Suite 5
Canton MA 02021
Hotline: 1(888) 821-0229
Fax: 1(508) 545-7580

Ordering Information:
Quantity sales.Special discounts are available on quantity purchases by corporations, associations, and others.For details, contact the publisher at the address above.

Printed in the United States of America.

ISBN-13:   Paperback   979-8-89356-540-9
                eBook   979-8-89356-542-3
                Hardback   979-8-89356-541-6

Library of Congress Control Number: 2024902483

Dedicated to

The Bereans among us.

TABLE OF CONTENTS

MAPS, DRAWINGS, AND CHARTS

FOREWORD

God inspired the Scriptures. Indeed He was their source. Therefore, they must tell His story, as He wants it to be told! God is a perfect author so the scripture must be consistent in all its parts; for only His viewpoint can be told. His story concerned the redemption of mankind by the means of the greatest price God could pay to accomplish that end. The story was of the Christ, and God chose the Christ to tell it. Then Christ commissioned just one angel to relay all of its parts to man. John recorded this commissioning and its purpose in these two passages. "The Revelation of Jesus Christ, which God gave Him to show to His bond servants, the things which must shortly take place; and He sent and communicated it by His angel to His bond servant John." Rev. 1:1 "I, Jesus, have sent my angel to testify to you these things for the churches. I am the root and the offspring of David, the bright morning star." Rev. 22:16

The revelation was of the Christ, so God gave Christ the authority to send this message to all of His servants, the prophets. Specific parts went to the other prophets, then John received his portion. And only one angel brought the unfolding message to each of these men of God.

How did he bring it? What method did he use, or what pattern did he follow? Since he was from God, he had to use God's methods, there was no other way to do it.

So how does God operate? Isaiah learned and taught us with these words: "To whom would he teach knowledge? And to whom would He interpret the message? Those just weaned from milk? Those just taken from the breast? For He says, "Order on order,

order on order, line on line, line on line, a little here, a little there." Isaiah 28:9,10

The word was sent; "tell this man such and such. Tell that man thus and so. Give them one item, and then explain it more Clearly." One man had a single fact explained. The story was clarified detail by detail, one piece at a time.

Sometimes the order for the angel to explain a fact was delayed because the angel was already busy on an important assignment. Such was the case with Zechariah. Near the end of one of his visions, as the angel was departing, another angel approached. As Zechariah explains, "And behold the angel who was speaking with me was going out, and another angel was coming out to meet him, and said to him, "Run, speak to that young man ..." Zech 2:3,4 So the angel returned to continue the vision, presenting another aspect.

This angel even had a distinct personality. Later that evening Zechariah saw him again. "Then the angel who was speaking with me returned, and roused me as a man who is awakened from his sleep." Zech.4:1 The angel then relayed a new part of the vision to Zechariah.

This angel went about his job very well. He gave all possible consideration to ensure his charge would understand. He always lingered after a vision in order to provide any interpretation required by the prophet.

When Daniel received the first of his visions, he was bolder than any of the other prophets. Because he was disturbed, he approached one of the angels who were standing by, watching with him. Daniel said, "I approached one of those who were standing by and began asking him the exact meaning of all this. So he told me and made known to me the interpretation of these things." Dan.7:16

Daniel had now met the special-delivery angel, who was standing closest to him. This angel had to see all the things about the vision were properly understood. The one who Daniel approached had to be that angel, because only one angel had been given this job. Daniel even learned his name!

As he was receiving his second personal vision, Daniel was not as bold as he had been with his previous vision. He did not approach as readily as before. An order was given for the angel to provide understanding for him. Daniel said, "and I heard the voice of a man between the banks of the Ulai, and He called out and said, Gabriel, give this man an understanding of the vision." Dan.8:16 Now Daniel has the name of this angel, and he can recognize him on sight. "While I was still speaking in prayer, then the man Gabriel, whom I had seen in the vision previously, came to me in my extreme weariness about the time of the evening offering." Dan.9:21

So Gabriel was the only angel charged to deliver and interpret the visions to the prophets. Another angel was allowed to assist Gabriel, although his primary duty was as the captain of the host. Gabriel said to Daniel, "But I will show thee that which is noted in the scriptures of truth: and there is none that holdeth with me in these things, but Michael your prince." Dan.10:21 KJV Michael knew what Gabriel knew, but Michael's primary duty was to serve as commander of the angelic army that protected Israel. Dan.12:1; Rev. 12:7

Gabriel did his job very well. One by one he gave each prophet his portion until the complete story was delivered. All that was necessary to understand the story was given as well. Unfortunately, current events and the cares and pride of life were more important to the men the prophets told their stories to, than the future events. So God sealed up the visions until the end time. Dan.12:4 But through Jeremiah He promised, "In the last days you will clearly understand it." Jer.23:20

Many of the events, which are the keys to insight, have already taken place, some entirely unnoticed by the Lord's people. It is as He said through Isaiah. "Who is so blind as he that is at peace with me?" Isaiah 42:19

Therefore, if you believe we are in the last days, and it is time to see clearly the prophetic events, let me guide you along the path I was led.

CHAPTER I

Rome Or Assyria

"Woe to Assyria, the rod of My anger and the staff in whose hands is My indignation, I send it against a Godless nation:" Isaiah 10:5.6.

While walking in the darkness that covered the earth, God said, "Let there be light," and there was light. He called the light day and the darkness He called night. Gen. 1:3,5 The light and the darkness existed together, but both of them did not rule over the same spot, for their prominence occurred in succession.

His people likewise walked in the light and then in the darkness. The light shone around His people when they listened to His words and followed His counsel. But darkness shrouded them when they turned from God to worship the strange impotent gods of the nations around them. In one particular period of darkness for the nation of Israel, during the Babylonian captivity, God again said, "Let there be light." This new light was not to be the physical light which He had already created, but the spiritual light that would illuminate the events that God's word was going to bring to pass.

The first time God created the physical light He did it for the whole world. This new spiritual light was sent to the whole world, too, not just for the nation of Israel, for Israel had failed to uphold the words and ways of God before the rest of this earth's people.

In the dark of the night, God sent the light to the heathen ruler, Nebuchadnezzar, whose mind began to see a vision. He received a dream from God. But what does the darkness know of the light? Either one exists or the other does. Nebuchadnezzar was not of the light. He did not comprehend the dream. In fact, he awoke with a start. Visibly shaken, as he realized that the dream had special meaning, Nebuchadnezzar set out to use the means of his kingdom to find out what it was.

He called on his union of magicians, conjurers, sorcerers, and master astrologers to tell him what the dream meant. He assembled them and said, "I had a dream and my spirit is anxious to understand it."

The master astrologers replied, "Oh king, live forever. Tell us your dream and we will declare its interpretation." Dan. 2:3,4 The master astrologers were filled with pride in their ability, and before they even knew the problem they were sure they could provide the solution. But before the king told them the problem again, he wanted to remind them of something.

The king replied, "The command from me is firm; if you do not make known to me the dream and its interpretation, you will be torn limb from limb, and your houses will be made a rubbish heap. But if you declare the dream and its interpretation, you will receive from me gifts, a reward and great honor; therefore, declare to me the dream and its interpretation." Dan. 2:5,6

His counselors, seeing the seriousness of the situation, said, "Let the king tell the dream to his servants, and we will declare the interpretation." Dan. 2:7

The king answered, "I know for a certain that you are bargaining for time, inasmuch as you have seen the command from me is firm, that if you do not make the dream known to me, there is only one decree for you. For you have agreed together to speak lying and corrupt words before me until the situation is changed; therefore, tell me the dream, that I may know that you can declare to me its interpretation." Dan. 2:8,9

Nebuchadnezzar had been very disturbed by the dream and suspected that his servants were not capable of giving him the information he sought, although they claimed, even as does a modern-day horoscope, that they could tell all. Eventually, like their modern counterpart, they claimed impotence because, "There is not a man on earth who could declare the matter for the king, inasmuch as no great king or ruler has ever asked anything like this of any magician, conjurer, or astrologer. Moreover, the thing which the king commands is difficult, and there is no one else who could declare it to the king except gods, whose dwelling place is not with mortal flesh." Dan. 2:10,11

As they could not tell what he sought, he commanded all the wise men to be killed. As Daniel was being taken into custody, he asked why. Receiving an explanation, he went to the king and requested time in order that he might declare the interpretation to the king. Dan 2:16

Why did the king honor Daniel's request? Time was one thing he would not give the others, neither did they seek it, for this was a situation they had never encountered before. Maybe the reason was Daniel's approach, not one of pride but of willingness to try. The king granted him time, so Daniel went home to get his companions and pray over the matter. God answered Daniel's prayer and gave him the dream and its meaning in a vision that night.

Daniel then went back to the king and explained the dream and its interpretation.

NEBUCHADNEZZAR'S DREAM

"You, O king, were looking and, behold, there was a single great statue; that statue, which was large and of extraordinary splendor, was standing in front of you, and its appearance was awesome.

"The head of that statue was made of gold, its breast and its arm of silver, its belly and its thighs of bronze, its legs of iron, its feet partly of iron and partly of clay.

"You continued looking until a stone was cut out without hands, and it struck the statue on its feet of iron and clay, and crushed them. Then the iron, clay, bronze, silver and gold were crushed all at the same time, and became like the chaff of the summer threshing floors; and the wind carried them away so that not a trace of them was found. But the stone that struck the statue became a great mountain and filled the whole earth." Dan. 2:31-35

Interpretation of the Dream

"You, O king, are the king of kings, to whom the God of heaven has given the kingdom, the power; the strength and the glory. Wherever the sons of men dwell, or the beasts of the field, or the birds of the sky. He has given them into your hand and has caused you to rule over them all. You are the head of gold. After you will arise another kingdom inferior to you, then another third kingdom of bronze, which will rule over the earth. Then there will be a fourth kingdom as strong as iron; inasmuch as iron crushes and shatters all things, so like iron that breaks in pieces, it will crush and break in pieces. In that you saw the feet and toes, partly of potter's clay and partly of iron, it will be a divided kingdom; but it will have in it the toughness of iron, inasmuch as you saw the iron mixed with common clay. As the toes of the feet were partly of iron and partly of pottery, so some of the kingdom will be strong and part of it will be brittle. In that you saw the iron mixed with common clay, they will combine with one another in the seed of men; but they will not adhere to one another, even as iron does not combine with pottery.

"In the days of those kings, the God of heaven will set up a kingdom which will never be destroyed, and that kingdom will not be left for another people; it will crush and put an end to all these kingdoms, but it will itself endure forever. Inasmuch as you saw that a stone was cut out of the mountain without hands and that it crushed the iron, bronze, clay, silver and gold, the great God has made known to the king what will take place in the future." Dan.2:37-45

An interesting aspect of this vision was the man who received it. Nebuchadnezzar was not a Jew, but he was ruling over the Jews by virtue of the power God had given him. The vision was not given in the normal manner to a Jewish prophet and then relayed to

Nebuchadnezzar; instead, it was given directly to him. This story belonged to the world.

This story has parts common to Daniel's later visions, and it is the first definite portrayal of those events. Nebuchadnezzar's vision was the first to deal at length with the way God was going to dispose of nations at the time of the end. It was something new. Consider the image. It had: 1) a head of gold, 2) arms and breasts of silver, 3) belly and thighs of brass, 4) legs of iron, 5) feet and toes of iron mixed with clay. Finally, the image was totally destroyed by a stone cut out of the mountain.

The light was given to the world. The world was warned that four kingdoms were going to arise in the earth. One by one they would pass away. Even the fourth would cease to exist upon the earth. However, in the last days ten nations would rise from the boundaries of the old fourth kingdom. When Christ, the stone from God, returns, He will destroy these ten nations, establish His kingdom over the nation of Israel, becoming the great mountain that grows to fill the whole earth.

Jesus said to them, "Did you never read in the Scriptures, The stone which the builders rejected, this same became the chief cornerstone; this came about from the Lord, and it is marvelous in our eyes?' Therefore, I say to you, the kingdom of God will be taken away from you, and be given to a nation producing the fruit of it. And he who falls on this stone will be broken to pieces; but on whomever it falls, it will scatter him like dust." Matt. 21:41-44

Daniel emphasized this to Nebuchadnezzar when he pointed out, "Inasmuch as you saw that a stone was cut out of the mountain without hands and that it crushed the iron, the bronze, the clay, the silver, and the gold, the great God has made known to the king what will take place in the future; so the dream is true, and its interpretation is trustworthy." Dan 2:45. This is God's cornerstone of this book. The rest of the Scriptures build upon this foundation.

The doom of these ten nations is sealed. Unfortunately, this vision by itself does not provide enough information to identify them. It does provide one fact which will be necessary to help identify them through information provided by the later visions. It establishes that Nebuchadnezzar was the head of gold; so the first kingdom of the four that held importance was his.

A literal interpretation of the Bible would require these four kingdoms to occur in sequence. This, in conjunction with Daniel's own visions, will help us to identify who they were. To this end, let's look at the rest of what Daniel saw.

The First Beasts

"I was looking in my vision by night, and behold, the four winds of heaven were stirring up the great sea. And four great beasts were coming up from the sea . . . . The first was like a lion and had the wings of an eagle. I kept looking until its wings were plucked, and it was lifted up from the ground and made to stand on two feet like a man, a human mind also was given to it. And behold, another beast, resembling a bear. It was raised up on one side, and three ribs were in its mouth between its teeth; and thus they said to it, 'Arise and devour much meat' . . . . And behold another one like a leopard which had on its back four wings of a bird; the beast also had four heads and dominion was given to it . . . . And behold a fourth beast, dreadful, terrifying and extremely strong; and it had large iron teeth. It devoured, crushed and trampled down the remainder with its feet; it was different from all the beasts that were before it, and it had ten horns. While I was contemplating the horns, behold, another horn a little one came up among them and three of the first horns were pulled out by the roots before it. This horn possessed eyes like the eyes of a man, and a mouth uttering great boats . . . . I kept looking because of the sound of the boastful words the horn was speaking. I kept looking until the beast was slain, its body destroyed, and given to the burning fire. As for the rest of the beasts, their dominion was taken away, but an extension of life was granted to them for an appointed period of time." Dan.7:2-12

"These great beasts which are four in number are four kings who will arise from the earth . . . . The fourth beast will be a fourth kingdom on the earth, which will be different from all the other kingdoms; and it will devour the whole earth, tread it down and crush it. As for the ten horns, out of this kingdom ten kings will arise; another will arise after them, different from the previous ones, and he will subdue three kings. He will speak out against the most high and wear down the saints of the Highest One, and he will intend to make alternations in time and law and they will be given into his hand for a time, times and half a time." Dan 7:17-25

Daniel saw four beasts rise from the sea. This sea was not literally a body of water, for even the angel said it stood for the earth. Further clarification of this symbology is provided to John. "He said to me, 'The waters which you saw, where the harlot sits, are peoples and multitudes and nations and tongues.'" Rev. 17:15 In other words, the sea Daniel saw represented mankind from which the beasts who were kings would come.

Daniel's vision was not very different from Nebuchadnezzar's. Daniel saw four beasts and there were four parts in Nebuchadnezzar's image. Each beast represented a king, even as each part had. The fourth beast possessed ten horns, even as the image had ten toes. But a new facet was added: A new king was going to arise among the ten. When this king grew in power; he was going to subdue three of the other kings. Then he would speak out against the God of Creation, who would give the saints or the Israelites into his hand for a three-and-one-half year period.

Both of these visions describe the same event. The significant difference is that Nebuchadnezzar saw an image while Daniel saw beasts. However, Nebuchadnezzar would not have regarded the beasts with as much awe as he regarded the image, for he was an image builder and the image he sought to build was his own. So God let Nebuchadnezzar see himself, and the image he saw was shocking.

On further examination, the two visions compare very favorably. Nebuchadnezzar's image had four parts and Daniel saw four beasts. Each part and each beast stood for a king or his kingdom. The head of gold of the image was defined as being Nebuchadnezzar. He was the first king of the four, which identifies territory that the ten nations at the end of time will come from. The first beast Daniel saw was the lion, the king of beasts. Therefore, the first beast, the lion, must also stand for Nebuchadnezzar. Who the rest represent we cannot yet say. We must continue to seek out understanding, even as Daniel did.

Daniel did not understand his first vision. He said, "My spirit was distressed within me and the visions in my mind kept alarming me." And again he said, "At this point the revelation ended. As for me, Daniel, my thoughts were greatly alarming me and my face grew pale, but I kept the matter to myself" Dan. 7:15,28

Now, if you were God and you wanted this man Daniel, whom you loved, to understand your plans, how would you go about it? Would you give him a different vision, with new material, or would you use a new vision to explain the point that led him astray from the plan of the last one? A wise God who builds his story line upon line would surely magnify and expand the problem area, and this is just what He did. He began the new vision with the identity of the fourth beast which had so awed Daniel.

The Ram and the Goat

"A ram with two horns was standing in front of the canal. Now the horns were long, but one was longer than the other, with the longer one coming up last. The ram butted westward, northward and southward and no other beast could stand before it; but he did as he pleased and magnified himself. Then behold, a male goat came from the west over the surface of the whole earth without touching the ground. The goat had a conspicuous horn between his eyes. In his mighty wrath, he rushed at the ram. He struck the ram and shattered his two horns, and the ram had no strength to withstand him. So he hurled the ram to the ground and trampled

8

upon it. Then the male goat magnified himself exceedingly. But as soon as he was mighty the large horn was broken, and in its place came up four conspicuous horns toward the four winds of heaven. Out of one of them came forth a, rather small horn which grew exceedingly great toward the south, east, and the beautiful land. It grew up to the host of heaven and caused some of the host and some of the stars to fall to the earth and it trampled them down. It magnified itself to be equal with the Commander of the host. It removed the regular sacrifice from Him and the place of His sanctuary was thrown down ... Because of the transgression the host will be given over to the horn along with the regular sacrifice!" Dan. 8:3-12

The Angel's Interpretation

"The ram which you saw with the two horns represents the kings of Media and Persia. The shaggy goat represents the kingdom of Greece, and the large horn that is between his eyes is the first king. The broken horn and the four horns that arose in its place represent four kingdoms which will arise from his nation, although not in his power. In the latter period of their rule, when the transgressors have run their course, a king will arise insolent and skilled in intrigue. He will be mighty, but not by his own power. He will corrupt to an extraordinary degree and prosper and perform his will. He will destroy mighty men and the holy people. Through his shrewdness he will cause deceit to succeed. He will magnify himself in his heart. He will corrupt many while they are at ease. He will even oppose the Prince of Princes, but he will be broken without hand:" Dan. 8:20-25

Look again to the words of the vision before this one. Consider how the lion, bear, and leopard attack their prey. They have claws to slash and tear and teeth powerful enough to dismember anything. The fourth beast was different, though; it had iron teeth with which it could bite and devour; then it could crush its prey; then it could stomp upon and trample the pieces.

9

The first three beasts, the lion, bear, and leopard, can surely devour. You might even say the bear could crush, but none of these three are capable of trampling their prey. An animal needs hard hooves for this. The ram and the goat are the only animals which Daniel mentioned that possess this physical characteristic. Significantly, they also possess another physical attribute which sets them apart from the first three; they possess horns with which they batter and crush their prey.

Either the ram or the goat could fulfill the description of the fourth beast. Both can crush with their horns, bite with their teeth, and trample their enemies with their hooves. The goat was not the fourth beast, though; it is mentioned because it killed the fourth beast, the ram.

Who was the ram with the two horns? "The kings of Media and Persia," a kingdom of combined rule. The first three beasts represented singular peoples. So the fourth beast, besides being different physically was also different in that it represented "the kings"—more than one king was being portrayed by the ram.

Consider also the changes the ram underwent. The first time that Daniel saw this beast it had two horns. It was killed. Then it rose again with ten horns. Then another little horn came forth from the ten and plucked out three of the others. No wonder Daniel was confused! He was so awed by what was taking place that he only described the action without giving the name to the fourth beast or revealing the territory which it represented. He did not do this until he got the second vision, which more clearly showed what was going to happen. The first vision described the three beasts, the lion, bear, and leopard, and described the actions of the fourth beast, the ram. The second vision named the fourth beast as the ram, and described how it was killed by the goat. Nevertheless, Daniel still did not understand his visions, because he did not relate the one to the other.

The second vision had the same effect upon Daniel as the prior one. He stated, "Then I, Daniel, was exhausted and sick for days. Then I got up again and carried on the king's business but I was astounded at the vision, and there was none to explain it." Dan 8:27

So Daniel used the orthodox means of his religion to enhance his chances of gathering understanding. He fasted. He prayed. He made what is probably recorded as the first New Year's Resolution. He did this at the beginning of the third year of Cyrus' rule.

"In those days I, Daniel, had been mourning for three entire weeks. I did not eat any tasty food, nor did meat or wine enter my mouth, nor did I any ointment at all, until the entire three weeks were completed." Dan. 10:2,3 Then on the twenty-fourth day of the first month, three weeks after he began to fast and pray, Gabriel returned.

He said, "Do not be afraid, Daniel, for from the first day that you set your heart on understanding this and on humbling yourself before your God, your words were heard, and I have come in response to your words. But the prince of the kingdom of Persia was withstanding me for twenty-one days; then behold, Michael, one of the chief princes, came to help me, for I had been left there with the kings of Persia. Now I have come to give you an understanding of what will happen to your people in the latter days, for the vision pertains to the days yet future." Dan. 10:12-14

Then he said, "Do you understand why I came to you? But I shall now return to fight against the prince of Persia; so I am going forth, and behold, the prince of Greece is about to come. However, I will tell you what is inscribed in the writing of truth. (Yet there is no one who stands firmly with me against these forces except Michael your prince. In the first year of Darius the Mede, I arose to be an encouragement and a protection to him.) Now I will tell you the truth: Behold, three more kings are going to rise in Persia. Then a fourth will gain far more riches than all of them; as soon as he becomes strong through his riches, he will arouse the whole empire against the realm of Greece!" Dan. 10:20-11:2

With these words of Gabriel, we now have enough information to put the names to the individual kings and identify their kingdoms and the sequence in which they would occur. Let us look at the kings from Nebuchadnezzar on. We have already seen that the lion, the head of gold, stood for Nebuchadnezzar. The bear, which was given to feasting, stood for the parts of silver and represented Belshazzar. The leopard with the heads of four victims, the parts of brass in Nebuchadnezzar's vision represented King Cyrus. Cyrus defeated Astyages of Media, Croesus of Lydia, Babylon, and Sardis, greatly expanding the territory over which he ruled. After Cyrus, three kings of Persia ruled. They were Cambyses II, Gaumata, and Darius. The ram represented the kingdom of the Medes and Persians at its greatest territorial size. The first of the two horns of the ram represented the king who obtained this great territory, and his name was Darius. Darius' son, Xerxes, represented the large horn which came up last. Xerxes became the richest Persian king of all, and he used his riches to stir up his whole kingdom against Greece. It took Greece many years to build up the materials and manpower and to await its first leader, Alexander the Great, to repay the attacks of Persia. From Xerxes to Alexander other Persian kings ruled, but they are of no consequence because the greatest king of Persian Empire had already come. Xerxes' attacks caused Greece to rise from its small status and become a great kingdom before which no others could stand.

Look at the maps of these empires (Maps 1 and 2) and see how they expanded. Look at the territory Nebuchadnezzar ruled. Belshazzar did not expand it for he was a parasite and feasted on what it contained, until the night it was given to another. That's why three ribs of the lion's carcass were in the mouth of the bear.

Cyrus did not mind fighting, though, and his father-in-law was his first opponent to fall. Then he conquered three other kingdoms, greatly expanding the land boundaries he ruled over.

12

Then other Persians ruled over all that Cyrus had possessed. Cambyses II, Guamata, and Darius added prodigious amounts of territory to the Persian Empire. Darius's son, Xerxes, grew rich from the tribute and taxes.

Darius began the Persian attacks against Greece; Xerxes continued them. He raised an army of about one million men and burned and looted Athens. Then he was forced to withdraw. Persia was not meant to rule over Greece. Eventually, it was to be the other way around.

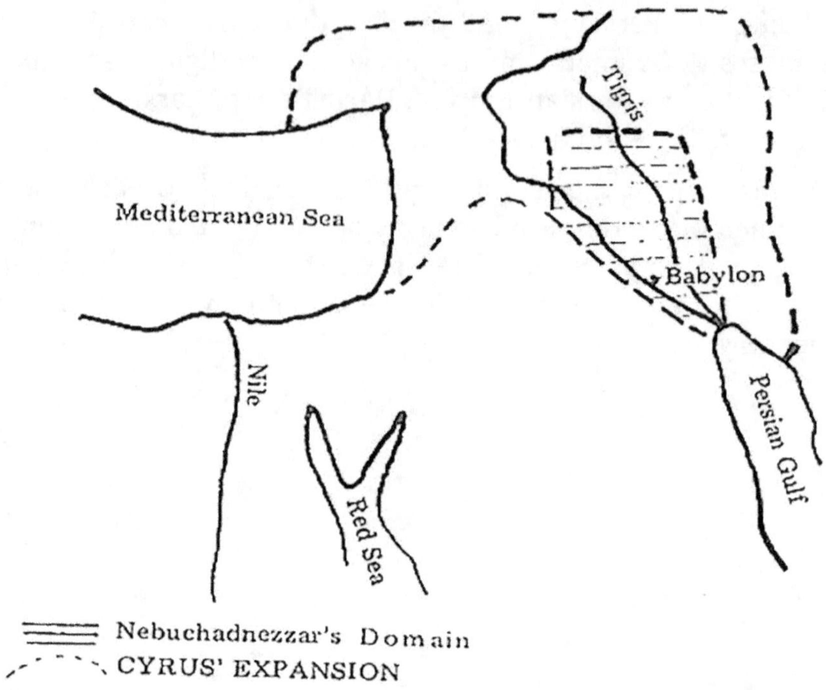

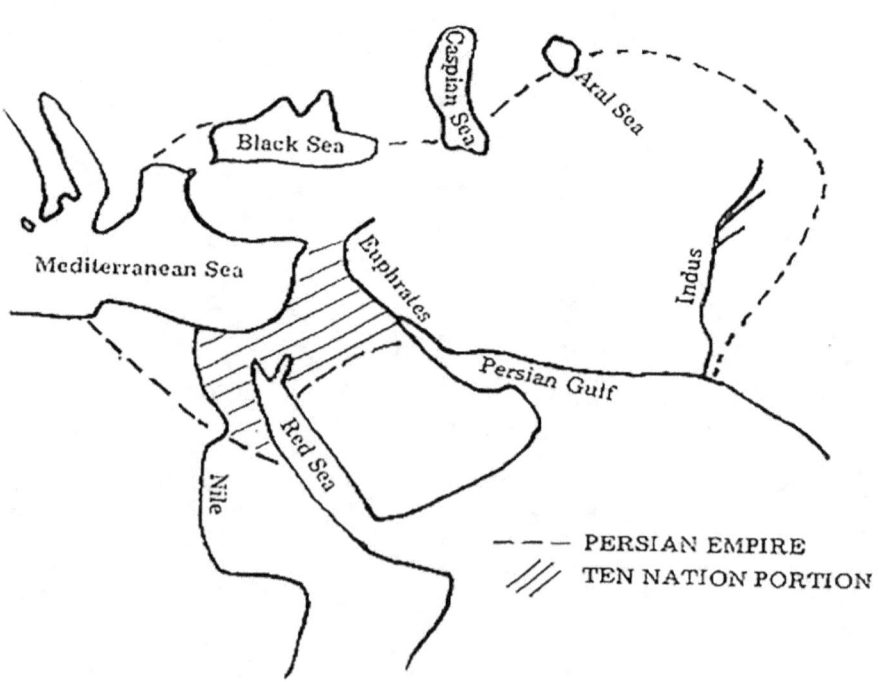

Mediterranean Sea

Tigris

Babylon

Persian Gulf

Nile

Red Sea

≡≡≡ Nebuchadnezzar's Domain
‒ ‒ ‒ CYRUS' EXPANSION

Caspian Sea

Aral Sea

Black Sea

Mediterranean Sea

Euphrates

Indus

Persian Gulf

Red Sea

Nile

‒ ‒ ‒ PERSIAN EMPIRE
/// TEN NATION PORTION

Hal Lindsey has ably put forth the theological seminaries' current viewpoints on the kingdoms in his book The Late Great Planet Earth. He labels the kingdoms as follows: first, Babylonia; second, Media and Persia; third, Macedonia (Greece); fourth, Rome.

There are two major errors in this listing. The first is that the first kingdom did not stand for a whole empire. "You are the head of gold," Daniel told Nebuchadnezzar. "You" was used in the singular form—"You" are the first kingdom. Therefore, the lion, the first beast, also stood for just one man and not a successive reign of kings, as was represented by the Babylonian empire. Then it follows that the other beasts, the bear and the leopard, also stood for singular kings. The next beast, the ram, stood for the kings of Media and Persia, thus changing the status of future beasts and the kings they represented.

The second major error is that the goat, which was the fifth beast mentioned by Daniel—the ram was the fourth—was described by the angel as representing Greece. But Lindsey would have us believe that the goat of the second vision and the leopard of the first vision are the same beast. This reasoning is based on the belief that the Macedonian empire was the third empire, because the Roman Empire was the fourth, and so the goat and the leopard would have to be the same beast. It might be said that the four horns of the goat stood for the four heads of the leopard; but for this reasoning to be valid, there would also have to be similarity between the two horns of the ram and some parts of the bear. There is no such similarity. Nor is there another beast in the second vision to compare with the lion of the first vision. A bear is not a ram nor is a leopard a goat. Each beast has its own distinctive identity which it shares with no other.

Great hope is placed in the ability of Rome to revive, but the visions do not support this contention. Nevertheless, if Rome is not to revive, just where does it fit into this story? To find out, let's look at the visions of another prophet, and see what John recorded.

"I saw a beast coming up out of the sea, having ten horns with ten diadems, and seven heads with blasphemous names. The beast which I saw was like a leopard, his feet were like those of a bear, and his mouth like the mouth of a lion. The dragon gave him his power, throne, and great authority. I saw one of its heads as if it had been slain, and his fatal wound was healed. The whole earth was amazed and followed after the beast. They worshipped the dragon, because he gave his authority to the beast; and they worshipped the beast saying, "Who is like the beast and who is able to wage war with him?" Rev. 13:1-4

The body of this dragon consisted of parts of Daniel's beasts, but they are mentioned in reverse order: the body of a leopard, the feet of a bear and the mouth of a lion. Why did the latter beasts (kings) have ever-increasing portions? Because the latter kings gradually increased the domain which the prior kings had ruled over. This description of the dragon shows it can't be the fourth beast because it does not possess the hard hooves it needs to be able to trample. It does not have the physical traits required of the fourth beast. Yet the dragon did come into possession of the special ten horn area of the fourth beast, the ram.

Both sets of ten horns represent the same ten-nation area. The visions of Daniel explained the special significance of these ten nations in the time of the end. Then they expound upon the ten and discuss the singular nature of the little horn, or fierce king, who will overcome three others from among the ten. Then the visions transfer this ten-nation area into the kingdom of the goat, as the goat kills the ram. Then the location of the little horn is identified as coming from the northern kingdom of the goat after it was divided into four parts (See Map 3)

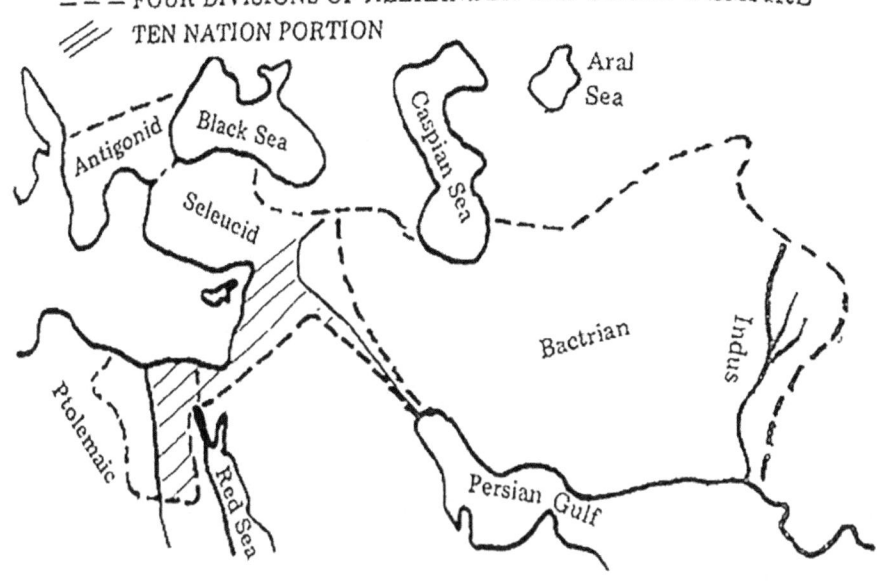

--- FOUR DIVISIONS OF ALEXANDER THE GREAT'S EMPIRE

/// TEN NATION PORTION

Aral Sea

Black Sea

Caspian Sea

Antigonid

Seleucid

Ptolemaic

Red Sea

Bactrian

Indus

Persian Gulf

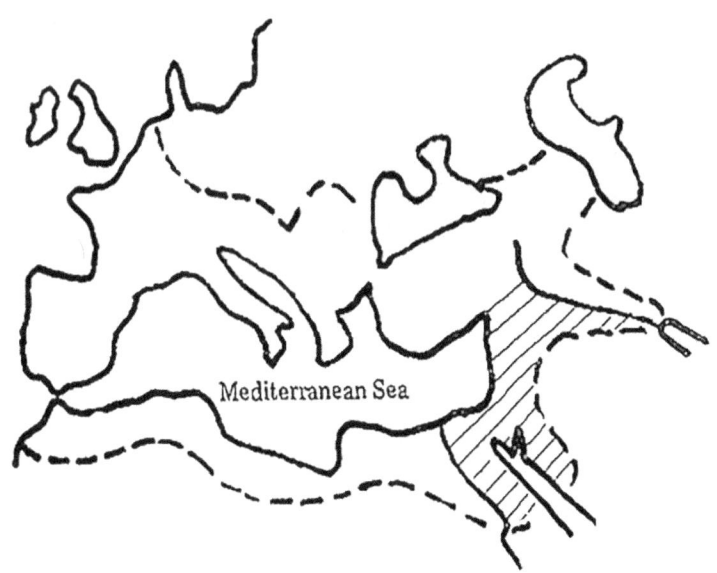

THE ROMAN EMPIRE

/// TEN NATION PORTION

Mediterranean Sea

John then traces these same ten nations into the dragon's empire, thus putting them under the rule of Rome. (See Map 4)

Therefore, the statement that Rome will revive has an atom of truth in it, in that Rome did rule over this special area. However, this area couldn't have been in Italy or Europe, because the *kingdom of the ram* did not extend to there. Let the next item in the discussion of this beast be its name: the dragon. It is so named because this beast which came out of the sea is the same as the one which was kicked out of heaven.

"Another sign appeared in heaven; and behold, a great red dragon having seven heads, ten horns, and on his head seven diadems."

"There was war in heaven, Michael and his angels waging war with the dragon, and the dragon and his angels waged war, and they were not strong enough, and there was no longer a place found for them in heaven. And the great dragon was thrown down, the serpent who is called the Devil and Satan who deceives the whole world; he was thrown down to the earth, and his angels were thrown down with him." Rev.12:3,7-9

The dragon had many aliases: the serpent, the Devil and Satan. His abode had been in heaven. He knew of God's plan to send a Messiah and set about to kill Him as soon as He was born, as is written in Revelation, Chapter twelve. The dragon did not have the power of God, though, so he failed and was kicked out of heaven.

To foil God's plan, he had founded an empire on the earth; to prepare to kill this male child. To do this, he had to attain control over some of the territory now ruled by the Greeks: just the special part that had been ruled by the ram. The dragon's final domain encompassed the necessary parts of the territories of the beasts which it gained through acquisitive territorial expansion, more aptly called war.

Each of the previous beasts represented definite kingdoms, but what did the dragon represent? To find this answer, we must turn to the seventeenth chapter of Revelation.

"He carried me away in the Spirit into a wilderness; I saw a woman sitting on a scarlet beast, full of blasphemous names, having seven heads and ten horns." Rev.:17:3

The scarlet beast which the woman rides is the same as the dragon previously described. The angel, in fact, helped to clarify this image. He said, "Why do you wonder? I shall tell you the mystery of the woman and of the beast that carries her, which has the seven heads and the ten horns. The beast that you saw was, and is not, and is about to come up out of the abyss and to go to destruction. Those who dwell on the earth will wonder, whose name has not been written in the book of life from the foundation of the world, when they see they beast, that he was and is not and will come. Here is the mind which has wisdom. The seven heads are seven mountains on which the woman sits, and they are seven kings; five have fallen, one is, the other has not yet come; when he comes he must remain a little while. The beast that was, and is not, is himself also an eighth and is one of the seven, and he goes to destruction. The ten horns are ten kings, who have not yet received a kingdom, but they receive authority as kings with the beast for one hour. These have one purpose and they give their power and authority to the beast. These will wage war against the Lamb, and the Lamb will overcome them, because He is the Lord of Lords and King of Kings, and those who are with Him are called and chosen and faithful. And the woman whom you saw is the great city, which reigns over the kings of the earth." Rev. 17:7-14,18

In other words, the woman stood for a city which the beast, the dragon, was using to accomplish his purpose. (Most interpreters identify this city as Rome.)

The dragon, the devil was wounded by the sword, but he lived. He was wounded as the heavenly host drove him and his angels out of heaven. The dragon did not die, for only one of its seven heads was wounded. It is this head and the empire it stands for that we need to identify. Satan's only concern is to exalt himself and become as powerful as God. All his efforts are expended toward this end. The Devil used the kingdoms of the lion, bear, leopard, ram, goat, and

19

dragon to further his goal. Look at the map of the Roman Empire (Map 3). It encompasses Nebuchadnezzar's domain. It includes the important parts of the other kingdoms as well.

This idea provides a new meaning to these words, "They are seven kings, five have fallen, one is, and the other has not yet come . . . the beast that was and not, is himself also an eighth and is of the seven." The five that have fallen are the lion, bear, leopard, ram, and goat; the one that is, is the dragon. There is one yet to come. The Devil, the serpent, is himself the eighth. The serpent is of the seven, because they existed only to serve him, and he worked through all of them. Though he was separate, he was of them all.

What of the devil right now? He is wounded. His authority to create and use empires is being restrained, but his wound is almost healed. It is almost time for him to bring a resurgence of power to ten nations from the boundary of the wounded beast; bringing forth a smaller empire, "like a lamb," for this last king to rule. This is the king who has not yet come (the seventh beast). John describes him as follows.

"I saw another beast coming up out of the earth; and he had two horns like a lamb, and he spoke as a dragon." Rev.13:11

Note first the origin of the beast. It came out of its grave, out of the earth. it was not a new beast coming up out of the sea. Reconsider for a moment the beasts Daniel described: the lion, bear, leopard, ram, and goat. How did each one die? Recall that the death of only one beast is recorded. This beast was attacked by a goat that crushed, trampled, and devoured it. This is how the ram perished, and the complete territory of the Medes and the Persians was eradicated. Therefore, it is the territory of the ram that will provide the ten nations of the last days. These ten nations will not occupy all the land previously ruled by the Medes and Persians, so this last beast will be smaller, "like a lamb."

This resurrected ram will be the fierce king whom Daniel saw. He will be the next king through whom the Devil will work.

The final order of all the beasts is now seen to be: the lion, bear, leopard, ram, goat, dragon, resurrected ram, and the serpent. We have seen that the ram was the fourth kingdom on the earth, and it did not represent the Roman Empire. Many people though, believe Rome will revive, and they base this belief upon several passages of Scripture. Let the Scriptures and history firmly put Rome in its grave forever.

The Seventy Weeks

"Seventy weeks have been decreed for your people and your holy city, to finish the transgression, to make an end of sin, to make atonement for iniquity, to bring in everlasting righteousness, to seal up the vision and prophecy, and to anoint the most holy place. So you are to know and discern that from the issuing of a decree to restore and rebuild Jerusalem until Messiah the Prince, there will be seven weeks and sixty-two weeks; it will be built again; with plaza and moat, even in times of distress. Then, after the sixty-two weeks, the Messiah will be cut off and have nothing, and the people of the prince who is to come will destroy the city and the sanctuary. And its end will come with a flood; even to the end there will be war; desolations are determined. And He will make a firm covenant with the many for one week, but in the middle of the week He will put a stop to sacrifice and grain offerings; and on the wing of abominations will come one who makes desolate, even until a complete destruction, one that is decreed, is poured out on the one who makes desolate." Dan.9:24-27

Now, let us consider the part of this vision that many interpret as Rome's revival. It is based on the phrase, "the people of the prince that is to come." Their reasoning goes as follows: Titus, the man who destroyed Jerusalem and the temple in 70 A.D., was a Roman. Therefore, Rome must revive to take part in Daniel's Seventieth Week. This hope is built on insufficient information. Just what do these words really say? Who will destroy the sanctuary—the people or the prince who is to come?

Let's clarify some terminology here. The prince who is to come is the Antichrist, Daniel's little horn and the fierce king. The people, then, must come from his nation. Now, Titus was a Roman and in no way can we imagine him being called a people. Therefore, the people must refer to the army Titus used. Just where did his army come from? Did the city of Rome have a great enough population to supply an army to fight every battle of the Roman Empire? History tells us otherwise. Langer documents it this way.

"Thereafter, auxiliaries were not employed in the country of their origin and the corps soon came to be composed of recruits of different nationalities. By this time (69-70 A.D.) the Praetorian guards were alone recruited in Italy; the legions drew from Roman settlers in the provinces or Romanized provincials, to whom citizenship was often granted to secure their enlistment." William L. Langer, An Encyclopedia Of World History, p.122

In other words, Titus did not use an army composed of native Romans. The citizenship of his soldiers was just a draft inducement. His army came from another country. Which one?

Gibbon tells us, "Under the successors of Alexander, Syria was the seat of the Seleucidae, who reigned over Upper Asia until the successful revolt of the Parthians confined their dominions to between the Euphrates and the Mediterranean. When Syria became subject to the Romans, it formed the eastern frontier of their empire; nor did that province, in its utmost latitude, know any other bounds than the mountains of Cappadocia to the north, and toward the south the confines of Egypt and the Red Sea. Phoenicia and Palestine were sometimes annexed to and sometimes separated from the jurisdiction of Syria." Edward Gibbon, The Decline And Fall Of The Roman Empire

In truth, Titus departed Rome alone and picked up his army along the way. He used the 10th Fretensis from Damascus, Syria and the 15th Appolonaris from Alexandria, Egypt. Rome will not revive, for its people are not those referred to. Even the physician Luke testifies that Israel was not under the direct rule of Rome. Luke recorded this: "Now it came about in those days that a decree went out from Caesar Augustus that a census be taken of all the inhabited earth. This was the first census to be taken while Quirinius was Governor of Syria." Luke2:1,2 Luke is speaking of the ruler of his homeland. Syria ruled Israel, while all were in subjection to Rome. God caused the truth to be recorded, but Satan distorted it. Rome is dead. The prophecies refer to Assyria and not to Rome.

The purpose of the goat in the visions was to establish this fact and designate the nation that the Antichrist would come from. Let us look once more at the passages regarding the goat.

Recall how the goat came from the west, virtually flying low until it charged into the ram. With its one horn it broke the rams two horns, tossed it into the air, trampled upon it and killed the ram. No one was able to rescue the ram, and it died.

Then the male goat magnified himself. When he did his proud horn broke as he died, and his four generals split the kingdom into four parts.

From one of these four divisions of the kingdom of the goat, came a small horn which grew very great, to the south, east, and Israel. And it grew up to the host of heaven and caused some of the host and some of the stars to fall to earth, and it trampled them down.

It proclaimed itself to be equal with the Commander of the host; and it removed the regular sacrifice from Him, and the place of His sanctuary was thrown down.

In explaining this vision, the angel said, "The shaggy goat represents the kingdom of Greece, and the large horn that is between his eyes is the first king. And the broken horn and the four horns that arose in its place represent four kingdoms which will arise from his nation, although not with his power. And in the latter period of their rule, when the transgressors have run their course, a king will arise insolent and skilled in intrigue. And his power will be mighty, but not by his own power. And he will destroy to an extraordinary degree and prosper and perform his will; he will destroy mighty men and the holy people. And through his shrewdness he will cause deceit to succeed by his influence; and he will magnify himself in his heart, and he will destroy many while they are at ease ... He will even oppose the Prince of Princes, but he will be broken without human agency." Dan.8:21-25

This means that the goat (Greece), with its great horn, would charge into the ram and destroy it completely. It would thus conquer and occupy all the territory the ram had possessed. So now, if we remember that the ten nations Christ would deal with in the final period of time were going to come from the boundaries of the fourth kingdom, we can see how they were annexed to Greece when they were captured by Alexander the Great.

When Alexander the Great died, his kingdom was split into four parts. Since Alexander had no descendants, his four generals took over and divided his kingdom. The four divisions are mentioned, not because they trace the ten nations, but rather because they pinpoint the nation in which the little horn, the fierce king, would arise. The part of this wording that identifies this nation goes as follows: 'Out of one of them came forth a rather small horn which grew exceedingly great toward the south, toward the east, and toward the beautiful land."

Alexander the Great's empire was split up into these four sections: Antigonid, Seleucid, Bactrian, and Ptolemaic. Look at the map of Alexander's empire (Map 2) to see where these four divisions were. Only two of the divisions, the Antigonid and the Seleucid, have a location that would permit travel to the south towards Jerusalem. Yet, the Antigonid section of the nation of Greece was not ruled over by the Persians. This leaves only the Seleucid section as the location from which the little horn could come. Can we pinpoint the exact nation of this little horn through what the rest of the prophets have to say? Yes, we can!

Two prophets have fingered the nation we are seeking. Isaiah said: "The Lord himself will give you a sign: behold, a virgin will be with child and bear a son, and he will call his name Immanuel. He will eat curds and honey at the time He knows enough to refuse evil and choose good. For before the boy will know enough to refuse evil and choose good, the land whose two kings you dread will be forsaken. The Lord will bring on you and your Father's house such days as have never come since the day that Ephraim separated from Judah even the king of Assyria." Isa.7:14-17

Micah agreed with Isaiah's identification. He said, "But as for you, Bethlehem Ephrathah, too little to be among the clans of Judah, from you One will go forth for Me to be ruler in Israel. His goings forth are from long ago, from the days of eternity. Therefore, He will give them up until the time when she who is in labor has borne a child. Then the remainder of His brethren will return to the sons of Israel. And He will arise and shepherd His flock in the strength of the Lord, in the majesty of the name of the Lord His God. And they will remain, because at that time He will be great to the ends of the earth. And this one will be our peace, when the Assyrian invades our land." Micah 5:2-5

The prophets do not argue with one another, nor do they lie. They recount the vision of God and declare His plan. They all say the Antichrist will be Assyrian. Only the Devil, in his self-magnification, has caused mankind to think he would be a Roman. That way, mankind would be looking the wrong way and be caught unawares by the event. Then they would say, "This could not possibly be the event spoken of in the Scriptures!" And they would, in effect, be blaspheming God because of their inability to piece the puzzle together.

"The Lord of hosts has sworn saying, 'Surely, just as I have intended so it has happened, and just as I have planned so it will stand, to break Assyria in My land, and I will trample him on My mountains. Then his yoke will be removed from them, and his burden removed from their shoulder. This is the plan devised against the whole earth; and this is the hand that is stretched out against all the nations.' For the Lord of hosts has planned, and who can frustrate it? And as for His stretched-out hand, who can turn it back?" Isa. 14:24-27

It may be said that this event has already been fulfilled, for Isaiah prophesied it before the Babylonian captivity which began through the efforts of Nebuchadnezzar, the Assyrian. This would have been its only application, except for the other words of Isaiah and Micah, which place Christ's birth before these events would take place. After Christ was born, the nation was to be distressed by the king of Assyria. This was accomplished when Syria, under the auspices of Rome, destroyed the temple and city and scattered the Jews in 70 A.D. Yet again Christ, personally, was to be the peace of Israel when (or after) the Assyrian invades the land. At this time, Christ is to be great to the ends of the earth. He was not this great in 70 A.D. The events at that time began the process of spreading the truth of Jesus to the world; but they did not complete it before the Assyrian invaded.

Titus used Syrian and Egyptian legionaires to attack in 70AD. They were Roman soldiers when they came. They were also Roman Citizens but only by draft inducement. Isa.7:18 The Assyrian is due to invade again. The "third time" of Micah will come. Ezekiel, too, said the sword would be swung a third time. So let's look at what will happen to Israel before then.

CHAPTER II

The Two Witnesses; Their Land, Their Temple

"Go therefore and make disciples of all nations, baptizing them in the name of the Father and the Son and the Holy Spirit, teaching them to observe all that I commanded you; and lo, I am with you always, even to the end of the days": Matthew 28:19, 20.

Once I met a famous preacher, and I listened to his sermon, which made reference to the Two Witnesses. After the sermon was over, I had a moment to begin to show him the Bible's definition of who the Two Witnesses are. But the preacher stopped me short by saying, "I believe that if God wanted us to know who the Two Witnesses are, he would have told us." God wants us to know who the Witnesses are or He would not have even mentioned them! Alas, at that point, I had just begun my research, so I did not have a ready answer; but his retort managed to spur me on to discover the truth of the matter.

No student of the Bible takes just one passage and builds a doctrine upon it, for the Bible is God's word.

Isaiah told us how God built His story and what its meaning was. "To whom would he teach knowledge? And to whom would he interpret the message? Those just weaned from the milk; Those just taken away from the breast? For he says, "Order on order, order on order, line on line, line on line, a little here, a little there!" Isa.28:9-10 The story is not built on one verse, but the one verse is a part of the story. It is the story of all the parts and verses which we are seeking.

The interpreter of the Bible must go about it even as Christ spoke to the Jews, "You search the Scriptures, because you think that in them you have eternal life; and it is these that bear witness of me." John 5:39 To interpret them one must search the Scriptures to find all the rest of that subject, which is hidden "a little here, a little there." He must go about his task even as Paul instructed Timothy to do. "Be diligent to present yourself approved to God as a workman who does not need to be ashamed, handling accurately the word of truth." 2 Tim. 2:15 The words of just one writer of a book of the Bible is not enough to establish the story; all of them must be consulted.

God established the law, which was his word. God, as well as man, must then abide by it to give it full meaning. God said in the law, "If anyone kills a person, the murderer shall be put to death at the evidence of witnesses, but no person shall be put to death on the testimony on one witness." Num. 35:30

Therefore, to have firm meaning and full validity, more than one person had to establish the truth. This applies to the whole Bible for every doctrine it contains. The testimony of every writer must be sought out in order to apply it to the doctrine and find the truth.

What bits and pieces does the Bible contain which can possibly identify who the "two witnesses" have been, are, or will be? The angel who came to John provided this definition, "These are the two olive trees and the two lampstands that stand before the Lord of the earth." Rev 11:4 This is the definition generations have ignored, so the witnesses remained unknown. How does the Bible identify these things? What does the language of the Lord say they mean?

One, like a son of man who was dead and is alive forevermore, told John, "As for the mystery of the seven stars which you saw in my right hand, and the seven golden lampstands, the seven stars are the angels of the seven churches, and the seven lampstands *are the seven churches* Rev. 1:20 A lampstand then stood for a church. Two lampstands then stand for two churches! Which two? The two olive trees! Who are they? Jeremiah provides the answer.

"The Lord called your name, 'A green olive tree, beautiful in fruit and form,' with the noise of a great tumult he has kindled fire on it,

28

and its branches are worthless. And the Lord of hosts, who planted you, has pronounced evil against you because of the evil of the house of Israel and the house of Judah, which they have done to provoke me by offering up sacrifices to Baal." Jer.1:16

God originally planted just one tree, the house of Israel. But through strife and dissension it split into two trees, one the house of Israel, the other the house of Judah. The two olive trees then stand for the houses of Israel and Judah. The two olive trees and the two lampstands then become the believers in God of all the children of Abraham to whom the covenant was given; even to the sons of Israel and then to the houses or nations of Israel and Judah. Is this in harmony with what the rest of the Bible states on this subject? Yes, it is! Turn to the words of Zechariah as recorded in his fourth chapter.

"Then the angel who was speaking with me returned and roused me as a man who is awakened from his sleep. And he said to me, 'What do you see?' And I said, 'I see, and behold, a lampstand all of gold with its bowl on top of it and its seven lamps on it with seven spouts belonging to each of the lamps which are on top of it; also two olive trees by it, one on the right side of the bowl and the other on its left side.' Then I answered and said to the angel who was speaking with me saying, 'What are these, My Lord?' So the angel who was speaking with me answered and said to me, 'Do you not know what these are?' And I said, 'No, my Lord.'" Zech. 4:4-5

The angel was surprised at Zechariah's lack of knowledge. He did not answer the question but rather ignored it for a while, as the teacher would when he wanted the student to reconsider it. And besides, he had to carry out God's commands before he could digress.

"Then he answered and said to me, 'This is the word of the Lord to Zerubbabel, saying: Not by might nor by power, but by My spirit, says the Lord of hosts.'" Zech. 4:6 This word, then, was going to Zerubbabel to strengthen him in his job and purpose, to let him know that God was with him and that God's Spirit would sustain the work no matter how difficult it would become. And the Spirit would sustain him as he superintended the building of the second temple.

Then Gabriel continued. "What are you, O great mountain? Before Zerubbabel you will become a plain; and he will bring forth the top with shouts of 'Grace, grace to it!' Also the word of the Lord came to me, saying, 'The hands of Zerubbabel have laid the foundation of this house, and his hands will finish it. Then you will know the Lord of hosts has sent me to you. For who has despised the day of small things? But these seven will be glad when they see the plumb line in the hand of Zerubbabel—these are the eyes of the Lord which range to and fro throughout the earth:" Zech. 4:7-10

The seven churches would then rejoice as the work progressed and finished, for the House of the Lord was the bowl that filled with oil and channeled the words of the Lord to the other seven churches. But Zechariah did not see this. So he asked, "What are these two olive trees on the right of the lampstand and on its left"; And the second time, "What are the two olive branches which are beside the two golden pipes, which empty the golden oil from themselves?" So he answered me saying, "Do you not know what these are?" And I said, "No, my Lord." Then he said, "These are the two anointed ones, who are standing by the Lord of the whole earth." Zech. 4:11-14

Zechariah understood the words he was to speak to Zerubbabel, but not the symbology. He again asked his original a question, 'What are these?" The angel was surprised again and replied, "Do you still not know?" The angel then replied with virtually the same words that he would later say to John, "These are the two ... that stand by the Lord of the whole earth." They are the whole host of Israel and Judah who serve the God who created this earth.

This vision of Zechariah is now clearly seen to reveal the process through which God sent His message to the world. His word flowed through the branch of Jesus Christ to the individual olive which was a servant of the Lord in Israel. The word overflowed from that servant even as the olive formed its drop of oil which fell and was caught by the golden bowl. In this manner, God channeled His word to the house of the Lord in Jerusalem. From the House of the Lord it then flowed to the seven other churches of the world.

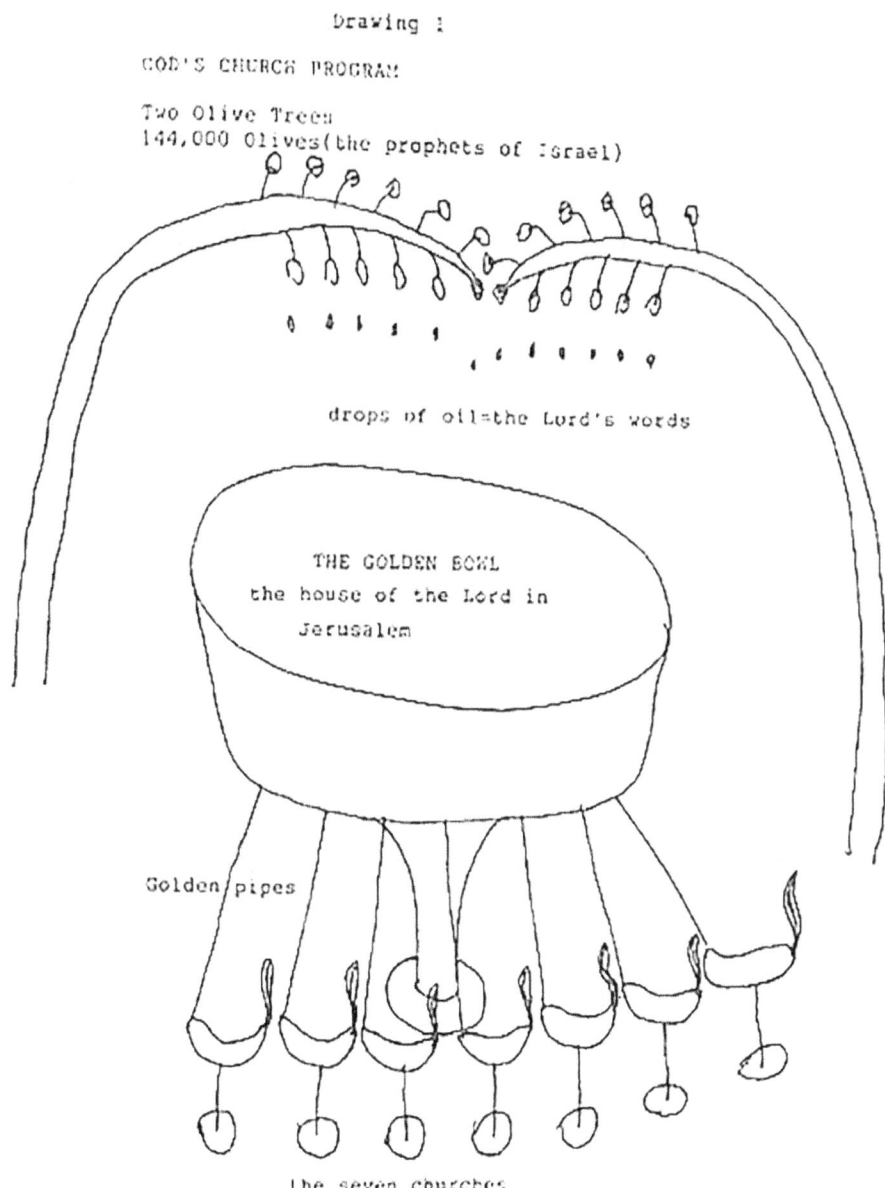

Drawing 1

GOD'S CHURCH PROGRAM

Two Olive Trees
144,000 Olives(the prophets of Israel)

drops of oil=the Lord's words

THE GOLDEN BOWL
the house of the Lord in
Jerusalem

Golden pipes

the seven churches

Zechariah lived when this process had stopped because the House of the Lord was destroyed. A cracked bowl cannot even hold oil, much less channel it to seven other lamps. Yet the seven were getting ready to rejoice, for the house was soon to be repaired to permit God's word to start flowing usefully once more. Even the trained theologian Paul taught the Romans about the olive tree "But if some of the branches were broken off, and you, being a wild olive, were grafted in among them and became partakers with them of the rich root of the olive tree, do not be arrogant toward the branches; but if you are arrogant, remember that it is not you who supports the root, but the root supports you. You will say, 'The branches were broken off so that I might be grafted in.' Quite right, they were broken off for their unbelief, and you stand only by your faith. Do not be conceited, but fear; for if God didn't spare the natural branches, neither will He spare you. Behold then the kindness and severity of God; to those who fell, severity, but to you, God's kindness, if you continue in his kindness; otherwise you also will be cut off. And they also, if they do not continue in their unbelief, will be grafted in; for God is able to graft them in again. For if you were cut off from what is by nature a wild olive and were grafted contrary to nature into a cultivated olive tree, how much more shall these who are the natural branches be grafted into their own olive tree? For I do not want you, brethren, to be uninformed of this mystery, lest you be wise in your estimation, that a partial hardening has happened to Israel until the fullness of the Gentiles has come in; and thus all Israel will be saved; just as it is written. The Deliverer will come from Zion, He will remove ungodliness from Jacob! And this is My covenant with them, when I take away their sins:" Romans 11:17-27

It is abundantly clear now that two witnesses are not just two people like Moses and Elijah! They are in fact all of God's chosen people from the houses of Israel and Judah. All other believers are added to their number and are partakers of their blessing through the seven other churches.

The witnesses have generations of Jews. The first generation to wear sackcloth was the one that saw Christ crucified, buried, and resurrected; almost totally rejecting Him. So He rejected them and they felt His wrath.

Titus was summoned. He came in charge of a Syrian division and an Egyptian division of the Roman Army. The people under him saw to the complete destruction of the temple and the start of a period of persecution throughout the world. In their tents in the wilderness, the Israelites put on the sackcloth because they did not have their beloved city any longer. They were not sorry that Christ was gone; they just wanted their beautiful land back. Some Jews did believe in Christ, and their dispersion was meant to spread the word. All wore sackcloth. All mourned for what they had lost. All sought repentance for their sins, but the times of the Gentiles was now upon them.

Their power was shattered; they were trampled underfoot. The only power they had left was the strength to hold fast to their testimony. They would not be able to perform any deed of valor until the period was over. Then, once again, they would don the robe of power and add the fulfillment of prophecy to their testimony. They would repossess Jerusalem. God enabled them to do this in 1967.

The fullness of the Gentiles is over. The time for these witnesses to wear sackcloth has passed. If they will recognize who they are, then through the Spirit of the Word, by prayer, they can lay full claim to the power God has in readiness for them.

The witnesses now have unlimited power. They can do whatsoever they desire; all they have to do is ask in concert and God will give their desire to them. Whether or not great things start to happen depends upon one single factor: desire to get something done.

"And if anyone desires to harm them, fire proceeds out of their mouths and devours their enemies; and if anyone would desire to harm them, they must in this manner be killed. These have the power to shut up the sky, in order that rain may not fall during the days of their prophesying; and they have power over the waters to turn them into blood, and to smite the earth with every plague as often as they desire." Rev. 11:5,6

The witnesses can tap the power that Elijah tapped. But while they have the ability to use this power and prove to all that their God does exist, one must wonder whether part of the reason for their coming deaths is the fact they are not doing so.

In spite of what their desires could accomplish, God still has His plan. They will turn the waters, that is, the nations, into blood as often as they will. No other nation in their vicinity has their power to fight and win, power to overcome and conquer. They have the power to expand their boundaries once more, just as God has planned. The land of their inheritance will fall to them. They will possess the boundaries recorded by Ezekiel.

Ezekiel's Israel Is Approaching

The words of the Lord came to the priest Ezekiel during the course of the Babylonian Captivity (605-536 B.C.) He relayed God's message to the rest of the captives and recorded them for posterity. Much of what he said was puzzling to the others, but one passage would have caused them to rejoice—his description of the land the people would possess when they returned as a national entity. The captives undoubtedly were elated by the thought that they would possess this land when they returned at the end of their appointed seventy years.

Unfortunately for that generation, God did not plan to reestablish the nation with them. They marched from Jerusalem as captives; they returned as servants of a strange king. Free men did not return! Those who returned were authorized to rebuild the temple, and later this permission was extended to the city itself.

They did not select a king or reform the nation. They did not have the political autonomy or authority necessary for them to allot the land as they were instructed. History records that they were still being ruled by others when Christ came. They observed His birth, watched Him mature, and pondered the miracles of His ministry. Some thought Him fit for death, so they crucified Him, buried Him, and entered the empty grave on the third day. Then Christ's generation felt God's wrath as they were persecuted and driven from the land without the nation ever being reformed.

Then, in 1948, the nation of Israel was reborn, as God began to fulfill these words.

"This shall be the boundary by which you shall divide the land for an inheritance among the twelve tribes of Israel; Joseph shall have two portions. And you shall divide it for an inheritance, each one equally with the other, for I swore to give it to your forefathers, and this land shall fall to you as an inheritance. And this shall be the boundary of the land. On the north side from the Great Sea by the way of Hethlon, to the entrance of Zedad; Hamath, Berothah, Sibraim, which is between the border of Damascus and the border of Hamath; Hazar-hatticon, which is by the border of Hauran. And the boundary shall extend from the sea to Hazar-enan at the border of Damascus, and on the north toward the north is the border of Hamath. This is the north side. And the east side, from between Hauran, Damascus, Gilead and the land of Israel, shall be the Jordan, from the north border to the Eastern Sea you shall measure; this is the east side. And the south side toward the south shall extend from Tamar as far as the waters of Meribath-Kadesh, to the brook, to the Great Sea. This is the south side toward the south. And the west side shall be the Great Sea, from the south border to a point opposite Lebohamath. This is the west side." Ezk. 47:13-21

Ezekiel described four borders, and some are difficult to understand; let's begin with the easy one and follow the border around the land.

The Western Border

This is that Great Sea, the Mediterranean Sea.

The Northern Border

This one is more difficult, but the passage contains two simple directions which aid us. They are: 1) the border of Hamath is north of the line. So Hamath cannot be included; 2) the line went inland until it reached the border of Damascus. Therefore, it would seem that the land which Hamath and Damascus ruled in Ezekiel's time is not included. (Today Syria rules the land which was previously ruled by Hamath and Damascus.)

A definite border begins to take shape as we examine the meaning of the descriptive words. The entrance of Hamath is a mountain pass at the northern border of Lebanon. Seagoing travelers disembarked on the Mediterranean coast to use this pass through the Lebanon mountain range to get to the high plain of Hamath. Zedad means "sloping place." After the pass, this must refer to the way the plain slopes up towards the mountains. Since we are not to go toward Hamath, in the north, we would have to follow the sloping terrain towards the south, going around the plain, turning east to the Anti-Lebanon mountain range, then north toward Hamath which we never reach, for we stop at Berothah, "a place with wells." Then we go to Sibraim, the two hills at the junction of the old borders of Hamath and Damascus. Then we proceed to Hazer-hatticon, the middle village between Hamath and Damascus. From here we cross the Hauran, the cave district of the Anti-Lebanon Mountains, so that we arrive at Hazer-enan, the fountain town which is the eastern end of the northern border.

The Eastern Border

This comes down between the cave district and Damascus, then it goes between Israel and Gilead. Gilead is the land east of the Sea of Galilee and the Jordan River. The intent seems to include the area which we know as the Golan Heights, for all the mountains of this ridge are given to Israel. From the Golan Heights it reaches the Jordan River, which it follows to the Dead Sea.

The Southern Border

This begins at the Dead Sea and goes to three places with doubtful historical locations: to Tamar, Meribath-kadesh, and to the Brook, before it returns to the Mediterranean Sea.

If we would have any hope of locating Tamar, we must consider the intended distribution of land allotments. Ezk.48. Seven tribes: Dan, Asher, Napthali, Manasseh, Ephraim Reuben, and Judah, are each to have an equal north-south division of the land between Jerusalem and the entrance of Hamath. This pass is at latitude 34-40N. Jerusalem is at latitude 31-47N. This is 173 nautical miles for seven tribes, so each part would be 24.7 nautical miles from north to south. The Scriptures state that every tribe must have the same portion. So to find Tamar, we must go south from Jerusalem the distance of the allotment to the Prince and add five portions for the tribes of: Benjamin, Simeon, Issachar, Zebulun, and Gad. The Prince's portion is 25,000 cubits or 6.25 nautical miles, if the cubit is 18 inches. (5 x 24.7 = 123.5. 123.5 + 6.25=129.75). This is on latitude 29-37N.

Elath is a little more than this far south of Jerusalem. Tamar means "palm," while Elath means "palm grove." Possibly these could be one and the same. However, this can't be the case, for Tamar and Elath are mentioned together. 1 Kings 9:18,26

The space program has provided satellite photography of this area. I have obtained and pieced together ten aerial photos of the region of Ezekiel's Israel. I have made the allotment measurements and expect to find Tamar buried on a hill about eight miles north of Elath. No one has ever looked for Tamar this far south of Jerusalem. (I did find Tamar. It is now called DOM PALM and is 11 kilometers north of Eilat.)

Meribath-kadesh, the site of holy contention between God and those of the Exodus who were disturbed because they were thirsty, is situated at Rephidim. Rephidim is located on the west side of the tip of the Sinai Peninsula. Numbers 33:14

Another identification should enable us to fix this border, so let's consider what Ezekiel meant by "the brook." We might start by pondering the responsibilities of a prophet to the visions of God. Consider in particular the case when the prophet sees a UFO (Unidentified Future Object). Does God have to tell him its name? Of course not, for it would only bring ridicule to the prophet who would speak the name for a thing which did not yet exist. What of the prophet then; can he invent a name? No, for then no one would ever understand. Rather, he must use the best knowledge of his day to describe what he has seen. Then, when someone looks back, understanding the knowledge of that day, he might see what God meant.

Ezekiel knew about the Nile River and the wadi in the middle of the Sinai Peninsula. If what he had seen had been either of these two bodies of water; he would have had to use its correct proper name. This he did not do! Therefore, since he only said "brook: maybe what he saw was in truth a third body of water which he did not recognize. It was smaller than the river and bigger than the wadi. This third waterway was fashioned in 1869 by the shovels of Ferdinand de Lesseps. He named it the Suez Canal.

The southern border thus goes from the Dead Sea to Tamar, around the Sinai Peninsula to the Suez Canal, and along it back to the Mediterranean Sea. These are the borders of Ezekiel's Israel.

This territory has never been obtained by Israel. There are three reasons why the prophecy has never been fulfilled.

1. Ezekiel, Chapter Four, describes a period of 430 years during which God would not permit Himself to look upon Jerusalem, hear a prayer, or answer a petition. Nothing proceeded from the city to Him or from Him to the city. The people bore the burden for their sin. They would have no word, vision or prophet to guide them. If you are able to accept it, this period began with the death of Malachi, the last Old Testament prophet, in 433 B.C. It ended after 430 years on the Jewish calendar with the birth of John the Baptist, in 6 B.C. By His word, God would not have given this inheritance to Israel during the interbiblical period.

2. The city Tamar, crucially important to establish the border and its allotment procedure, must be identified to establish and confirm the circumference of the inheritance. Tamar itself was build by King Solomon and inhabited only about 300 years. I had thought, Nebuchadnezzar's army destroyed it and removed all its people to Babylon, and no one who returned from Babylon knew where it was. Yet this study gave me hope of a most promising location for it. As the Lord provides it shall be uncovered and identified to affirm God's continuing faithfulness to this promise. It was during the rule of King Ahaz that the Syrians captured Elath. (2 Kings 16:6) Since the Syrians destroyed Eilat, they must also have destroyed Tamar, and while King Uzziah rebuilt Eilat he did not rebuild Tamar which was already covered by wind blown sand.

3. Ezekiel did not name the Nile or the Sinai's stream as the waterway of his vision. This was not a sin of omission. Ezekiel faithfully described what he saw to the best of his ability. He disclosed the third waterway the vision presented but whose existence he never knew. Thus, he could use no name for it but only described it as the brook. The brook he prophesied is now reality, and named the Suez Canal.

Israel's Rebirth

God began to fashion Ezekiel's Israel in 1948. In 1957 Israel occupied the Gaza strip. The tents of Judah were established before the city of Jerusalem, but, in 1967, Jerusalem was restored to Israel as the clans of Judah consumed all on their right and left. Zech 12:6-8. In a six-day war, Israel occupied the Golan Heights, Jerusalem and the West Bank, and all the Sinai right up to the Suez Canal. Right now Israel owns all but a small portion of this promised territory. That which remains to fall to her is the exact shape of Lebanon.

No one in this world doubts that there shall be another Middle East War. Everyone is pondering what the outcome of it will be. God's word cannot be shaken! A coming war will see the nation of Lebanon rechristened and found no more. God is not dead nor is His hand weak. He has stated what He is going to do, and even now He is accomplishing it. Thus, the 1967 war took only six days; for God will always rest on His Sabbath after He performs a week of labor. When the time is right, He will give Lebanon to Israel. Give God the glory when this happens. Proclaim to those around you, "God did that! Praise His holy name!"

Pause for a moment; let the significance of what you have read sink in. For if the words of Ezekiel were recorded for this generation, we shall see them as they are fulfilled, and their fulfillment is fast approaching.

Israel is still the pride of God's eye. He is cultivating, watering, and pruning it. If His words mean anything, Israel must grow again. The living God has power to make it grow. When it does, you will have His proof that He still exists and cares for the people.

Since I first published this in 1979, some border changes to Israel have occurred. First in 1979 Jimmy Carter, the President of the United States thought it would be good if he could have Israel gave up the Sinai Peninsula to Egypt for peace with Egypt. So the words of the prophet Hosea 5:10 were activated. It said the princes of Judah or the leaders of My people, have become like unto those who move a border. This will cause God's wrath to be poured out upon them. Also in 2007, Israel walked away from Gaza.

This is a direct affront to the Lord God of Israel. His own people don't know or appreciate His work or His words. He is not a happy camper. Now He must act twice to get the job done. Do not marvel over the increased military actions in Gaza and Lebanon. Israel must reoccupy Gaza, clean out the West Bank once more, retake Lebanon, kicking Syria out. Then when Syria does not recover Lebanon, they will force Egypt to co-ordinate an attack, which will cost Egypt the Sinai Peninsula. God will give the land of Ezekiel's promise to Israel.

If you don't accept the message and its meaning, and you laugh and malign it, what will you do upon hearing it is fact and Israel now looks like Map 5?

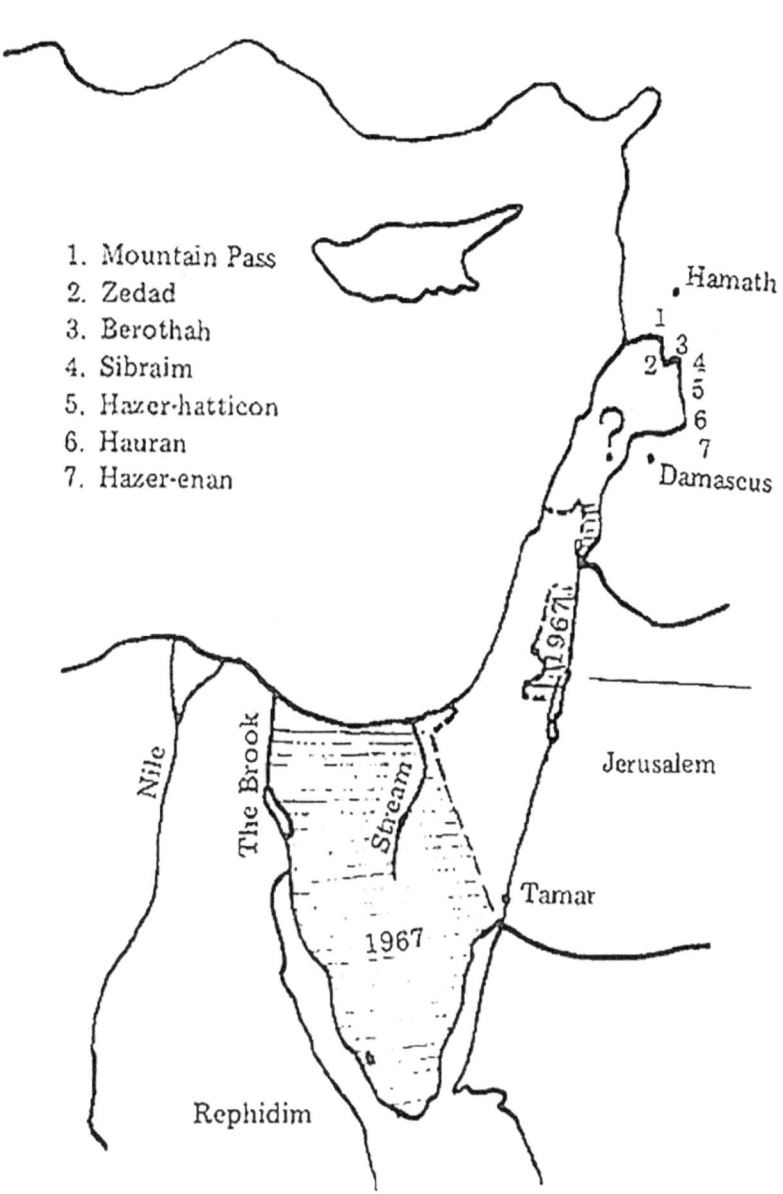

1. Mountain Pass
2. Zedad
3. Berothah
4. Sibraim
5. Hazer-hatticon
6. Hauran
7. Hazer-enan

Hamath

Damascus

Nile

The Brook

Stream

Jerusalem

Tamar

1967

Rephidim

Prophecy is a sign for believers, a sign to those who understand, watch, and wait for it to come to pass.

Do you realize the prophetic meaning of this? Can you see the hand of God at work today? Can you see from current events the way the Spirit is moving upon the waters to cause the word of God to come to pass? That which was promised WILL FALL to the nation of Israel; she will not have to seek it.

Israel has already its inheritance numerous times. Once she destroyed valuable aircraft at Beirut International Airport in retaliation after Arab terrorist blew up one El Al airliner at Athens, Greece. Recently, Israelis killed sixty Arabs and inflicted heavy destruction on some villages which the terrorists, who killed eleven Israeli Olympic athletes, were thought to come from. More recently, they killed selected Arab leaders in their homes in downtown Beirut. And then—you just keep watching the news.

The terrorists exist because God is using them to provoke Israel. The only way that Israel can stop the terrorists' activities is to take over the whole nation which is providing them shelter. Pity poor Lebanon! Once more there will be a short war in the Middle East. The Jews will not desire it, but God will force it upon them. More Arabs will be dispossessed. The world will scream and shout, but Israel will perform valiantly. Israel will possess her inheritance. God will see to it! When Israel does possess her inheritance, the land will be divided by the tribes, in accordance with the allotment procedure shown in map 6.

THE ALLOTMENT PROCEDURE

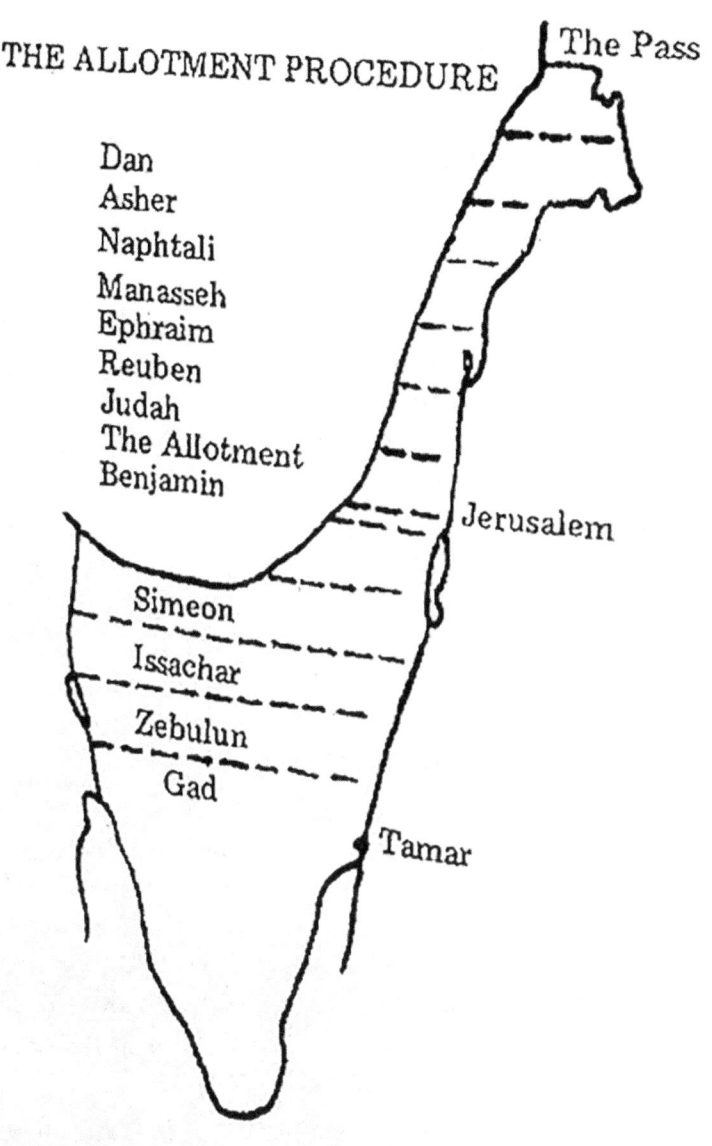

The Pass

Dan
Asher
Naphtali
Manasseh
Ephraim
Reuben
Judah
The Allotment
Benjamin

Jerusalem

Simeon

Issachar

Zebulun

Gad

Tamar

Centered over Jerusalem is a special area reserved for the Prince of Israel who is soon to come. This area shall provide a special blessing for Israel and all the rest of the world.

The Location of Ezekiel's Temple

Ezekiel expounded at length upon the details of the interior and exterior of a magnificent temple. His explanations enable scholars to make architectural drawings of the building and even erect model structures of what it will look like. Discussion of the temple is reaching fever pitch as the day to begin construction is rapidly approaching.

My main question is, where will the real temple be built? Ask anyone and he will answer: upon the site of Solomon's temple. Search with me and see if this is the scriptural location. It will not be found if it was meant to fill a seeming gap in God's word. Then it is prone to be presumptive and assertive, thus hiding the truth of the word by ending the search for it.

Jews have returned to Jerusalem. Allelujah! This event was unheard of in the annals of Christendom. Only a few had foreseen such an event, but the majority of mankind was unimpressed and did not heed what was taking place. This unseeing generation will see probability of the construction of the temple become imminent practicality. Only there is one little problem—there is a temple already standing on Solomon's old site.

The Mosque of Omar sits on the rock. Arabs built and revere it. This magnificent structure would have to be destroyed to construct Ezekiel's Temple on Solomon's choice land. Should a Jew tear it down, the Arabs would start the fiercest Holy War yet. So, between brothers, what's the hurry? Maybe, as one put it, an earthquake will occur to eliminate the problem. News of a new Jewish Synagogue planned for downtown Jerusalem is even regarded by some as fulfillment of the prophecy.

Yet all the while, the word is clear. Ezekiel did describe the temple's location, but the place he cited is easily overlooked, for it requires diligent study to find it.

The allotment portion runs from the Mediterranean Sea to the Dead Sea and the Jordan River. It is 25,000 cubits from north to south. This is about Four Nautical miles. Located in the allotment portion is the sacred allotment square. This area is the heart of our study.

The allotment square has three significant divisions. Ezekiel's description of them provides the basis for this sketch, which is presented so that you can more readily understand this holy area.

The northern area is for the sanctified sons of Zadok, because they kept the ordinance of the previous temple when the sons of Levi slighted their duty. The temple's sanctuary shall be in this area, a most holy place. It is possible for the temple to be located anywhere in this portion.

The middle area is set aside for the Levites who do remain.

The southern area will have two open spaces of 10,000 cubits, one on either side of a special 5,000 by 5,000 cubit square. On this holy square there shall be a city 4,500 by 4,500cubits. The city permits a clear area of 250 cubits all around it. There are twelve gates to the city, one for each tribe of Israel. The name of the city boldly proclaims, "The Lord Is Here." As we continue to examine the temple's location, we find it is surrounded by a wall which measures 500 reeds on each side. This is a 5,000 by 5,000 foot square, about 443 acres. Ezekiel puts all of it onto the land set apart for the sons of Zadok.

If these scriptures were all we had to consider, there would still be room for the tradition that Mount Moriah will be the site, except our troubles have multiplied, for much more than the Mosque will have to be destroyed. Mount Moriah is only twenty-six acres, so a considerable portion of Jerusalem would have to be razed to clear out the whole area for the temple. But would such a clearing make the site holy?

In man's eye it would be possible. However, God's word will not permit it, for it labels Mount Moriah a profane place. Ezk.43:7-11

While the kings committed harlotry there.

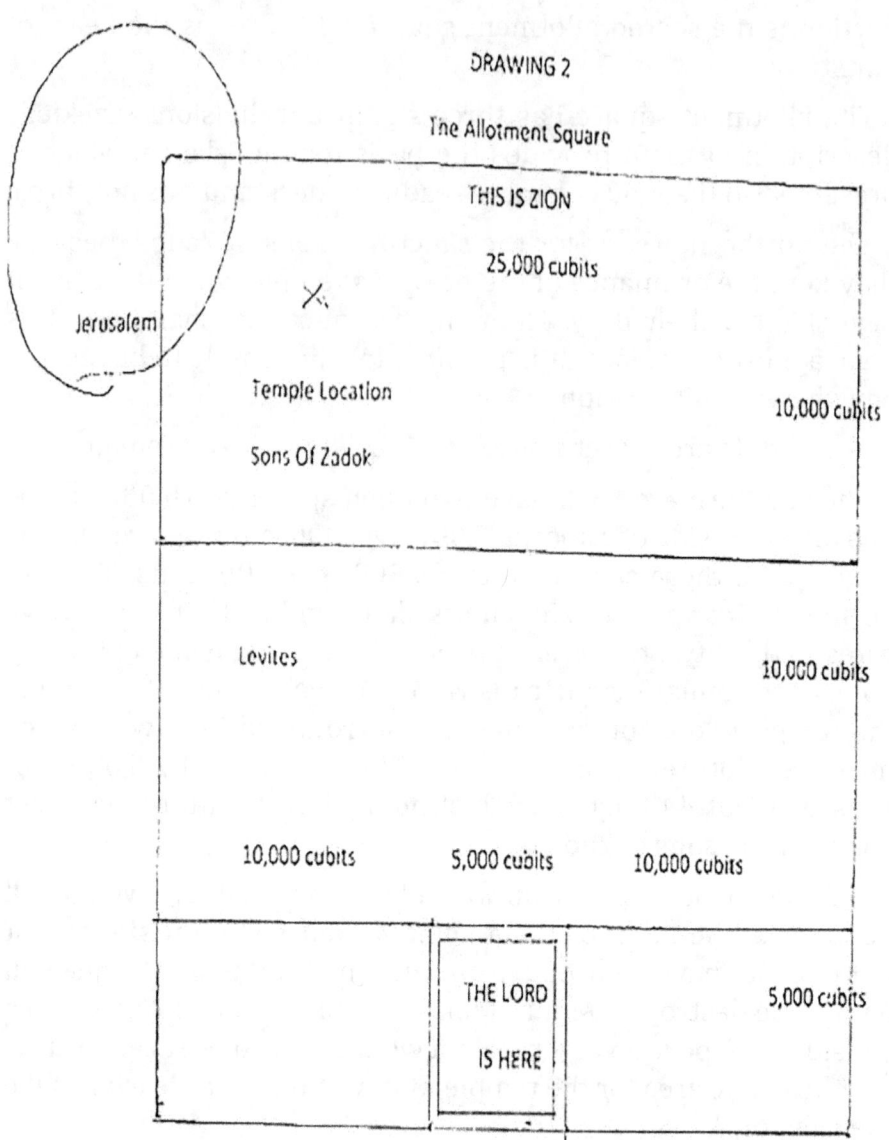

DRAWING 2

The Allotment Square

THIS IS ZION

25,000 cubits

Jerusalem

Temple Location

Sons Of Zadok

10,000 cubits

Levites

10,000 cubits

10,000 cubits   5,000 cubits   10,000 cubits

THE LORD

IS HERE

5,000 cubits

The Lord is There

46

When they expired, their corpses were interred within the temple to proclaim a monument to the dead, instead of leaving holy the dwelling place of the living God. Meanwhile, the people listened to a real-estate promoter who harped upon the necessity of developing the land, until it was built up doorpost to doorpost to the temple and no one could say which house you were going to enter as you walked down the street. Search hard; but still you would not find a better neighbor than the uncomplaining God who lived next door.

Only God was not there, for He could not dwell among iniquity; so the glory of the Lord departed the midst of the city. Ezk. 11:23 Ezekiel's temple will not be built within the city. His location has been consistently overlooked, although he described it before he spoke of the temple. The temple's structure "like a city" will be on the south slope of a mountain in Israel. Ezk.40:2

The terminology, "like a city," will not permit it to be built on the old site, for then it would be surrounded by a city and could not be described as a city set apart. Rather, it is at a new location selected by God Himself, for when the glory of the Lord departed the middle of the city it came to rest over the mountain which is east of the city. The entire area of this mountain from its top all around is most holy. Ezk.43:12

Look no more to Mount Moriah. The Mount of Olives is the scriptural place. This location will bring real meaning to the saying, "My house shall be called a house of prayer" Isa.56:7

The Mount of Olives also has the divine sanction of the life of Christ. This is where Christ went to pray when He was in Jerusalem. Luke 22:39 This was the point where His triumphal ride as the Messiah began. Matt.21:1 This was where He rose from the earth forty days after He rose from the grave. Acts 1:9-12 This is the spot to which He will return as He establishes His kingdom. Zech.14:4

It is of this use for the Mount of Olives that Isaiah writes, "In the last days, the mountain of the house of the Lord will be established as the chief of the mountains, and will be raised above the hills, and all the nations will stream to it. Isa.2: 2 May God permit you to come, pray and worship His holy name, in His house, which will be in front of Jerusalem to the east.

What of the temple itself? When shall it be built? Will it be before or after Christ returns? Again, the Scriptures state the plain truth. The temple will not be built until our Lord returns because it is He who will build it.

Zechariah heard, "Then say to him, 'Thus says the Lord of Hosts, Behold a man who name is Branch, for He will branch out from where He is; and He will build the temple of the Lord. Yes, it is He who will build the temple of the Lord, and He who will bear the honor and sit and rule on His throne, and the counsel of peace will be between the two offices:" Zech 6:12,13

This reference to the Branch does not refer to Joshua or any of his friends. Nor could it refer to the temple that Zerubbabel was going to build.

It is in these areas that we have had our greatest troubles with the prophecies. For instance, when Isaiah spoke about the rebuilding of the temple and the city, it was easy to infer that Cyrus was the one who would fulfill the prophecy. This interpretation disturbed all those people who knew what the rest of the Scriptures contained because the records disclose that Cyrus was only concerned with rebuilding the temple. 2Chron.36:23 He never did issue any decree concerning the rebuilding of Jerusalem.

Woe, woe, woe. Why did God permit such flagrant disobedience from his chosen servant, Cyrus? Isn't He concerned with the exactness of His word? How our troubles multiply when we do not know just what God has planned! We cannot find the truth of this matter until we know the whole of God's plan. Yet Ezekiel has described a new city and temple, and those who love the Lord look forward to it. Isaiah looked ahead to the days of their reality and he spoke of God's righteous one who would rebuild them. Also there is an event coming that would require them to be rebuilt during the reign of Christ, not before He comes. Ezekiel was blameless in recording what he saw. I would be at fault, though, if I did not offer you this further thought. Daniel's seventieth week begins with a peace treaty between Israel, Syria and Iraq. What need is there for a peace treaty if there is no fighting going on? Syria's actions in entering Lebanon and fighting there, when the terrorist leaders were killed, leads me to believe that Syria will not appreciate Israel's takeover of Lebanon. Syria will not sit idly by and watch Lebanon be invaded. She will reason that, if Israel wants to, what will stop her from growing strong enough to annex Syria in the ensuing years? So Syria will fight Israel over, and for, Lebanon, but she will not take it back. Up to this point it is all Syria, but then they see the face that is ruling Iraq. The one who is blind in his right eye and his right arm is useless. They ask him to join in the fight to get Lebanon back, and he does. The peace treaty that will mark the end of this war will also mark the beginning of Daniel's Seventieth Week. This generation will see all these things come to pass.

God is angry at Israel's shortcomings. He is dissatisfied with her lack of concern about fulfilling His commands. This is why Daniel's seventieth week will come upon Israel—the week begins with the treaty signed by a treacherous man who does not regard the God of Israel but magnifies himself as god.

The treachery of this treaty will go beyond the intentions of the Assyrian who signs it, for it will also signify the loss of the power of the witnesses. With it, the witnesses have completely turned from the words of their God to the promises of men. The nation of Israel will believe that peace has come. The peace will be the result of the works of their hands. This will result in a temporary cessation of battle, but a sword will be at their throats because the treaty will not have been the work of their God. Let Israel trust in Him and not in a piece of paper. They seal their doom when they fail to do this.

"And when they have finished their testimony, the beast that comes up out of the abyss will make war with them, overcome them, and kill them." Rev. 11:7

They prophesied, clothed in sackcloth, for 1260 days. Then they were given time to put off their rags of repentance and don the robe of power. Nevertheless, their period for testimony draws to a close and they are killed. They are not assassinated or slain, as the rest of the prophets were because they are not just one or two prophets. They are many. It is necessary for the Antichrist to make war, to fight against many, to kill them. Thus, their testimony comes to a close.

The end is hastened because of the incompetence of the ruler of their nation. For if the ruler of the nation had known at what time of the night the thief was coming, he would have been on the alert and would not have allowed his house to be broken into. Matt.24:43 But he believes in the treaty, not the words of his God, and does not consider an attack to be imminent, even when he sees Egypt begin to provoke Assyria. He may go to sleep with a satisfied soul that night, thinking, "Peace, sweet peace." His restful repose will be rudely interrupted by the insistent pounding of the Assyrian artillery outside his door. His defenses will be breached. The enemy will be within before his presence is known.

Pity poor Israel! The Abomination is standing in their midst. Their national period of great tribulation now begins. Its woes begin with the deaths of many witnesses.

The church—that is, the worldwide association of believers— does not go through Israel's tribulation. This escape is not because they have been taken out of the world; rather, it is due to the limited geographical location in which the tribulation occurs. All the believers in the world do not live in Israel, and it is only this limited host, the holy people of the beautiful land, who are severely persecuted by the Assyrian. This truth is what Gabriel revealed to Daniel when he asked: "Then I desired to know the exact meaning of the fourth beast ... and the meaning of the ten horns that were on its head, and the other horn which came up, and before which three of them fell, namely, that horn which had eyes and a mouth uttering great boasts, and which was larger in appearance than its associates. I kept looking, and the horn was waging war with the saints and overpowering them until Ancient of Days came, and judgment was passed in favor of the saints of the Highest One, and the time arrived when the saints took possession of the kingdom.

"Thus he said; "The fourth beast will be a fourth kingdom on the earth, which will be different from all the other kingdoms, and it will devour the whole earth and tread it down and crush it. As for the ten horns, out of this kingdom ten kings will arise; and another will arise after them, and he will be different from the previous one and will subdue three kings. And he will speak out against the most high and wear down the saints of the Highest One, and he will intend to make alternations in time, times, and half-a-time. But the court will sit for judgment, and his dominion will be taken away, annihilated and destroyed forever. Then the sovereignty, the dominion, and the greatness of all the kingdoms under the whole heaven will be given to the people of the saints of the Highest One; His kingdom will be an everlasting kingdom, and all the dominions will serve and obey Him. Dan.7:19-27

We have already discussed the identity of this little horn which had so bothered Daniel. We scripturally identified the horn as representing the coming Assyrian ruler variously referred to as the Antichrist, The Abomination of Desolation, and the son of destruction. This man is going to gain authority over the saints or witnesses in Israel when he overcomes the three nations of Israel, Egypt, and the Sudan.

When the Assyrian rules over Israel, he will have the power to change the times and the laws by which the Jews live and worship. Those who survive his rule will exist under him for times, time, and half-a-time, or a three-and-one-half-year period. This is a literal earth period. It is the last literal one to be mentioned by Daniel and John as they relay the time sequence of the Second Coming. The 2300-day time period, which marked the time switch to the heavenly calendar, was the next one to be mentioned.

When this earth period of three and one-half years is converted to the heavenly standard, it becomes known as three and one-half days, and this how it is cited for the rest of the story. It is the last half of the seventieth week, the time when the Assyrian will rule over Israel. During this time, he will cause many deaths and much suffering.

It is of this period that Christ said that one half the population of Jerusalem would die, killed by the flood of Assyrians overflowing their country. Matt.24:37-43. Zechariah also supports this view as he says, "For I will gather all the nations against Jerusalem to battle, and the city will be captured, the houses plundered, the women ravished, and half of the city exiled, but the rest of the people will not be cut off from the city." Zech.14:2

When all the nations referred to come against Jerusalem, the fighting will be fierce. The Jews will fight to defend their city. Their enemies will have to be strong to overcome them. They will be strong, though, and they will capture the city, killing many. The half that will be exiled will be those banished from the city by death, having perished in the fighting.

A terrible aspect of their demise will be the type of weaponry that will be used against them. The Assyrian will have paid a great sum from his national treasury to purchase these weapons from the god of fortresses whom he honors. Dan.11:38 This type of weaponry is among the most horrible that mankind has ever devised. Its effects are foretold in two significant announcements of woe. The first is, "Woe to those who are with child and to those who nurse babes in those days!" Matt.24:19 The second is "And their dead bodies will lie in the street of the great city which mystically is called Sodom and Egypt, where also their Lord was crucified. And those from the people and tribes and tongues and nations will look at their dead bodies for three days and a half, and will not permit their dead bodies to be laid in a tomb. Rev.11:8,9

The reason for both of these statements lies in the ability of these weapons to pollute long after they are expended, because their explosion releases great amounts of radioactivity. The greatest fear expressed by two famous scientists in their report on the case against nuclear power plants is based on the genetic damage radiation causes. (John W. Goffman and Arthur Tamplin:Poisoned Power) This damage will be quickly apparent in the newly born and the fear of deformities will be ever present in expectant mothers.

The radiation will also prevent anyone from coming near the dead bodies to bury them. Anyone who would come would receive a sufficient amount of radiation to cause his own death within a short time. A burial detail would have to have the proper protective clothing and equipment to protect their lives. However, the Assyrian will not care to spend his money for this aspect of warfare.

So the witnesses—that is, a great many Jews—will die and remain unburied. The Assyrian may not care but God will. He will extend mercy to these Jews.

"And after the three days and a half, the breath of life from God came into them, and they stood on their feet; and great fear fell upon those who were beholding them. And they heard a loud voice from heaven saying to them, 'Come up here: And they went up into heaven in the cloud, and their enemies beheld them. And in that hour there was a great earthquake, and a tenth of the city fell; and seven thousand people were killed in the earthquake, and the rest were terrified and gave glory to the God of heaven. Rev.11:11-13

Israel's tribulation will be over. The testimony of the witnesses will be complete. A partial Resurrection will bring them into the presence of God.

It is my hope that the 7000 who will be killed in the earthquake that will destroy one tenth of the city will belong to the army of Assyrian, who will be camped on the mountain to the east.

Here then is how Daniel framed prophecy.

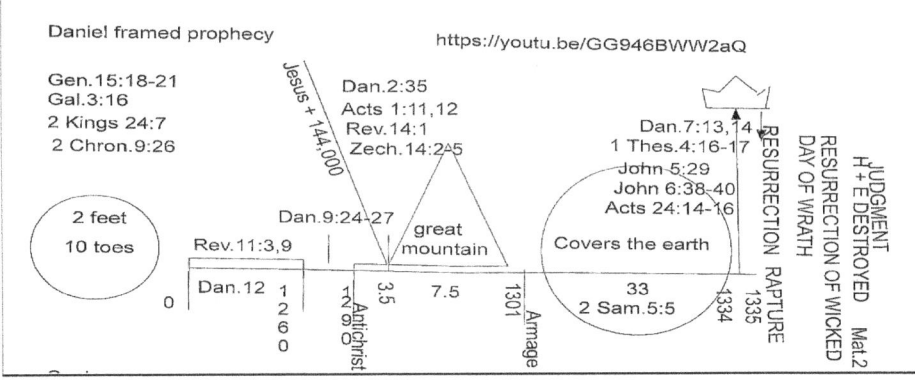

CHAPTER III

The Assyrian

"Now it will come about in that day that the remnant of Israel, and those of the house of Jacob who have escaped, will never again rely on the one who struck them, but will truly rely on the Lord, the Holy One of Israel": Isaiah 10:20

Ateacher must know what to teach and how he is to instruct before he will ever succeed in that subject. When we look closely at what most modern teachers instruct about the events and personalities of the scriptural references concerning the Last Days, we discover a unique approach. It is different from the usual approach to all other theological and Biblical studies in that preachers are able to find personal relevant, effectual application for nearly everything the Bible contains. But they approach this subject with the attitude that there is no personal application for these scriptures and so it is not necessary for them or anyone else to understand them. They acknowledge that they do not understand these scriptures and have no hope that anyone will.

It has become convenient to group all these obscure events into a period referred to as Daniel's Seventieth Week or Israel's Tribulation, then further instruction is discouraged because none of these events are pertinent. You see, all the Christians are going to be taken out of all this trouble. So, since it does not apply to you or me why should we be concerned with it? If no Christian is able to be concerned, how could any sinner ever be? Faith comes by hearing and hearing by the word of God. Romans 10:17 What then does the word of God contain?

The Scriptures refer to the Assyrian, the fierce horn, the cruel master, the Abomination of Desolation, the Antichrist, the son of destruction, and still more. How can one hope to ever understand what so many people are going to do? When this is our approach, all we can find is confusion. But if we say that, in assessing all that the prophets speak about one man, there is indeed just clarification from each prophet's segment, then indeed we can begin to find order, insight, and understanding of what God's word proclaims.

This approach has assured us that Rome will not revive. If not Rome, then of what do the Scriptures speak? Do we just destroy one tradition and leave a vacuum? If there was no hope, this book would never have been written. In a vacuum, nothing exists. Yet the Scriptures are something; they speak of positive events and a singular person. They cannot produce a vacuum. Their systematic study may reveal much about the Assyrian.

The visions have already taught us that four kingdoms will rule over a special part of the earth. They identify the fourth kingdom as the Medes and the Persians. Ten nations will rise from the boundaries of this empire in the period known as the Last Days. Then a fierce king is going to arise among these ten and overcome three of them.

The visions relayed how the goat (Greeks) killed the ram (Medes and Persians). They described how the goat trampled on all the pieces of the ram, occupying all the ram had ruled. They foretold that at the death of Greece's first king his kingdom would be split into four parts. Then they explained that a fierce king would come from the northern or Seleucid division and named him as the Assyrian.

Many scriptures discuss the singular nature, personality, and activity of the man who is to be the Antichrist. Most current theological reports on these scriptures include a note for the reader not to confuse the Antichrist with the Assyrian. Other than this passing reference, no real study has been done to clarify who the Assyrian is or why he is even mentioned. It is impossible to understand fully the Antichrist until we understand the Assyrian.

The tradition of Rome's revival has misdirected this search of the Scriptures and bears the responsibility for this lack of information.

Since the Antichrist is supposed to be a Roman, what need is there to apply the scripture about the Assyrian to the same time period as that of the Antichrist? It only leads to confusion. One man can't have two nationalities, so why bother?

The Antichrist will not be a Roman. The scriptures give him only one nationality—that is, Assyrian! Failure to note this equivalence can only lead to the conclusion that two different kings will attack Israel during the same time period. Both must then be individually successful over Israel.

Greater meaning comes to the term Assyrian when we reconsider the resurrected ram with its two horns. We know one horn stands for one king, so these two horns represent two kings. One of them is the king of Syria. Syria is but a portion of Assyria, so the other horn must stand for the rest of the territory subsumed under this term. Now we can begin to appreciate why Babylon reemerged in Revelation. It takes modern Babylon—Iraq—plus Syria, to give full meaning to the word Assyria.

It will take the political union of Iraq and Syria, led by the king of Assyria, for the devil to become strong enough to pluck out three of those ten nations.

It is unfortunate that we have not previously known these things from the Scriptures, but another tradition has prevented it. Some have taught and still teach that Babylon was a code word that John used to mean Rome. This teaching implies that when God told John to say Rome, John said Babylon because he was afraid of Roman retribution. John was already a prisoner of Rome. Therefore, he lied about what God wanted him to speak because he was afraid of further punishment. Belief that John lied so blatantly completely demolishes all that the Book of Revelation discloses. Thus it can't be understood, for it is the work of a man and not his God. Also, since it was written by a liar, how can you expect to believe or understand anything it contains? Where else did John lie? I cannot find that he did. John spoke exactly as God wanted him to speak. May the understanding this book provides enable those teachers to lay aside their traditions that detract from the glory and exactness of God's word.

In all of God's word there is but one name given that ties the Antichrist to a nation and that name is the Assyrian. The Devil's attempts to shroud this fact has resulted in much searching and twisting of the Scriptures, so everyone will have eyes and mind directed toward Rome. All searching of the Scriptures to prove that basic assertion was thus misdirected. However, God's Spirit is a Spirit of Truth and in His sure course the meaning of His words has come to you. Rome shall not revive! A portion of the kingdom of Assyria shall.

What else can we learn from the Scriptures about this man? Will his background be completely Syrian? Or will he also be a Jew, as others have stated from their studies of the Scriptures that he would be? Daniel said, "And he will show no regard for the gods of his fathers or for the desire of women, nor will he show regard for any other god; for he will magnify himself above them all." Dan.11:37 This means that since he does not regard the god of his fathers, namely Abraham, Isaac, and Jacob, that he has to be a Jew. This is further reinforced by the way he disregards the desire of the Jewish women to be the mother of the Messiah, since Christ is not commonly recognized as being the one that was promised to them. So young Jewish women still have this hope of being the Messiah's mother. This idea of his being a Jew is reinforced by the words of Zechariah, "Woe to the worthless shepherd who leaves the flock!" Zech.11:17

Was this man singled out because he was going to leave the nation of Assyria, which he ruled over, in order to attack the other three nations? Or is this passage instead informing us that he left Jewish beliefs in order to rule over Assyria? Besides describing this man's religious disassociations, Zechariah also io provides a physical description. "A sword will be on his arm and on his right eye. His arm will be totally withered, and his right eye will be blind." This is the appearance of the Assyrian ruler that the world must look out for—a man physically handicapped and spiritually muddled.

He will not come to power in a time of peace but in a time of turmoil. The Middle East, which knows no peace, will see none. The turmoil will increase until Israel is forced to take over the nation of Lebanon to stop the terrorists activities. When Israel does occupy Lebanon the ten nations will begin to exist, for at that time only ten nations will remain between the Nile and the Euphrates. The Antichrist, the Assyrian, will then be allowed to come into power.

This fighting will continue between the Arabs and the Jews until the peace treaty between Israel and Assyria signals the start of Daniel's seventieth week; the start of the Last Seven prophesied years before Christ comes and the world will say, "Peace, Peace!"

Jeremiah called this peace one of treachery. He said, "Ah, Lord God! Surely Thou has utterly deceived this people and Jerusalem, saying, 'You will have peace'; whereas a sword touches the throat." Jer.4:10-11 A sword does touch the throat, a sword of treachery, held in the hand of the Assyrian.

Daniel records this period as follows: "And he will make a firm covenant with the many for one week, but in the middle of the week he will put a stop to sacrifice and grain offerings and on the wing of abominations will come one who makes desolate, even until a complete destruction, one that is decreed, is poured out on the one who makes desolate." Dan.9:27

The nation of Israel will live in this period of false hopes until the middle of the week. Then this peace will be shattered by fighting among their Arab neighbors. "And at the end time, the king of the south (Egypt) will collide with him; and the king of the north (Assyria) will storm against him with chariots, with horsemen, and with many ships; and he will enter countries, overflow them, and pass through ... He will also enter the beautiful land, and many countries will fall; but these will be rescued out of his hand: Edom, Moab, and the foremost of the children of Ammon." Dan.11:40-41

So, in the middle of the seventieth week, Egypt begins the strife that rouses the Assyrian to attack in order to repay this affront. Look at the point where the attack originates and consider the route which he follows. He enters the beautiful land, or Israel. Therefore, he has to be a close neighbor, for how could Israel expect peace if the treaty was not signed with a neighbor? It is the Jews and the Arabs who are fighting!

Nevertheless, this Assyrian does not proceed directly into Israel, for the northern border is well guarded. Instead, he uses a route that is much easier and goes right to the heart of Israel. He uses the route of the passerby, that is, the way of the people who traveled by land around the Mediterranean Sea. A part of this route goes east from Jerusalem by the Mount of Olives, across the Jordan River, then turns north towards Damascus. This is the route the Assyrian will follow, but he will travel it in reverse. This is the reason the foremost of the children of Ammon escape from his path, as he cuts across the north-western part of the nation of Jordan, going directly to Jerusalem. That is why the rest of Jordan (which is the nation of the children of Ammon) and Edom and Moab (the people to the east and south of the Dead Sea), escape his wrath. It is his purpose to go to Egypt, and he must cross Israel to get there.

Christ explained the next events very clearly. He said, "Therefore, when you see the Abomination of Desolation which was spoken of through Daniel the prophet, standing in the holy place (let the reader understand), then let those who are in Judea flee to the mountains; let him who is on the housetop not go down to get the things out that are in his house; and let him who is in the field not turn back to get his cloak. But woe to those who are with child and to those who nurse babes in those days! But pray that your flight may not be in the winter, or on a Sabbath; for then there will be a great tribulation, such as has not occurred since the beginning of the world until now, nor ever shall. And unless those days had been cut short, no life would have been saved; but for the sake of the elect those days shall be cut short." Matt.24:15-22

This period of great tribulation for Israel begins when the Antichrist, the Abomination of Desolation, the Assyrian himself, stands in the holy place. The holy place is widely regarded as being in the rebuilt temple. But this viewpoint is based on superficial study of the Scriptures and lacks the insight provided by the vision of all the prophets. Nevertheless, this passage is used to proclaim that the new temple must be built upon Mount Moriah, and that the Mosque of Omar, which currently stands there, must be torn down. Only in this way could the Assyrian possibly stand in the holy place in the temple.

Paul seems to support this view when he says, "Now we request you, brethren, with regard to the coming of the Lord Jesus Christ, and our gathering together to Him, that you may not be quickly shaken from your composure or be disturbed, either by a spirit or a message or a letter as if from us, to the effect that the day of the Lord has come. Let no one in any way deceive you, for it will not come unless the apostasy comes first, and the man of lawlessness is revealed, the son of destruction, who opposes and exalts himself above every so-called god or object of worship, so that he takes his seat in the temple of God, displaying himself as being God." 2 Thess.2:1-4

The Assyrian then will seek to exalt himself as the highest object of worship, and he will take his seat in the temple of God, which is not necessarily Ezekiel's temple. Nor need it be a building for Daniel 8:11 only requires the overthrow of the place of the sanctuary, not the sanctuary itself.

Just what do the Scriptures record of Satan's plan? Isaiah said, "How you have fallen from heaven, O, star of the morning, son of the dawn! You have been cut down to the earth, you who have weakened the nations! But you said in your heart, I will ascend to heaven; I will raise my throne above the stars of God, and I will sit on the mount of assembly in the recesses of the north. I will ascend above the heights of the clouds; I will make myself like the Most High." Isa.14:12,13

Our earlier study showed that the location of Ezekiel's temple was to be on the uplifted south slope of the Mount of Olives. Ezekiel also explained that, according to law, the whole top of this mountain was the most holy place. Ezk.43:12 Lucifer intends to establish his throne on its north side with the aid of the Assyrian, who will encamp upon the most holy place.

60

The new temple will not be built there before Christ comes. The Assyrian will not enter the actual building. Paul told the Thessalonians that the Lord will not come before the son of destruction, the Abomination of Desolation is revealed. Neither will we be raptured, or gathered to the Lord, before he is revealed. Therefore, when we understand these additional words of Zechariah, we know that the temple is not built until after Christ returns. "Then say to him, thus says the Lord of hosts, 'Behold a man whose name is Branch, for He will branch out from where He is; and He will build the temple of the Lord. Yes, it is He who will build the temple of the Lord, and He who will bear the honor and sit and rule on His throne. Thus, He will be a priest on His throne, and the counsel of peace will be between the two offices:" Zech.6:12,13

The temple will not be built until after Christ returns for Christ Himself shall build it, and all the Assyrian will have to stand upon will be the Mount of Olives itself. When this occurs, Israel had better look out. It will be even as Christ said, "For the coming of the Son of Man will be just like the days of Noah. For as in those days which were before the flood they were eating and drinking, they were marrying and giving in marriage, until the day that Noah entered the ark, and they did not understand until the flood came and took them all away, so shall the coming of the Son of Man be. Then there shall be two men in the field; one will be taken, and one will be left. Two women will be grinding at the mill; one will be taken, and one will be left. Therefore be on the alert, for you do not know which day your Lord is coming. But be sure of this, that if the head of the house had known at what time of the night the thief was coming, he would have been on the alert and would not have allowed his house to be broken into." Matt24:37-43

This passage is not a description of the Rapture, as some have inferred. To see its truth, we must understand what happened to the people in Noah's day. When the flood came, they were taken away, not by the Rapture, but into the captivity of death. The only people left were those the Lord held dear. Death is what is coming upon Israel. Two thirds of its people will also be taken away by death, caused by the overflowing army of the Assyrian. Zechariah 13:8

This is why, when the Assyrian crosses the Jordan River and stands upon the Mount to the east of Jerusalem, the inhabitants are called upon to flee.

The resistance of Israel will come too late to stop the onslaught of the Assyrian's army. It is God's plan that the Assyrian will continue on through the nation. Daniel said, ""then he will stretch out his hand against other countries, and the land of Egypt will not escape. But he will gain control over the hidden treasures of gold and silver, and over all the precious things of Egypt; and Libyans and Ethiopians will follow (or rather be) at his heels." Dan.11:42,43

What is the purpose of this battle of the Assyrian? Daniel stated that it was to pluck out and take over three other nations. Two of these nations are directly named in the Scriptures, Israel and Egypt. It is now easy to identify the third one.

When the Assyrian enters Egypt, he will split his army into two parts and plunder all the treasures of Egypt. One part of his force will go toward Ethiopia. One part of his force will go west toward Libya. Each section of his army will then be poised at the borders of these two nations, ready to step across. Now, Libya borders Egypt directly on the west. However, Ethiopia does not border Egypt at all. The nation called Sudan is between them. Then, if his army is to cross into Ethiopia, it will be treading upon the Sudan. But before his armies go on, for this is the Assyrian's intention, he will receive some very bad news.

"But rumors from the East and from the North will disturb him, and he will go forth with great wrath to destroy and annihilate many. And he will pitch the tents of his royal pavilion between the seas and the beautiful holy mountain; yet he will come to his end and no one will help him." Dan.11:44,45

The nations that yelled, "Peace, peace, at last" will only look in shock, as the Middle East once more erupts into warfare. They will be powerless to do anything but watch, because this sequence of events will not take long. Zechariah times it. "Then I annihilated three shepherds in one month, for My soul was impatient with them, and their soul also was weary of Me." Then I said, "I will not pasture you. What is to die, let it die, and what is to be annihilated, let it be annihilated; and let those who are left eat one another's flesh." Zech.11:8,9

Fortunately, though, two nations do have influence over this Man. Nations from the east and north interfere with his actions. They are the ones referred to as "the god of fortresses." They will be the nations to which this man paid his gold and silver; costly stones and treasures. He did it in order to obtain their weapons.

The United States reacted when Cuba obtained these same weapons, but will the world know or care when the Assyrian obtains them?

Tidings eventually will reach the ears of the Assyrian. This is an approximation of what he will hear: "We are glad that you removed the power of the thorn of Israel. We are pleased that you have quieted the impertinent nation of Egypt. But we are concerned that you have taken over the Sudan also, and wonder when you intend to stop. We have reserved the continent of Africa for ourselves in our plan of world conquest. Therefore, we bid you to stop. We have supplied you with our weapons of war. If you continue, we will withdraw them from you. If you continue, we will also stop you ourselves. Keep what you have, but go back home."

So in anger, he will rejoin his armies, destroying anyone and anything that strikes his fancy. He will set up his new operations headquarters on the north side of the Mount of Olives. This will be his location when the seventieth week ends. This is where he will meet his death from a sword not wielded by a man. Isa.31:8,9

WHY DO YOU KEEP USING THE NAME OF A MAN WHO IS ALREADY DEAD?

I watched the same news you saw. I saw him surrender from a hole in the ground. I watched the trial. I heard him sentenced to death by hanging. But this I know from Isaiah chapter 14. He is called the king of Babylon. He was rejected by his grave. He despoiled his country. He killed his own country men. And a place of slaughter was prepared for his sons. HE WAS DEAD WHEN THE ROPE WAS REMOVED, BUT HE WAS PLACED IN A TRAUMA RECOVERY UNIT AND RESTORED TO LIFE. Also he had a body double who has not been seen again since the day the lid on the coffin was nailed shut.

When Syria is kicked out of Lebanon, the Syrians will seek him out and ask him if he will help them fight their common enemy. He is more than happy to join forces with them to fight Israel. So I say,"SADDAM HUSSEIN IT IS TIME FOR YOU TO SHOW YOUR FACE TO THE WORLD AGAIN. YOUR TIME HAS COME!"

CHAPTER IV

Locusts, Living Beings and Cherubin

Bring up the horses like bristly locusts. (Jer.51:27)

God has a special purpose and calling for every person who is born upon this earth. It is his purpose and calling, so he comes near to present every individual with that person's particular service.

When my uncle Ray (a God-fearing man) returned from World War II, he spoke to my father about the Lord Jesus. An organization known as Youth for Christ was about to hold a rally in the Cudahy and Silverdale area of Wisconsin, so my uncle urged my father to come and bring the family. We all went.

That night, at the age of seven, I went forward and met the Lord He became my spiritual father as I was born again. This was the only conversion of any of his children which my father witnessed. I will be forever grateful to my uncle, and to his caring persistence. Even more now that I have witnessed the salvation of my children.

We attended services at Grace Chapel in Silverdale I enjoyed singing songs and memorizing Bible verses. That winter one of the men of the church, Mr. Brach, came to the house and asked my father if you would permit him to take me shopping for a suit. My father was proud, but he knew I did not have any clothes for the winter. So, because of a child's necessity, he allowed Mr. Brach to take me shopping with him.

For the first time in my life I was to receive a new item of clothing, and not just another hand-me-down. (I was the fifth child of seven children.) I skipped along the sidewalk with him for the entire mile or two we traveled.

Mr. Brach bought me a blue wool suit. On that day, the gift was all could think about for the joy of having it. Today I can fully appreciate the kindness and generosity that motivated him to buy a gift for me. Over time the gift was worn out and outgrown. Eventually it perished, but the kindness of the man of God will live on and the memory of what he did will be passed on to others.

Life goes on. We moved. Mother sought a new church. Its motto was, "The church that preaches what the Bible teaches." when I was 12, John Rogers, a man concerned with the development of young people, gave me my first Bible, at the East Troy Bible Church in East Troy, Wisconsin. I read it and reread it. I studied portions which were of interest to me. It was not the only book I read, yet its influence was so pervasive that my high school teacher could recognize, by my hand in assignments, that the King James English had become foundational structure of my sentence arrangement.

When I was 16, John's locusts of Revelation chapter 9 came alive. To me, it seems as though I knew what he had described. It was so real to me, I thought it was common knowledge for everyone and I never mentioned it. It was significant to me and started my search for understanding. When I was 30, and home on leave, I went to church with an older sister, Sandra. The Bible class was going to study in Revelation chapter 9, that very day; so I asked them if they would let me teach the class. They were kind enough to let me do so. This provided my first opportunity to teach the locusts identity. The class marveled to see what the locusts look like. Then they began to ask questions about other items in the Bible. Suddenly aware of how much I did not know, even after 18 years of reading the Bible, I proposed in my heart to seek the answers I could not give. I found that I had a good knowledge of all that the Bible contained, except for the book of Revelation.

When I returned home, I raced through the Scriptures from Psalms to Revelation, looking for any passages speaking of things to come. I put them into the groupings they spoke of. Then for the next two years I studied to find and categorize all the Scriptures which spoke of things to come. The Scripture would prompt a question and I would go seeking the answer This search would prompt new questions before the answer was found. Then the search for other answers would begin. Finally, I could clearly see what the Scriptures present as a last days scenario. I published my first book The Vision of All in 1979 to proclaim the sequence of prophetic events. I merged that book into this one, to provide a complete portrayal of prophetic events.

Are we in the last days? Yes, you may say. Do you understand the plan of God in prophecy? No. You know any preacher who does? Do not answer that. Just examine the attitude he displays as he teaches his messages of Bible prophecy. Probably he clearly admits that he does not understand the overall picture of events, but he is sure that the Lord will return. You listen attentively no matter what his message. Yet he does not know, so you don't either.

The Old Testament prophet Jeremiah said, "the anger of the Lord will not turn back until he has performed and carried out the purposes of his heart; in the last days you will clearly understand it." Jeremiah 23:20 Now, through the pages of this book someone comes and says, I clearly understand. It is God's time and it still took me years to study the Scriptures. I don't expect you to fully comprehend everything with just one reading. I simply ask you to do your part. Open your mind and try to understand what these pages teach. So let us examine John's locusts and see the bugs whose eyes give understanding.

John's locusts

A test of the worth of any study of the book of Revelation is based on the careful attention given to seek the literal meaning of the passages. Most works fail to attain this standard because more imagination than care is applied to the words. The real problem may be that we have not considered how it is possible for a prophet to intelligently describe to us in terms of our knowledge just what it was that he envisioned. It is evident that a man who lived 2000 years ago would have difficulty in verbally portraying the appearance, the skill needed to use, and the purpose for almost any item invented since the turn of the 20th century. Yet, in the visions of the last days, the prophets had to see every item visible to the eye. God did not censure the visions.

The prophet was faced with an almost insurmountable problem. Although the vision was the best documentary presentation ever seen, it did not go into specifics for any of the items the prophet saw.

No name was mentioned for any mechanical contrivance. If a name was spoken for a thing, the word would have no meaning to the prophet or to his generation, for the thing was not yet in existence. Therefore the prophet could not pick a name, but he had to diligently attempt to describe it. Only in this fashion could anyone in the future hope to understand what the man of God was saying. God only asked, "What do you see?" He never told the prophet what it was.

So let us approach this task by looking at what the man knew and trying to see how he applied this to his writing. Then we stand a chance of seeing the objects which his words attempt to describe. Then we will appreciate the difficulty of his task and God's necessity to preserve seemingly useless information so that it would arrive intact to this generation.

Revelation nine describes a part of the trumpet judgments. Four trumpets have already blown. We will study them presently, but for now we want to present the eye-opener for four different men: John, Ezekiel, Joel, and Jeremiah.

The fifth angel blew his trumpet and a presentation was made to star already present on the Earth. In John's writing a star was a symbol which represented an angel. Revelation 1:20. This particular star represented Satan, who is also called Lucifer because he shown with heavenly brilliance. He was called "the star of the morning, son of the Dawn." His fall from heaven was lamented for he sought to weaken the Earth. Isaiah 14:12. The

Lord was present at his fall, for he said, "I was watching Satan fall from heaven like lightning." Luke 10:18

Satan is called the fallen Angel because he rebelled against God and was driven from heaven. John writes, "and there was war in heaven, Michael and his Angels waging war with the Dragon. And the Dragon and his Angels waged war, and they were not strong enough, and there was no longer a place found for them in heaven.

"And the great Dragon was thrown down, the serpent of old who is called the devil and Satan, who deceives the whole world; he was thrown down to the Earth, and his Angels were thrown down with him.) Revelation 12:7-9.

So the presentation was made to the Angel Satan who was already upon this Earth. At God's appropriate time, he was given the key to the bottomless pit. The bottomless pit is something which can never be filled up without ever changing its size. In the Scriptures only greed is given this status. Jesus taught, "beware, and be on your guard against every form of greed; for not even when one has an abundance does his life consist of his possessions" Luke 12:15 So the bottomless pit is a storehouse of the items to lust after, which have not yet been made manifest upon the Earth. Receiving the key Satan mused, it's about time, I know my time is running short and I need to give the eyes something to feast upon. So taking the key, John tells us that he opened the bottomless pit, and smoke went up out of the pit, like the smoke of a great furnace; and the sun and the air were darkened by the smoke of the pit. And out of this smoke came forth locusts upon the Earth, and power was given to them as the Scorpions of the earth have power. Revelation 9:2,3

Did John know what a furnace was? Probably not, you guess. Yet the Scriptures speak of how the Lord brought Israel out of the iron furnace, out of Egypt. Deuteronomy 4:20. Since iron working was a skill known to Egypt, John would have known what a furnace was. He would know of fire hot enough to melt the metal ore and to keep it molten long enough to fashion something from it. When the furnace was being used, the furnace would produce a dense smoke. Whatever the purpose of the furnace, its product came out of the smoke, out of the fashioning process. Yes, John knew what a furnace was. But how big was the biggest furnace he had ever seen? It was nothing to compare with this great furnace which was polluting the air. What he saw was a furnace being used to manufacture something; something which he likened to a locust, for he did not know its name.

What does a locust look like, and what are the lifestyles of the actual insects? Its body is shaped like the end of your thumb brittle shell, large glassy eyes, and some have wings and can fly. They can also make a high-pitched ringing sound when the urge comes upon them. The majority of its life 7, 10, or 21 years, is spent below the ground grubbing for existence. Then it emerges for a short 1 to 3 month period as the mature pest we recognize, hopefully in numbers we can count.

Insects are not born in furnaces that are operating, so the product of the furnace could not have been an insect. And, to this end, John specifically states that they are not alive, for they do not have the insects voracious appetite. John said, "and they were told that they should not hurt the grass of the earth, nor any green thing, nor any tree, but only the men who do not have the seal of God on their foreheads." Revelation 9:4

So what John was describing was not born or hatched, but manufactured into existence, specifically created to hurt men of two possible groups: one group of mankind has the seal of God protecting them, the other group does not. Just what is this seal of God and how is it obtained? When you search for this concept, one Scripture stands out.

"Hear, O Israel! The Lord is our God, the Lord is one! And you shall love the Lord your God with all your heart and with all your soul and with all your might. And these words, which I am commanding you today, shall be on your heart; and you shall teach them diligently to your sons and shall talk of them when you sit in your house and when you walk by the way and when you lie down and when you rise up. And you shall bind them as a sign on your hand and they shall be as frontals on your forehead. And you shall write them on the doorposts of your house and on your gates." Deuteronomy 6:4-9

This code of responsible action towards God's word and love is the only way an individual can attain unto God's good housekeeping seal of approval. What it takes is a consummate loving effort to preserve and promulgate God's words through one's life, moment by moment, day added to days, and years multiplying in his service. Do you know anyone who measures up? Therefore, not everyone in God's family is protected from this power to hurt. The protection applies to those with more than just a religion of convenience. The seal is not a garment you put on when you leave your house. It is not the tattoo of a signet ring. It's the inward love which extends outward.

Consider the locusts power, "and they were not permitted to kill anyone, but to torment for five months; and their torment was like the torment of the scorpion when it stings a man. And in those days men will seek death will not find it; and they will long to die and death flees from them. Revelation 9:5,6.

These locusts can hurt severely, but they are never held responsible for anyone's death. The duration of their power is not reckoned on Earth's calendar but on the heavenly calendar, which we shall study in the heavenly days chapter.

We are told that "the appearance of the locusts was like horses prepared for battle." John 9:7

How does one compare a locust with the horse? If one is discussing size, there is no comparison. But John is not talking about an insect here; rather, he is talking about something made in the furnace. John is saying this thing he likened to an insect is as big as the horse. Like the Roman warhorse, it also has armor plating from side to side, from front to back, and from top to bottom. It also performs the function of the horse: it is a beast of burden, a means of transportation, and a vehicle of war. As they come close to John, he is able to describe more clearly all of their features.

He writes, "and on their heads, as it were, crowns like gold." Revelation 9:7

Gold has always been considered a precious metal because of its unique characteristics and its rarity. Almost every atom of impurity can be removed from it. It is a soft metal. It can be readily fashioned into any form. Most important of all, it never tarnishes, but shines continually. So a crown like gold could be made out of any substance, but it must possess an inherent shine. John continues: "and their faces were like the faces of men. And they had hair like the hair of women, and their teeth were like the teeth of lions." Revelation 9:7,8

When in human history, has biology recorded any human head which was separated from or connected to anything but a human body? In times past, heads have been severed from their bodies, resulting in an immediate cessation of life for both head and body. Headless bodies do not move around, nor do bodiless heads. Nor have the supporters of this theory of evolution ever found a human head on inhuman body. Yes, John saw a human face, for there's nothing else on earth like one. As they approached within 50 feet, under the shiny crown, in the glass eye, John saw a human face suddenly appear. The face also had a body connected to it, but the construction of this entity from the furnace prevented him from seeing the rest of the body. John could also see the hair distinction of the male-female difference; but without the confirming evidence of the rest of the body, John could not state a gender.

Then John saw the teeth of these people. My, how white and shiny! Never in any of his days had John Ever Seen an Actual Living Person with these Pearly White Teeth. They were as clean and white as a lion's. The Bible gives only two reasons for white teeth: you got white teeth from much use of milk; or the Lord gave you clean teeth in the middle of the famine. Genesis 49:12; Amos 4:6

John continued, "and they had breast plates like breast plates of iron; and the sound of their wings was like the sound of chariots, of many horses rushing to battle." Revelation 9:9 The reason John could not comment upon the body now becomes clear. The body was protected by a breast plate which looked like iron.

Concentrate upon the picture described by John. Imagine a crown over the heads, and the body protected, like the warhorse, by the breast plates in front, back, and on both sides: breast plates like iron. One could walk up to this locust, conceived in fashioned in the furnace, and rap it with his knuckles. Then it would give off the ringing sound, common to iron. That sounds like iron. But it has a protective coating over the iron which John had never seen before, it was painted. John had never seen iron any color but natural color. He did not know enough to ascribe the shine to the paint the glass and chrome. If John had also been an artist, he might have painted a picture like this of one of his locusts.

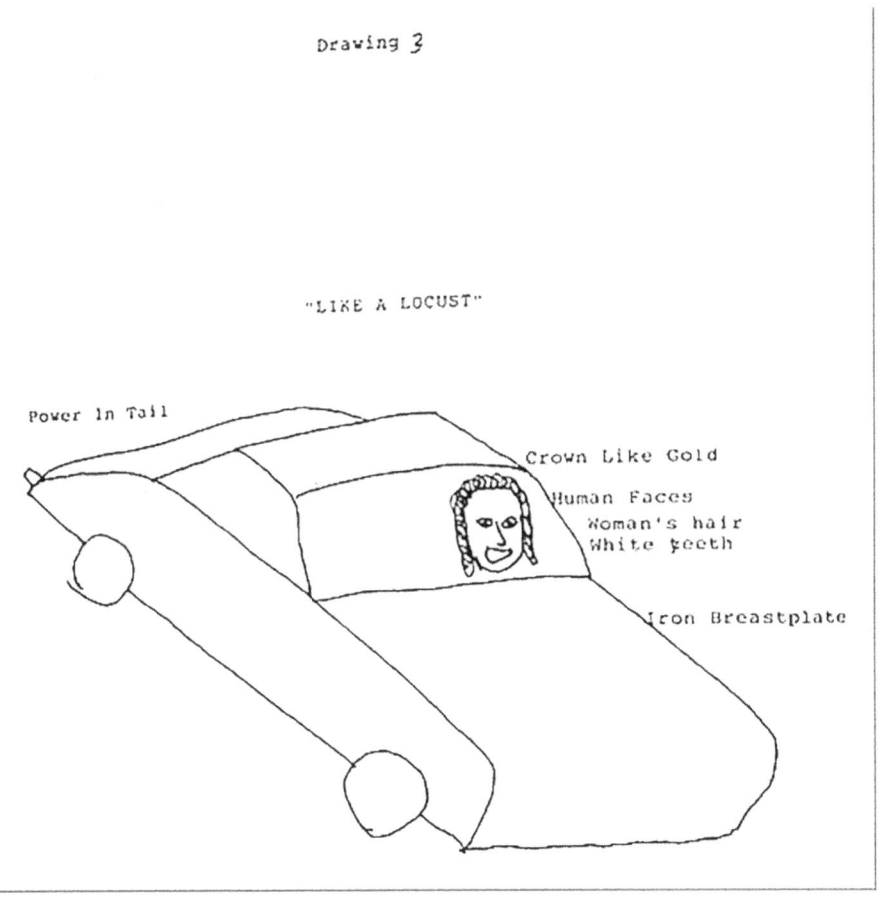

Drawing 3

"LIKE A LOCUST"

Power In Tail

Crown Like Gold

Human Faces
Woman's hair
White teeth

Iron Breastplate

This picture would show John's locust to be man's modern means of land transportation: the car, truck, bus, train, and airplane.

Are you astonished at this? Or do you, perhaps, laugh at this concept? Go backwards in time, you contemporary man, and in the language and knowledge of 2000 years ago, describe an automobile more clearly than this passage does, to Peter. Then by your verbal description expect Peter to understand what you're talking about. Peter's reaction to such an affront might bring him right to the verge of exorcising that evil spirit which he perceives to be in you.

John did not understand what he saw in the vision. Off in the distance it looks like something round and pudgy. It had a brilliant exterior, and large glassy eyes. It was as big as the horse grazing in the field. With awe he witnesses the distinctive Doppler effect of its sounds as it approaches and passes by. Coming within 50 feet, John sees human faces through the glassy eye. Some of the heads display a full womanly head of hair. All who smile present their white teeth, as they go by. Then John is made aware of the power their tails possess as he locates the source of the sound emanating from the mechanical locusts, on which are painted the colors of the rainbow. What glory!

Some of the locusts even possess wings and can fly. Just one of them passing by sounds like the thundering of an army charging into battle. John continues, "they have as King over them, the Angel of the abyss; his name in Hebrew is Abaddon, and in the Greek he has the name Apollyon" Revelation 9:11. "Destruction" and "destroyer" are the names of their kings and the purpose for which they were created and brought into your life. Surely they provide you a benefit. Their mobility enables you to work and to live wherever you want. With them you can run swiftly and far, and not be tired.

But they exact a price. The high price of owning and operating a personal locust keeps many from setting something aside for their future. Careless maintenance and reckless operation endanger life and limb. Yet the locust is not to blame, for it has no power of its own. The people who use it bear the responsibility for its safe or recklessness use.

Its power comes from the lubricant found in the bowels of the earth. A liquid oil is pumped out and refined into gasoline, kerosene, oil, and other petroleum products which are essential to the operation of the mechanized locusts.

The price for this oil is clamped down like a cork on a champagne bottle which is greatly agitated. When the cork finally pops, no one will be fast enough to catch it and stop it from reaching the height to which the pressure will propel it. Just like this cork the price of oil is rocketing up. Nevertheless, as long as it is available, people will pay whatever price is asked; not knowing that these oil revenues are providing the basis for the economic Assyrian rebirth of the Assyrian Empire. The oil will provide this Assyrian ruler with enough wealth to fully equip the best army to ever launch an attack against Israel.

"And the word of the Lord came to me saying, what do you see Jeremiah? And I said, I see a rod of an almond tree. Then the Lord said to me, you have seen well, for I am watching over my word to perform it. And the word of the Lord came to me a second time saying, what do you see? And I said, I see a boiling pot, facing away from the North. Then the Lord said to me, out of the North the evil will break forth on all the inhabitants of the land. For, I am calling all the families of the kingdoms of the North, declares the Lord; and they will come, and they will set each one his throne at the entrance of the gates of Jerusalem, and against all its walls roundabout, and against all the cities of Judah. And I will pronounce My judgments on them concerning all their wickedness, whereby they have forsaken Me and have offered sacrifices to other gods, and worshiped the works of their own hands." Jeremiah 1:11-16.

With these words, Jeremiah was called into service for the Lord. He saw the pot being emptied, but he did not describe what the throne looked like. However, his captive contemporary, Ezekiel, saw exactly what it was that issued from the pot when God called him into service: "now it came about in the 30th year, on the fifth day of the fourth month, while I was by the River Chebar among the exiles, the heavens were opened and I saw visions of God. (On the fifth of the month in the fifth year of king Jehoiachin's exile, the word of the Lord came expressly to Ezekiel the priest, son of Buzi, in the land of the Chaldeans by the River Chebar; and there the hand of the Lord came upon him.) And as I looked, behold, a storm wind was coming from the north, a great cloud with fire flashing forth continually and a bright light around it, and in its midst something like glowing metal in the midst of the fire." Ezekiel 1:1-4.

Look at the characteristics of this description: a great cloud generating the storm, a terrific wind, a bright aura around the cloud, and a searing heat source in its center. No natural cloud ever contained all these parts at the same time. In this vision they are grouped together, having lain dormant for over 2,500 years. If you do not see what Ezekiel was looking at, you never learn anything else from this chapter. When I read this, I said to myself, "My God, I was trained to drop that thing!" Ezekiel is looking at an atomic bomb going off over the land of Israel.

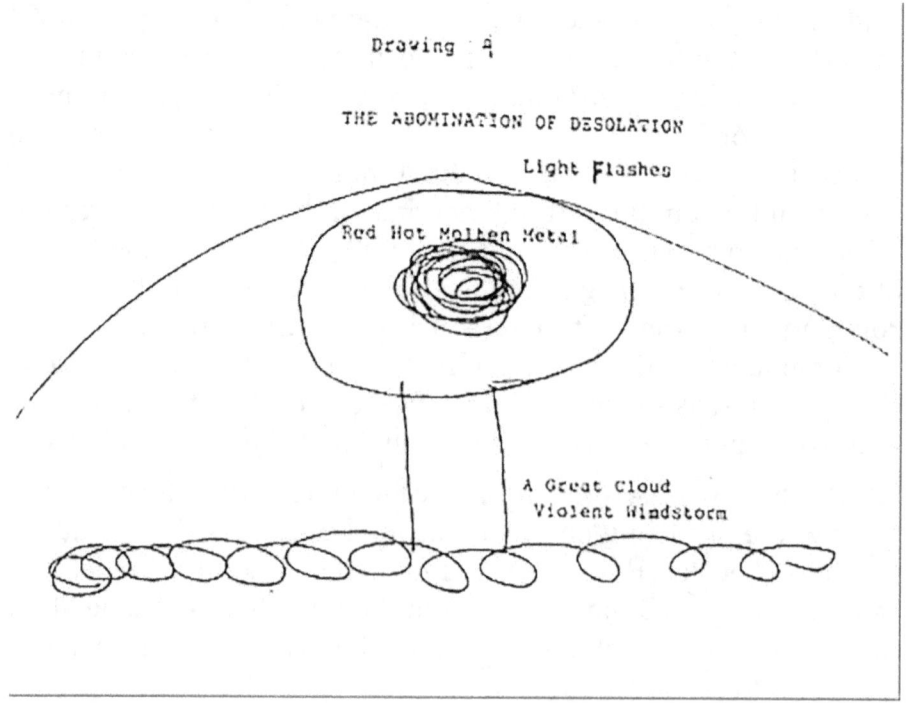

Drawing 4

THE ABOMINATION OF DESOLATION

Light Flashes

Red Hot Molten Metal

A Great Cloud
Violent Windstorm

In the middle of the 20th century, mankind learned how to assemble the components which are able to produce this distinctive cloud. Twice they have been called upon to produce this cloud over Hiroshima and Nagasaki. Countless thousands died in the heat of the fireball and its light flash melted their flesh away. The rushing wind from the blast claimed more lives. The great cloud formed around the fireball as it climbed skyward.

The bombs did not kill everyone outright. Many on the fringes of its awesome power were injured by this new instrument of destruction but survived in lingering pain. They became known as a new class of people: the Hibakusha. Learn of them and translate the name into to Hebrew, for Israel shall be the next nation to see the cloud over its people, as the Army of the Assyrian Antichrist approaches. He will have purchased one dozen limited tactical nuclear weapons to use in the Middle East. With them he will overrun Israel, Egypt, and the Sudan, in 30 days. When the cloud rises, the living beings draw near.

"And within it there were figures resembling living beings. And this was their appearance: they had human form. Each of them had four faces and four wings. And their legs were straight and their feet were like a calf's hoof, and they gleamed like burnished bronze. Under their wings on their four sides were human hands. As for the faces and wings of the four of them, their wings touched one another; their faces did not turn when they moved, each went straight forward. As for the form of their faces, each had the face of a man, all four had the face of a lion on the right and the face of a bull on the left, and all four had the face of an Eagle. Such were their faces. Their wings were spread out above; each had two touching another being, and two covering their bodies. And each went straight forward; wherever the Spirit was about to go, they would go, without turning as they went." Ezekiel 1:5-12

2500 years ago, why did a man call something alive? What was the primary criteria, the main reason? What's the difference between you and the tree? What can you do that the tree cannot do? You can move! The things Ezekiel saw were moving, therefore he called them alive. But they did not possess animal type flesh and muscle powered movement.

Take a break. Pick up a Bible and then read Ezekiel chapters 1 and 10.

I am going to look at what Ezekiel saw, but I will unite the visions the way a modern prophet would speak of them.

Their legs are straight: that is, there was no hip action, no knee bending, no ankle flexing, no toe wiggling. The leg never goes backward or forward, but it keeps coming closer and closer. Have you ever seen a straight leg that moved? This is the problem, you know this thing by its right name and you would never think to call it a straight leg. But the prophet does not have the benefit of your wisdom and experience.

The leg did support the weight of the main body. The whole body—from front to back—was rigid as well. It always pointed straight forward, even when it turned. So it was unlike an animal, whose head is mounted upon a neck, permitting the head to initiate a turn by pointing in a new direction and letting the rest of the body follow until it comes into alignment. This thing that moved, whose legs were straight, never flexed like an animal. Wherever it was pointed, it went. Since it moved, it was fitting for Ezekiel to call it a "living being".

Four distinct types could be recognized as they came closer, as the cloud lifted. They each revealed the face of a man, and as in John's description, the rest of the body was still connected. Ezekiel even comments upon the human hands which were under the wings. They carried men. They 'gleam like burnished bronze' means they reflected sunlight as a modern mirror does. (Burnished bronze was the original mirror.) Their feet were like a calf's hoof, soft and pliable because the calf's hoof has not taken the set yet and hardened.

The living being on the left looks like a bull (cherub), with head lowered and back muscles straining to support the supply burden it is carrying. When Ezekiel sees this side profile, he notices something else—it has a wheel for each of its four sides. And the appearance of the wheel is like there is a wheel within the wheel.

The appearance of the wheel within the wheel was like a tarshish stone, or sparkling beryl, or beryllium, or shiney aluminum; in modern terminology. They were called the whirling wheels in my hearing; that is, they did not just roll over the surface of the ground like every other wheel before them. These wheels could actually spin under their own power. Now, tell me the truth, you have already done this with your own wheels haven't you?

By the way, what is the shape of the straight leg? What Connects the body of a JEEP to the ground and permits it to move around? It's a wheel! See, I told you, you knew it by its right name. The straight leg is the frontal view of the wheel. Do You know how close to the frontal view of the wheel you must be before the roundness of the wheel comes into perspective? You must be within about 25 feet. Beyond that it is just a straight leg and You can't even say it's turning. But you know what it is and bow it operates.

On the right one was one with the face of a lion. From Revelation chapter 9, it is a lion's mouth. When or how does a lion's mouth get your attention? When it's open. What's it doing, just picking its teeth? No, it's growling. A lion is not a dog. What do you call the noise he makes as he announces he has selected you for his supper? A roar! Now mind you, this lion's mouth is in a viper's head upon a serpent's body. A viper's head is something with slits and pits in it. A serpent's body is long and round. When the roar of an attack comes out of the lion's mouth, the mouth smokes, then hyacinth or a flash of purple appears (as the gunpowder finishes burning) and what was roared at goes up in fire and brimstone.

In the air, above these three, is a new eagle like bird helping the others along. Such a bird had never been seen before! It had four wings, two of which touched each other where they were joined together. This eagle flew, but unlike any other bird, for the four wings were always pointed straight out and they never moved or flapped. If the wings did not move, where did the power to fly come from? Ezekiel did not know, yet in awe he said two of the wings were on this side of the body, two were on that side, and two were joined together touching one another They fly as fast as lightning flashing from the east to the west. The noise of their rings was awesome, like the noise of an abundant waterfall, the tumult of an army camp, or the voice of God Almighty.

Over the heads of the living beings was the appearance of another expanse or a different atmosphere. Ezekiel has never seen glass that he could see right through. And the curvature of the glass canopy shifts the atmospheric blue until it appears to be bluer than blue.

The Wheels of the living being were really special. They were connected to it. When the living being rose up from the Earth, the wheels rose up with it. Then they changed position and moved so close to the body that you could not see the wheels anymore, as the landing gear was being retracted.

When this living being approached the Earth to land, it dropped its wings. This does not mean the wings fell off, but Ezekiel saw a part of the wing that lowered, when the flaps came down.

Then Ezekiel saw up there in the air, high up, something that resembled a throne, Lapis lazuli or emerald green in color. And on that throne there was a figure that resembled a man; not just the face anymore but the whole body! This throne does not have any wings or wheels, yet it is flying in the sky. There is an amber glow of light surrounding the man, from his head to his feet. Ezekiel has never seen sunlight reflected by a curved windshield.

By this time, I hope you are able to see the modern Army that Ezekiel and I saw. But just in case you need little help, this is the picture his words caused me to see.

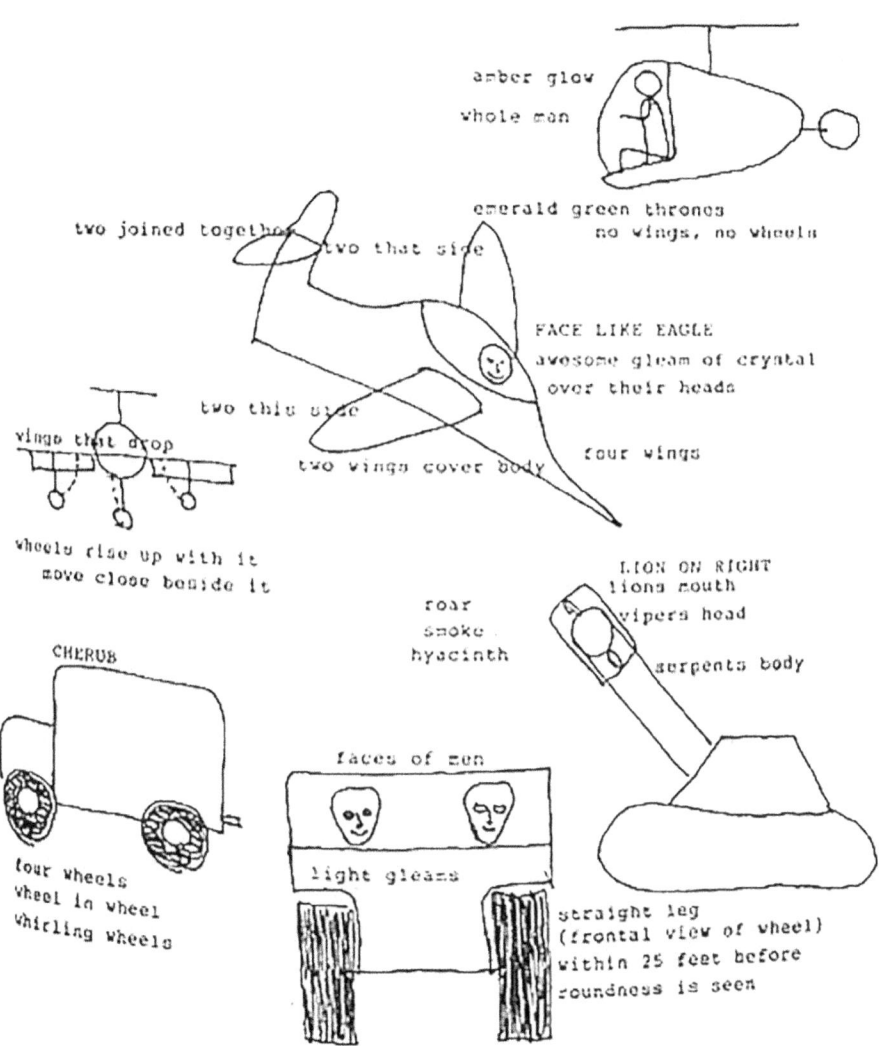

amber glow

whole man

emerald green thrones
no wings, no wheels

two joined together
two that side

FACE LIKE EAGLE
awesome gleam of crystal
over their heads

two this side

wings that drop

two wings cover body

four wings

wheels rise up with it
move close beside it

LION ON RIGHT
lions mouth
vipers head

roar
smoke
hyacinth

serpents body

CHERUB

faces of men

four wheels
wheel in wheel
whirling wheels

light gleams

straight leg
(frontal view of wheel)
within 25 feet before
roundness is seen

Jeremiah had a vision of a pot being emptied and saw the thrones which would come and surround cities of Israel, starting with Jerusalem. The armies of the North would come, each with the kingdom power of life and death from a throne, which could be moved to bring wrath against Israel. The power of the Kings of old

81

is now vested in the tank commanders and pilots of the world's armies. 10 nations from the ram's Empire are starting to prepare their armies for a victory over Israel. Their victory will come after Ezekiel's Israel is established. Ezekiel saw how the thrones moved and identified enough of their features so that today, when the Army is imminent, we might know with certainty what he saw.

Now we can understand that the locusts and living beings described by the prophets are actually modern means of land transportation, the car, the truck, the train, and the airplane, helicopter, and tank. Once we see this, we can better understand the call of Joel to God's service. Joel saw the tanks that he called 'locusts' destroy the land and buildings of Israel, by making the land quake and the vegetation burn. Look at the two-pronged attack of the atomic bomb and the tank corps.

Joel said, "The word of the Lord that came to Joel, the son of Pethuel. Here this, all elders, and listen, all inhabitants of the land. Has anything like this happened in your days or in your father's days? Tell your sons about it, and let your sons tell their sons, and their sons the next-generation. What the gnawing locust has left, the swarming locust has eaten; and what the creeping locust has left, the stripping locust has eaten. Awake, drunkards, and weep; and wail, all you wine drinkers, on account of the sweet wine that is cut off from your mouth. For a nation has invaded my land, mighty and without number; its teeth are the teeth of a lion, and it has the fangs of a lioness. It has made my vine a waste, and my fig tree splinters. It has stripped them bare and cast them away; their branches have become white. Wail like a virgin girded with sackcloth for the bridegroom of her youth. The grain offerings and the libations are cut off from the house of the Lord. The priests morn, the ministers of the Lord. The field is ruined, the land mourns, for the grain is ruined, the new wine dries up, fresh oil fails. Be ashamed, O farmers, wail, O vinedressers, for the wheat and barley; because the harvest of the field is destroyed. The vine dries up, and the fig tree fails; the pomegranate, Palm also, and the Apple tree, all the trees of the field dry up. Indeed, rejoicing dries up from the sons of men. Gird yourselves with sackcloth, and lament, O priests; wail, O ministers of the altar! Come, spend the night in sackcloth, O ministers of my God, for the grain offerings and the libations are withheld from the house of your God. Consecrate a fast, proclaim a solemn assembly; gather the elders and all the inhabitants of the land to the house of the Lord your God, and cry out to the Lord. Alas for the day! For the day of the Lord is near, and it will come as destruction from the Almighty. Has not food been cut off before our eyes, gladness and joy from the house of our God? The seeds shrivel under their clods; the storehouses are desolate, the barns are torn down, for the grain is dried up. How the beasts groan! The herds of cattle wander endlessly because there is no pasture for them; even the flocks of sheep suffer. To thee, Lord, I cry; for the fire has devoured the pastures of the wilderness, and the flame has burned up all the trees of the field. Even the beasts of the field pant for thee; for the water brooks are dried up, and fire has devoured the pastures of the wilderness. Blow a Trumpet in Zion, and sound an alarm on My holy mountain! Let all the inhabitants of the land tremble, for the day of the Lord is coming; surely it is near, a day of darkness and gloom, a day of clouds and thick darkness. As the dawn is spread over the mountains, so there is a great and mighty people; there has never been anything like it, nor will there be again after it to the years of many generations. A fire consumes before them, and behind them a flame burns. The land is like the Garden of Eden before them, but a desolate wilderness behind them, and nothing at all escapes them. Their appearance is like the appearance of horses; and like war horses, so they run. With a noise as of chariots they leap on the tops of the mountains, like the crackling of a flame of fire consuming the stubble, like a mighty people arranged for battle. Before them the people are in anguish; all faces turn pale. They run like mighty men; they climb the wall like soldiers; and they each march in line, nor do they deviate from their paths. They do not crowd each other; they march everyone in his path.

When they burst through the defences, they do not break ranks. They rush on the city, they run on the wall; they climb into the houses, they enter through the windows like a thief. Before them the earth quakes, the heavens tremble, the sun and the moon grow dark, and the stars lose their brightness. And the Lord utters His voice before His army; surely His camp is very great, for strong is he who carries out His word. The day of the Lord is indeed great and very awesome, and who can endure it? "Yet even now," declares the Lord, "return to Me with all your heart, and with fasting, weeping, and mourning; and rend your heart and not your garments." Now return to the Lord your God, for He is gracious and compassionate, slow to anger, abounding in loving kindness and relenting of evil. Who knows whether He will not turn and repent, and leave a blessing behind Him, even a grain offering and a libation for the Lord your God? Blow a trumpet in Zion, consecrate a fast, proclaim a solemn assembly, gather the people, sanctify the congregation, assemble the elders, gather the children and the nursing infants. Let the bridegroom come out of his room and the bride out of her bridal chamber. Let the priests, the Lord's ministers, weep between the porch and the altar, and let them say, Spare thy people, O Lord, and do not make Thine inheritance a reproach, a byword amoung the nations. Why should they amoung the peoples say, 'Where is their God?'" Joel 1:1-2:17

These words by the prophet Joel provide a complete description of how the Army of tanks, fighter aircraft, supply trucks, and personnel vehicles announced the start of the last half of Daniel's 70th week, the time of Israel's great tribulation.

Yet this is not a conventional army; it is a tactical, nuclear force. Look again at the destruction the land undergoes: before the Army arrives, the ground is shaken and noise fills the atmosphere; the fire before them and the flame behind them cause the life-sustaining fertility of the land to disappear; all the vegetation is utterly ruined and wasted; every tree is shattered and denuded, but not as if the tanks were deliberately taking aim at each one. The Army is intent on killing the people who are before it, as many as it can. Yet the types of weapons it possesses includes one which is capable of destroying all the vegetation above and below the ground, and able to blanch with light all the branches that did not burn. It even destroys the seed which is in the ground. The harvest of the field is totally ruined by it: the lush vegetation gives way to the desolate wilderness. These mechanical, warhorse like locusts strip the land clean. Nothing like it has ever been seen before.

When one gains insight and understanding about the words of these visions, one is able to envision the Army which the words describe. Yet, just in case you still think that this lion like living being does not represent a tank, let me share the vision that established it in my mind.

Mouth power

John wrote, "and this is how I saw in the vision the horses and those who sat on them: the riders had breastplates the color of fire and hyacinth and of brimstone; the heads of the horses are like the heads of lions; and out of their mouths proceed fire and smoke and brimstone. A third of mankind was killed by these three plagues, by the fire and the smoke and the brimstone, which proceeded out of their mouths. The power of the horses is in their mouths and in their tails; for their tails are like serpents and have heads, and with them they do harm." Revelation 9:17-19.

The head was on the tail. The tail was like a serpent long and round. Their breastplates, their protection was the color of fire, and hyacinth which is a flash of purple, and brimstone which is the odor of burning sulfur. These three make up the mane of the lion's head, which appears when the mouth roars and disappears when it is quiet. Like the lion, it always roars before it attacks its prey. Consider the rider upon the horse, protected by its mouth in the lion's head on the serpent body. While this passage of Revelation pertains to the battle of Armageddon, I present it here because of what it is. Look at the modern picture and consider this portrayal.

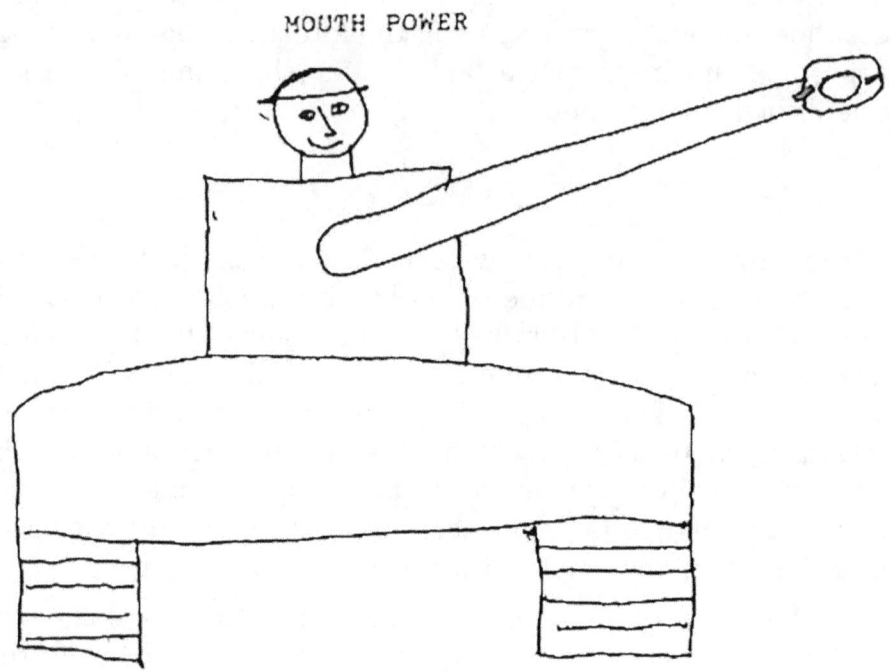

MOUTH POWER

Ezekiel saw four faces in what he called the living beings. The first time he named the four as a man, a lion, a bull, and an Eagle. Then he called them a cherub, a man, a lion, and an Eagle. The cherub thus becomes the one that looked like the bull, the beast of burden. (One is a cherub, two or more are cherubim.)

Cherubim are not a class of Angels. Angels have the power to give a man a vision or take him by a lock of his hair and transport him by the spirit. Ezekiel 8:3. But King David said, "and he rode on a cherub and flew; and he appeared on the wings of the wind. 2 Samuel 22:11. So a cherub has always been something which could provide transportation to carry one to his destination.

The cherubim also have power other than the mere transportation, for from their initial reference they also had military might. Moses said, "so He drove the man out; and at the East of the Garden of Eden He stationed the cherubim, and the flaming sword which turned every direction, to guard the way to the tree of life." Genesis 3:24. This flaming sword which turned every direction had to be a laser.

John wrote, "and before the throne there was, as it were, a sea of glass like Crystal; and in the center and around the throne four living creatures full of eyes in front and behind. And the first creature was like a lion, and the second creature was like a calf, and the third creature had a face like that of a man, and the fourth creature was like a flying eagle. And the four living creatures, each one of them having six wings, are full of eyes around and within; and day and night they do not cease to say, "Holy, holy, holy, is the Lord God, the Almighty, who was and who is and who is to come." And when the living creatures give glory and honor and thanks to him who sits on the throne, to him who lives forever and ever, and will cast their crowns before the throne, saying, "Worthy art Thou, our Lord and our God, to receive glory and honor and power; for Thou did create all things, and because of thy will they existed, and were created." Revelation 4:6-11.

Therefore, the cherubim are the Lord's means of heavenly transportation, and their sightings, with power to accomplish specific purposes have been recorded throughout the Scriptures. Moses records one. Let me introduce it with a short poem.

At the tip of the flame

rides the rocket with no name.

ringing sound fills the Ears,

paralyzes you with fears.

The mountain smokes,

shakes and grows quiet.

Then it speaks

and you hear God!

About 2 million people watched this with Moses, "so it came about on the third day, when it was morning, that there were thunder and lightning flashes and a thick cloud upon the mountain and a very loud trumpet sound, so that all the people in the camp trembled. And Moses brought the people out of the Camp to meet God, and they stood at the foot of the mountain. Now Mount Sinai was all in smoke because the Lord descended upon it in fire; and its smoke ascended like the smoke of a furnace, and the whole mountain quaked violently. When the sound of the trumpet grew louder and louder, Moses spoke and God answered him with thunder. And the Lord came down on Mount Sinai, to the top of the mountain; and the Lord called Moses to the top of the mountain, and Moses went up." Exodus 19:16-20.

But the people were not permitted upon the mountain to see what the Lord had arrived in, and what sustained Moses in his presence for 40 days. When he entered the cherub, Moses saw all the glory of the Lord God and all the patterns of the things which he was to construct upon the Earth for the Lord's worship. Exodus 25:40. The thunder, the streak of light, and the trumpet roar was the landing phase of one of the cherubim.

The fire and the light were associated with the parting of Elijah and Elisha, "Then it came about as they were going along and talking, that behold, there appeared a chariot of fire and horses of fire which separated the two of them. And Elijah went up by a whirlwind to heaven. And Elisha saw it and cried out, "my father, my father, the chariots of Israel and its horsemen!" 2 Kings 2:11, 12

Throughout Elijah's ministry they remained close to assist and protect him. On one occasion he asked that his servant might see them!

"Now when the attendant of the man of God had risen early and gone out, behold, an army with horses and chariots was circling the city. And his servant said to him, "Alas, my master! What shall we do?" So he answered, "Do not fear, for those who are with us are more than those who are with them." Then Elisha prayed and said, "O Lord, I pray, open his eyes that he may see. And the Lord opened the servant's eyes, and he saw; and behold, the mountain was full of horses and chariots of fire all around Elisha. 2 Kings 6:15-17.

May your eyes be opened to see them.

Jesus took Peter, James, and John to the top of a mountain and was transfigured there. Jesus spoke with Moses and Elijah, who appeared to them. Peter remarked that they should build three temples there. In response to this, Matthew records what happened: "while he was still speaking, behold, a bright cloud overshadowed them; and behold, a voice out of the cloud, saying, "This is My beloved Son, with who I am well pleased; listen to him! Matthew 17:5.

The glory cloud which hid this cherub also hid the one which received the Lord when he departed from this Earth. Luke wrote, "and after he had said these things, He was lifted up while they were looking on, and a cloud received Him out of their sight." Acts 1:9

The Lord has used His cherubim in mighty ways. From them, He rained fire and brimstone on Sodom and Gomorrah. Genesis 19:24-26 Jacob's ladder descended from one. Genesis 28:10-17. From them fire consumed a soaking wet altar with its sacrifice. 1 Kings 18:38 They also destroyed by fire two captains of 50 with their 50. 2 Kings 1:9-15.

The heavenly cherubim do not cease to praise God. They have the power to execute the desires of the Lord God. Therefore, it behooves us, here upon the Earth, to use the counterfeits which the destroyer has provided for us to use with greater respect then we have been. Through misuse, these things are killing us both literally and economically.

Your "locusts" will not provide the blessings of your future: you should not place your hope in them. Your locusts, living beings, and cherubim were created to harm you; and if your heart, your words, and your dreams are not fully committed to the word and the will of the Lord, they will do so.

CHAPTER V

The abomination of desolation:
the nuclear issue of the 70th week.

Therefore when you see the abomination of desolation which was spoken of through Daniel the prophet, standing in the holy place (let the reader understand). Matthew 24:15.

In 1962 I completed the NAVIGATOR-BOMBARDIER training course at Mather Air Force base in California. When the background checks of the members of the class were completed by the FBI, and our top-secret nuclear clearances were granted; we were trained in the construction, the operations, the ballistics, and the devastation resulting from the use of the atomic bomb. When the course was finished and the time came to select an assignment, only two options were available. You could select either a hole in the ground or a hole in the sky. That is, you could become a missile man in a silo or a bombardier in the B-52. Neither of these two choices appealed to me. Why would you want to do something that no one in their right mind would ever permit or encourage you to do?

Once you have received this training and all the safety measures associated with it, you do not just say, I want to drop an atomic bomb today. Oops what a pity, one bomb, one city! While practice makes perfect, this was one thing you were never able to practice.

Therefore, hugging my career to the bomb did not appeal to me. Just before these assignments were selected, the Tactical Air Command called for three navigators to go operational in KB50J tankers used to refuel fighter aircraft in the air. My standing in the class was high enough to permit me to select an assignment going to England AFB, Louisiana. So I became an operational navigator, departing the bomb and all it entails. Since I had received this training I can recognize how these events are spoken of in the Bible.

Understanding must begin with the subject that Jesus said we would have to understand. Jesus said, "when you see the abomination of desolation spoken of by Daniel the prophet standing where it ought not, let the reader understand." Matthew 24:15, Mark 13:14. The first thing one must see about the abomination of desolation is how big is it? Is it something you can hold in your hands? Is it as big as a man? Is it as big as this house? Is it bigger than a house? Then you realize Jesus told you how big it was through the rest of the words he spoke. "Then let those who are in Judea flee to the mountains; let him who is on the housetop not go down to get the things out that are in his house; and let him who is in the field not turn back to get his cloak." Matthew 24:16-18

So I asked myself, how many people are there in the land of Israel? Is there just one house and one field? This thing could be small then, but the population of Israel is over 9 million people now. So how big does something have to be to enable 9 million people to see it at the same instant of time and recognize it for what it is?

A sailor on a ship on the ocean can see 7 miles due to the curvature of the earth. Someone in an airplane flying at 10,000 feet can see 100 nautical miles due to the curvature of the earth.

This means that if you are 100 miles away from where the event occurs it must rise to a height of 10 to 20,000 feet for you to be able to see it. What do we have in the Scriptures that is this big?

I put this question in the back of my mind as I continued to search the Scriptures. I found the answer to the question as I read these words of Ezekiel. "And as I looked, behold, a storm wind was coming from the North, a great cloud with fire flashing forth continually and a bright light around it, and in its midst something like glowing metal in the midst of the fire." Ezekiel 1:4.

When I read this, I said, "My God I was trained to drop this thing, Ezekiel is looking at an atomic bomb going off in the land of Israel! THE ABOMINATION OF DESOLATION IS A NUCLEAR DEVICE DETONATING OVER THE LAND OF ISRAEL! The first device to be detonated in the Trinity test, produced a cloud which rose to a height of 40,000 feet. The flash of light produced was seen 250 miles away. When the hydrogen bomb was set off, its cloud rose to 125,000 feet. If you use the Trinity figures and draw a 250-mile radius from Jerusalem, the resulting Circle will encompass all of Israel. When the first flash of light is seen, everyone in Israel will know what it is, as they watch the cloud rise.

Daniel made two references to the abomination of desolation. The first time he mentioned it he said, "and he will make a firm covenant with the many for one week, but in the middle of the week he will put a stop to sacrifice and grain offering; and on the wing of abominations will come one who makes desolate, even until a complete destruction, one that is decreed, is poured out on the one who makes desolate." Daniel 9:27. Then Daniel wrote, "and from the time that the regular sacrifice is abolished, and the abomination of desolation is set up, there will be 1290 days!" Daniel 12:11.

From these two passages I concluded that the 70th week is sitting on day 1290 like goalpost! Day 1290 occurs in the middle of the 70th week. When that flash of light is seen it is day 1290.

Now that you have seen what it is, look at how it operates. "And he performs great signs so that he even makes fire come down out of heaven to the Earth in the presence of men. Revelation 13:13. This is how it operates. It is sent up into the atmosphere in the nose of the rocket. As it descends toward its target, at a predetermined altitude above the ground the device is activated. The searing heat of the chain reaction reaches from that point to the ground, and the cloud rises.

"And the Lord God of hosts, the one who touches the land so that it melts, and all those who dwell in it mourn, and all of it rises up like the Nile and subsides like the Nile of Egypt:" Amos 9:5.

"Because of this will not the land quake and everyone who dwells in it mourn? Indeed, all of it will rise up like the Nile and it will be tossed about, and subside like the Nile of Egypt." Amos 8:8.

Before the first atomic bomb went off only an earthquake would seem to have been the cause for what Amos was looking at. Not only does the atomic bomb melt the land it also causes the land to rise up and settle back down like a River.

This is also the first part of the curse found in Deuteronomy. "The Lord will make the rain of your land powder and dust; from heaven it shall come down on you until you are destroyed." Deuteronomy 28:24.

"And it will come about in that day, declares the Lord God, that I shall make the Sun go down at noon and make the Earth dark in broad daylight." Amos 8:9

You just read from the Bible the first things that an atomic explosion produces. The land rises up, only to settle back down; but parts of it were melted and particles have been lifted into the heavens. This produces a cloud so black no light can shine through it, and then particles from the cloud begin to fall out of it, back to the land and even upon the bodies of the people. In the book of the law God was telling man the penalty for not obeying his laws and commands. In the beginning he told them disobedience would bring his wrath upon them, and the atomic bomb would be that wrath. So as the end of this planet approaches, so do the nuclear weapons that are about to end it.

"And the fourth angel poured out his bowl upon the sun; and it was given to it to scorch men with fire. And the men were scorched with fierce heat; and they blasphemed the name of God who has the power over these plagues; and they did not repent, so as to give him glory. And the fifth Angel poured out his bowl upon the throne of the beast; and his kingdom became darkened; and they gnawed their tongues because of pain, and they blasphemed the God of heaven because of their pains and their sores; and they did not repent of their deeds." Revelation 16:8-11.

The flash of light is brighter than the sun. It is followed by a heat that cannot be measured, a heat that melts everything. Then because the land has been lifted up like powder and fine dust, the light of day is so blocked out by the pollution in the air, that high noon looks like midnight. "Therefore all hands will fall limp, and every man's heart will melt, and they will be terrified, pains and anguish will take hold of them; they will writhe like a woman in labor, they look at one another in astonishment, their faces aflame." Isaiah 13:7,8

Imagine at the moment of the flash, you are looking at your wife, and she is looking at you. You see her face on fire and she sees your face on fire; and that is the last thing you see before the rest of your body also burns and your ashes fall to the ground. "Their flesh will rot as they stand on their feet, and their eyes will rot in their sockets, and their tongues will rot in their mouth." Zechariah 14:12. This is getting gruesome, isn't it? But you don't need to worry, before you can even speak a word your spirits will be departing.

Perhaps, you will not be in the blast radius of the bomb, and you will wonder what you should do? If you remember the words of the prophet Isaiah, you will, "enter the rock and hide in the dust." Isaiah 2:10. "And men go into caves of the rocks and into holes of the ground: Isaiah 2:19. It takes 3 feet of dirt to protect you from the radiation emitted by the bomb. Then because of the powder and fine dust that has been lifted up by the bomb into the atmosphere and turned radioactive and now it is falling down upon you, there's another thing you must do. Radioactive fallout chemically bonds with hair. You cannot wash it out. Because you cannot wash it out, the radioactivity will continue to penetrate into your body until it has destroyed your tissues and killed you. So you must shave off all your bodily hair.

"Everyone's head is bald and every beard is cut off." Isaiah 15:2. The fallout also causes another problem. It has so polluted the land that all sexual activity is brought to a stop. The men and women of every family are separated and the men are living by themselves and the women are living by themselves. Zechariah

12:1-14. No children are permitted to be conceived and born in the areas where the radiation remains hot.

Two thirds the population of the land of Israel and one half the population of the city of Jerusalem are going to be killed by the modern army that brings the atomic bomb into the land of Israel and uses it. Zechariah 13:8; 14:2.

Finding the ground zeros for these bombs proved to be a real challenge. I started to make progress when I encountered the words of Amos, "and the summit of Carmel dries up." Amos 1.2

Then Nahum put Mount Bashan in the same situation as Mount Carmel, Nahum 1:4. Then Isaiah added the Plain of Sharon to the situation that Mount Bashan and Mount Carmel were in. Isaiah said, "Sharon is like a desert plain, and Bashan and Carmel lose their foliage." Isaiah 33:9. When you look at the situation of Mount Carmel you see that it establishes the bay that the city of Haifa is situated in. Mount Bashan is where Amman, Jordan was built. King Hussein of Jordan was a good friend to Saddam Hussein during operation Desert Storm. But then their friendship cooled, other events troubled the Iraqi ruler. Saddam's 2 sons-in-law and their wives fled Iraq to Jordan, making Saddam very angry. "My good buddy, who stood beside me during the Desert Storm warfare, has done gone and signed a peace treaty with my enemy. And my sons-in-law are telling him all my secrets, I have to kill that cat before he blabs to the world what I am doing. So he lied to his sons-in-law saying all was forgiven and they could return home; but he shot them as soon as they stepped across the border. Then Jordan's King died of natural causes. But Saddam's anger remains, and Amman, Jordan will receive the destructive end of an atomic explosion.

The plain of Sharon has the distinction of being the location of the Valley of Dry Bones. Ezekiel chapter 37.

Why do you never see a bone in a Valley? Do you have a dog? If so, this is what you should do tonight. Cook a shoulder roast that has a bone. After supper is over bring the bone to your dog and let him smell it. Then take the bone to your door and throw it out as hard as you possibly can. 5 minutes later bring the dog to the door and command him to fetch the bone. How long does it take your dog to find the bone? Why doesn't the dog see the bone when he goes out the door? The dog has eyes, doesn't it? Why does he need to sniff for the bone until he sees it? What color is your yard and how tall is it. It's green, and it is taller than any bone lying there. Valleys and yards are filled with greenery. You never see a bone in a Valley until you're standing right on top of it. What happened to the greenery? It disappeared in a flash of light.

Ezekiel said, "the hand of the Lord was upon me, and he brought me out by the spirit of the Lord and set me down in the middle of the Valley; and it was full of bones. As he caused me to pass among them round about, and behold; there were very many on the surface of the Valley; and Lo, they were very dry. And he said to me, Son of Man can these bones live? And I answered, Oh Lord God, thou knowest. Again he said to me, prophesy over these bones, and say to them. 'O dry bones, hear the word of the Lord. Thus says the Lord God to these bones, behold, I will cause breath to enter you that you may come to life. And I will put sinews on you, make flesh grow back on you, cover you with skin, and put breath in you that you may come alive; and you will know that I am the Lord. So I prophesied as I was commanded; and as I prophesied, there was a noise, and behold, a rattling; and the bones came together, bone to its bone. And I looked, and behold, sinews were on them, and flesh grew, and skin covered them; but there was no breath in them. Then he said to me, prophesy to the breath, prophesy, Son of Man, and say to the breath, thus says the Lord God, come from the four winds, O breath, and breathe on these slain, that they may come to life. So I prophesied as he commanded me, and the breath came into them, and they came to life, and stood on their feet, and exceedingly great Army." Ezekiel 37:-10.

Whose Army was this? It was Israel's army. They were at ground zero, for atomic bomb number two. Mount Bashan at Amman, Jordan gets hit with atomic bomb number three. The fourth bomb hits Tel-aviv. The fifth bomb strikes Cairo. The sixth bomb blows the Aswan dam. The number seven bomb destroys Khartoum.

When the Aswan Dam is blown, the flood of waters washes Cairo away giving it its new name, the city of destruction. Isaiah 19:18. The onrush of waters from the Dam will also cut seven new pathways for the water flowing from the dam, so that the Nile River will never flood again. Isaiah 19:7

Daniel records the progress of this attack. "And at the end time the King of the South will collide with him, and the kingdom of the North will storm against him with chariots, with horsemen, and with many ships: and he will enter countries, overflow them, and pass through. He will also enter the beautiful land, and many countries will fall; but these will be rescued out of his hand: Edom, Moab, and the foremost of the sons of Amman. Then he will stretch out his hand against other countries, and the land of Egypt will not escape. But he will gain control over the hidden treasures of gold and silver, and over all the precious things of Egypt; and Libyans and Ethiopians will follow at his heels. But rumors from the East and from the North will disturb him, and he will go forth with great wrath to destroy and annihilate many. And he will pitch the tents of his Royal Pavilion between the seas and the beautiful holy mountain; yet he will come to his end, and no one will help him." Daniel 11:40-45.

When the Russian and Chinese emissaries catch up with Saddam in the Sudan, this is what they will say to him. "Hello Saddam, we knew when we sold them to you who you wanted to use them against. We did not mind. We thought everyone would think that you had them buried in the sand, and no one could find them when they looked; not that we sold them to you last month. We even understood when you slapped the Egyptian down because he did not help you get Lebanon back. But you have also taken the Sudan and we have reserved Africa to ourselves in our plan of world conquest, which we have not given up. Furthermore, your armies look like they are going to attack Ethiopia and Libya. Unfortunately we can't let you do this, because the United States has informed us that they will put one on Moscow if you cross either of these borders. We can't afford to let that happen. By the way, this telephone is live and Moscow is listening to our conversation. Should something happen to these ambassadors, or should this phone go dead, the button will be pushed.

Moscow already knows all the types of vehicles you have here and how far you can get in each one while the rockets are coming. You have seen what these little firecrackers can do. Well we've got a biggie. Every place you could possibly be is going to go up in smoke and dust.

We know how many we sold you. We have counted each one you used. We know what you have left and you will not get any more. We will let you keep the lands you have already taken, but you must go back home.

With great anger and wrath, Saddam returns, and encamps on the north side of the Mount of Olives, making the land west of the Nile River so polluted that no foot of man or beast can cross it for 40 years. Ezekiel 29:10,11.

Child of Abraham, Citizen of Israel, when the flash of light occurs, maybe your flesh will be instantly vaporized, or you'll watch your flesh burn, or shave off all your hair; be separated from your family, have no more sex, and find there are places you cannot walk upon. So repent while you can. Get down on your knees and pray. Do you want to be alive or dead when Jesus, your Messiah returns?

CHAPTER VI

Was HE or Wasn't HE?

"There are many devices in a man's heart; nevertheless, the counsel of the Lord, shall stand": Proverbs 19:21.

As we study the Scriptures, the stumbling block for the Jews of Christ's day can be quickly understood, as the prominent division in them is seen. That is, there is a distinction between those which were pre-kingdom and those which are kingdom. Christ's countrymen stumbled and took offense for they could not see the difference, nor find a fitting answer to the question, "How can the kingdom of a murdered man last forever?"

If Christ was the Messiah, He should have established His kingdom. Since He didn't, He wasn't! However, they did not understand that the Messiah had to die. They had never searched out the limited number of the pre-kingdom prophecies and put them into order. If they had, they would have acknowledged these claims which Christ fulfilled:

—Born of a virgin: Isaiah 7:13, 14: Matthew 1:18-25; Luke 1:26-35.

—Of the line of David: II Samuel 7:12-17; Psalms 89:3, 4; Matthew 21:9; John 7:40-42.

—In Bethlehem: Micah 5:2; Matthew 2:3-6.

—Out of Egypt have I called My Son: Hosea 11:1; Matthew 2:15.

—He shall be called a Nazarene: Isaiah 11:1; Matthew 2:23.

—Coming riding upon a colt: Zechariah 9:9; John 12:12-16.

—Betrayed: Psalms 41:9; Mark 14:43-49.

—For thirty pieces of silver: Zechariah 11:12, 13; Matthew 27:3-10; John 18:1-5.

—Smitten: Isaiah: 50:6; Matthew 27:27-31; Mark 14:65; John 19:1.

—He opened not His mouth: Isaiah 54:4-7; Mark 15:2-5; Acts 8:32-35.

—His hands and feet are pierced: Psalms 22:16; Zechariah 12:10; 13:6; Acts 2:22, 23.

—Given gall and vinegar to drink: Psalms 69:20, 21; Matthew 27:33, 34.

—They gamble for His clothes: Psalms 22:1-21; John 19:23, 24.

—Messiah cut off: Isaiah 53:8; Daniel 9:26; Luke 23:46.

—Dies with sinners: Psalms 22:16; Luke 23:46.

—Buried with the rich: Isaiah 53:9; Matthew 27:38, 57-60.

—Thou wilt not leave my soul in hell: Psalms 16:10; Luke 24:1-7.

The preceding list of pre-kingdom prophecies, which also gives the reliable testimony of one to two eyewitnesses, should firmly establish that Christ has fulfilled them. According to the Law of Moses, the testimony of two was fact and acceptable truth (Deuteronomy 17:6). Therefore, on this basis alone, the pre-kingdom claims of Christ must be acknowledged and those prophecies accepted as being fulfilled.

The Scriptures state that God is true, and in any contest between God and men, it is better for every man to be proved a liar than it is for God to be one (Romans 3:4). Then let us accept the fact that the word of God regarding His prophecies is true, and if they have not already been fulfilled, they shall be. Now if on this basis we reexamine the claims of Christ, the reasoning could proceed like this.

Isaiah spoke of a son born of a virgin. Matthew and Luke testify to the fulfillment. The idea of a virgin birth is difficult for some to accept. Nevertheless, they accept that God fashioned Adam from the earth's clay and later fashioned Eve around a rib taken from Adam. Surely, if God had such power in the beginning, no man has lessened it and God is still able to fertilize any woman whom He might choose. Two men, one of whom was a doctor, testify to the birth and the testimony of two is true.

But was He, or was He not? If Christ was not born in fulfillment of this prophecy, two men have lied. Consider how you regard this claim, for if you don't believe it, could you ever believe any man's claim to a virgin birth? Luke was a physician and as such he would only testify to what he knew was true; surely a doctor should be able to identify virginity. Today the words artificial insemination describes what took place, and any modern doctor could cause a virgin to give birth in this manner if his ethics would permit him to do so. Surely God had more power than a doctor.

Zechariah said the Messiah would come riding upon a colt. Matthew and John say He did.

But did he, or did He not? You would be hard put to find this animal in today's Jerusalem. Wouldn't He be more likely to come riding in a bullet-proof limousine; only to be blown up by a grenade? Wouldn't the Middle East's terrorists take any opportunity to assassinate Him to remove this source of goodness from our midst, because they can't have Him? How can He hope to live? He has to be killed when He is revealed; if Christ was not the one.

The Psalmist said He would be betrayed and Zechariah sets the fee as thirty pieces of silver. Mark and John record the betrayal while Matthew mentions the price.

But was He or was He not? Two men record the betrayal. Who has the power to set their testimony aside? If He was not betrayed, then He must be. Child of Abraham, what do you think of yourself and your neighbors? If He was not betrayed, then one of you must do it and become a little richer; and how far shall your thirty pieces of silver go?

Isaiah said He would be beaten. John and Mark say He was.

But was He or not? If not, do you regard it lightly that one of You must do the job? Is there that much anger in your soul?

Isaiah said He wouldn't even open His mouth. Mark and the writer of Acts said He did not.

But did He or did He not? Can you take comfort from the knowledge that no matter what you do to Him, He won't condemn you? Will that make you fiercer?

The Psalmist and Zechariah said His hands and feet would be pierced. Luke said they were.

But were they or were they not? What would prompt you to use a cruel and unusual punishment that hasn't been practiced for almost two thousand years? Do you take joy in using hammer and nail to position a body of flesh upon a tree? Child of Abraham, why don't you get it over quickly and just shoot Him?

The Psalmist said He would be given gall and vinegar to drink. Matthew says He was.

But was He or was He not? Just what does the army of Israel get to drink, anyway? Is this why you are such good fighters? Would you ever think of treating an Egyptian that way? Could you really despise a new Messiah more than you despised Christ?

The Psalmist said soldiers would gamble for His clothes. John says they did.

But did they or not? Remember, in accordance with your Scriptures, if it was not it shall be. Are your wages so little and your clothes so tattered that you have to take the clothes off a dying man to keep warm? Not only that, are you proud you stripped Him naked before you killed Him, just so that you wouldn't bloody the clothes?

Child of Abraham, consider your Scriptures, watch, and pray. These are not kind thoughts to you as they come your way, and come they must. Either Christ is the Messiah or He is not.

Think back now to see if you were ever taught a course on all the Messianic prophecies. Your scriptures do contain them, so why are they not taught? Are prophets false prophets because the events they predicted have not happened yet? Are they not upon us now?

When you study them, you will note a separation factor. There are those prophecies which must be fulfilled before the kingdom is set up, and those which will be fulfilled during the kingdom rule. The Messiah was to be born, serve for a time, be killed and buried, rise from the dead, and come again as a mature man of power to set up and rule over the kingdom. The Messiah can't be killed after the kingdom is established or it would not endure forever (Daniel 2:44).

Before the kingdom is established He must come and perish for the iniquity of His people. Faithful witnesses record that Christ did this. But did He or not? For a moment, let's accept the word of the witnesses and say that you were among the group of those who fulfilled the prophecies upon Christ. After you slew God's sacrifice, He convicted you of your iniquity, but you hardened your heart. You would not be shamed. To protect your dignity you would seek to: discredit the birth—say He wasn't the man; bring iniquity upon Him—claim that He must have been a malefactor, for He was crucified with some; deny His resurrection—hold that He was stolen from the grave, He wasn't dead anyway; strike the testimony of the witnesses from the record—assume they were fanatics who could not be believed; prohibit the Messianic passages from being taught in a related fashion; in short, anything practical to say the Scriptures were not fulfilled. Then you raise your hands to heaven, proclaiming they are clean, and expressing your desire for God to send the right one.

On the other hand, if your religious rulers were right and Christ was not the man, just remember that your Scriptures still need to be fulfilled. The word of God cannot fail! Since this is the case, Child of Abraham, you must persecute another man in the way your Scriptures record. Or both you and your Scriptures are nothing but vanity.

You know your heart and soul. Are they really as depraved as Your forefathers say they must be?

Your Scriptures testify to the worth of your ancestors and the way they incessantly worried their God with their iniquities; and how He punished them, time and time again. Isn't it easier to believe that after the murderers performed the recorded acts that they became scurrilous liars as well to cover their tracks? Either they lied, or you will, or all our words are worthless.

Child of Abraham, it is not enough to condescend to today's thoughts and say that Christ was a great man when you do not know what made Him great. It is not enough to say He was a great teacher when you do not know what He taught. It is not enough to say He was a great leader when you have never done a word that He said. It is not enough to say He was a prophet when you do not read or record any prophecies He made. Must you lie just because your fathers did?

Child of Abraham, you know your removal from the land of God's promise has always been because of your sinful behavior. What sins of your fathers were so great that God drove them out of His land and scattered them to the world from 70 A.D. until 1948? Just possibly could it have been because they did kill the Son of God just as it is recorded?

God has always told His people about important events before they happened, so that when they were fulfilled, mankind would have to say, "God did that!" All those who believe this search the Scriptures to learn God's plan before He implements it. There is joy in watching God's greatness unfold. Do you know the Scriptures or only what men have told you about them? As you read this book and search the Scriptures, do you see that the Messianic kingdom is imminent and that Christ was the one who was to come to die for your iniquity? Then He was crucified, dead, and buried; but God would not leave His soul in hell so He resurrected Him from the grave. Soon He is coming again—after Israel changes the name of Lebanon; after Assyria overcomes Israel, Egypt, and the Sudan.

Child of Abraham, will you be one of those whom God purges from the land before He announces the kingdom? For what cause is your punishment coming? Is it due to your unbelief? Is it because you seek your own goodness, your continual attempts to follow the letter of the law, yet never being able to do it? Is it not because you claim to have rebuilt your nation by yourself, that is through the power of your own hand, in direct opposition to the words of Zechariah who said the sons of David were not to glorify themselves but recognize God working in their midst? Is it not because with the hope you vest the kingdom prophecies, as expressed in the Zionist movement, you believe that you can bring them to pass through your own deeds? Implying by bring them to pass through this both that you do not really need the Messiah anyway and also that since you only look to the kingdom prophecies you acknowledge that all the pre-kingdom prophecies have been fulfilled or done away with?

Is not this the reason God showed you your sins were not atoned by permitting the Arabs to strike you on Yom Kippur, your Day of Atonement?

We could go on but it would become fruitless. It would be as misdirected and pointless as the last twenty centuries which saw Christians persecute Jews because of what their fathers had done. Yet through all this, the Jews deserve to be praised, for they were like a fortress. No matter how fierce the attack, they held to their Scriptures. They stood firm in the traditions they had been taught. They preserved the words of their God and they think they understand them.

They do not desire Christians to instruct them for they have felt the whip of anger often enough. They have no need to be patted on the back and hear, "It is unfortunate you are going to go through the time of Jacob's trouble, but we'll pray for you as God Raptures us out of it." Do we show real love in this manner? Do we not isolate them even more?

Once before when they were isolated, six million of them perished in Hitler's chambers. That was about one third of the world's population of Jews. We thought it was shocking but how many of our hearts were tender enough to shed just a few tears? And when the Assyrian again shepherds the land of Israel so that

106

you see six million more of the children of Israel die, will you shed tears then? And if you do, will they only be because you were not raptured yet? Will your adherence to your traditions be strong enough to sustain your faith? Or will you lose yours as they grow to look forward to the appearance of their Savior. The One who said, "You search the Scriptures, because you think that in them you have eternal life, and it is these that testify of me and you are unwilling to come to me, that you may have life

John 5:38, 40

Only Israel's Messiah is able to provide life, for He alone overcame death. This is better understood when you understand the difference between a prince and a king. A prince is the heir to the throne, while the king ruler upon it. Daniel said Messiah the Prince was to be killed. If this death ended His life there could never be Messiah the king. Yet the heir was killed, even buried. Continuity of life was guaranteed by God's promise that this One would be king.

Christ is the Messiah. Are you ready to meet Him face to face?

CHAPTER VII

Israel's Messiah

"For since the beginning of the world, men have not heard, nor perceived by the ear, neither hath the eye seen, 0 God, beside Thee, what he hath prepared for him that waits for him": Isaiah 64:4.

Pity poor Israel! Israel has always been blessed or cursed by the prophets of God. Their prophecies have always been explained beforehand, but few tried to understand, to prepare and be ready. All through the history of the Bible, Israel has been punished for not listening to the words of God, disobeying Him, and sinning against Him. The Jews now have the ability to reverse a part of this history. They can turn to the words of their God and act upon them. They must remember, though, that the prophets have always been killed for speaking the words that the Lord has given them. They have been killed for using the power of God to explain or accomplish His will.

The nation of Israel is now a witness for God, whether she desires it or not. The Jews have the choices of the prophets. They can speak or hold their peace. If they hold their peace and do not the words of their God, they will perish. If they turn to the words of God and heed them they shall meet the fate of the prophets and be killed. Either way, they perish as a nation one more time! It would be so much more glorious if they would take the power God has waiting for them, use it, and then be killed by the nations around them than it would be if they were to be headstrong and perish having done nothing. Why should that be?

Yet the ending of the nation of Israel shall be just like its beginning. It was born in captivity; it will go out the same way.

"The Word of the Lord came unto him saying, 'He that shall come forth out of your own bowels shall be your heir. Look now to the heavens and see if you are able to number the stars. So shall your seed be .... And God said to Abraham, 'Know of the certainty that your seed shall be a stranger in a land that is not theirs, and shall serve them and be afflicted for four hundred years:" Genesis 15:13.

Thus, Israel was born in captivity and bondage, and it shall go out in the same manner before Christ returns. Israel was being ruled by people who were not Jews when Christ came the first time. Even so shall it be when He comes again. What need do the Jews have for a Savior, when they have nothing to be saved from?

Understand what the nation of Israel is: It is represented by John as the "Two Witnesses." The prophets Jeremiah and Zechariah, and the apostles John and Paul, provided for identification of the Two Witnesses as the believers of God in the House of Israel and the House of Judah. Today, they are represented by the believers in the nation of Israel. God is with Israel today! Israel came into existence according to His plan, which He is still working.

The nation of Israel was reborn as Zechariah recorded: Zechariah 12:6,7 from the world's wilderness the tents of Judah first; then the restoration of the house of David or the city of Jerusalem. The hands of the Jews did not do this! God caused the world to drive them out of the countries they inhabited during World War II. Then the world, in shock and shame at their tortures and deaths, permitted them to travel to Palestine. The Jews had not sought it, God forced the trip upon them. Palestine became the only place where the Jews felt they could obtain peace, so they went there. Then God caused the Arabs to start three major battles; the first established the nation, the second caused expansion of the territory to protect it; and the third, the Six Day War, repossessed Jerusalem. The times of the Gentiles had ended. The cleansing of the sanctuary was complete. The nation of Israel now has the promise and the power to do whatsoever she desires upon the earth. John stated that the Jews could cause the rain to stop would they but ask it of God. Revelation 11:6.

But Israel does not have much time. They have put off their sackcloth and wear the robe of power, but will they call upon God, nationally, for power to do what they wish? The timetable is running out. John's "beast from the abyss," Daniel's "little horn," is due to overcome them.

We have seen how the Assyrian will deceive Israel with a peace treaty, after Israel takes over Lebanon. We have seen how the Egyptian will provoke the Assyrian, causing him to break the treaty, attack, and overcome the nations of Israel, Egypt, and the Sudan. We have seen how political pressure will cause the Assyrian to return and camp upon the Mount of Olives, where he will proclaim that he is a god and worthy of worship.

His camp upon the top of the Mount is the location from which he will fulfill these words of Daniel. "Through his policy he shall cause craft to prosper in his hand; and he shall magnify himself in his heart, and by peace shall destroy many; he shall also stand up against the Prince of Princes; but he shall be broken without hand." Daniel 8:25. The Assyrian and Christ will stand face to face in his camp upon the mount.

This personal confrontation will take place at the end of the seventieth week. It will be more than the Assyrian can take, and he will die there. His death may be caused by a heart attack brought on by the earthquake, but that view is not supported by the meaning of the words "Broken without hand." These words speak of a death that is caused by someone. The Assyrian does not just die; he is cut off. Note that it is said that no man kills him. This leaves only God to do it through the power of the returned Christ. Let's see how He will do it by reexamining the piecemeal revelations about Christ's return.

We have seen what the Assyrian will do to the witnesses during the last half of the seventieth week; he will kill them, leave their bodies unburied, and change the worship services of those who remain. Then, at the end of the seventieth week, the dead will receive the breath of life again, stand on their feet, and rise to heaven following the command, "Come up here!" In fear, their enemies will watch them rise. Their nerves will start shaking; their bodies will, too. Their fear will, seemingly be transmitted to the earth itself and it will start to shake.

Then, in that same hour, there will be an earthquake that will destroy one tenth of the city of Jerusalem and kill seven thousand men. Then those who remain will give glory to the God of Heaven! Why? Because Christ will be here upon the earth! He will have finally returned! You see, this earthquake which John recorded will be the result of what Zechariah saw. Zechariah explained its cause this way.

"And His feet shall stand in that day upon the Mount of Olives, which is before Jerusalem on the east, and the Mount shall cleave in its midst thereof toward the east and toward the west, and there shall be a very great valley; and half of the mountain shall remove toward the north, and half of it toward the south. And you shall flee to the valley of the mountains for the valley of the mountains shall reach unto Azel: yea, you shall flee, like as you fled before the earthquake in the days of Uzziah, king of Judah: and the Lord my God shall come, and all the saints with Thee." Zechariah 14:4,5.

When Christ returns, He will stand right in front of the Assyrian, upon the top of the Mount of Olives, in the middle of his camp, to personally cut him off from the land of the living.2 Thessalonians 2:7-10. And one of His angels standing by will capture Satan as he attempts to flee the mortal body.

The full import of this first return as a thief, unaccompanied by the Rapture, is brought home by two Scriptures. The first is part of Nebuchadnezzar's vision. In it, he saw a stone prepared by God come through the air to smash the ten toes and the whole image. Then the stone underwent a transformation. It grew into a mountain at the place where it came to rest, and then it expanded until it filled the whole earth. The second was spoken on the top of the Mount of Olives. "Men of Galilee, why do you stand looking into the sky? This Jesus, who has been taken up from you into heaven, will come in just the same way as you have watched Him go into heaven!' Acts1:11.

Christ rose from the top of the Mount of Olives through the air into heaven, as men watched him go. Gabriel's words about his return will also have him come from heaven, through the air to the top of the Mount of Olives, as men watch His complete return. At this time, they will not see Him pause in the air to gather His own to Him. His journey will be nonstop.

A geological rift runs through the Middle East. Right now, it is just lying there, awaiting the pressure of that special footprint to trigger the movement and cause the Mount to split in half. When it does, that Man standing on its top will not have to claim to be Christ. He will be! Doubting Thomas's proof will be seen.

It is this event that the living Jews are waiting for. Those whom the Assyrian does not kill will be fully aware of the Scriptures. They will have been brought through the tribulation because they know God. They will await the sign of this special earthquake, because they will recognize the One standing upon the top of the Mount. Their actions will say they know; otherwise, they will seem crazy. Just look at what they will do after the quake occurs: They will run right into the crevasse! They will flee from the city by the way of the crevasse as they run to the top of the mount. They will know who is there! This will be the quickest way they can get out of the city to meet Him. It will be even as Zechariah recorded.

"And I will pour upon the house of David, and upon the inhabitants of Jerusalem, the spirit of grace and of supplication. And they shall look upon Me whom they have pierced, and they shall mourn for Him as one mourns for his only son, and shall be in bitterness for Him, as one that is in bitterness for his firstborn." Zechariah 12:9,10.

Those who remain will look upon the Messiah. They will see the scars from the nails and the spear. They will realize that He is the Man that their fathers rejected and killed. They will be overcome with feelings of ancestor hate, not ancestor love. They will be bitter about what they were taught and what they believed. Their eyes will behold the truth.

Hallelujah! Praise be to God of Heaven! Israel's Messiah is here! Bless the nation of Israel, for Christ will! It will be a nation without the ability to sin.

Zechariah spoke "of the spirit of grace and of supplication." Isaiah said, "In that day man will have regard for his Maker and his eyes will look to the Holy One of Israel." Isaiah 17:7. Jeremiah also spoke of this, "'Behold the days are coming' declares the Lord, 'When I will make a new covenant with the house of Israel and with the house of Judah, not like the covenant which I made with their fathers in the day I took them by the hand to bring them out of the land of Egypt, My covenant which they broke, although I was a husband to them. But this is the covenant which I will make with the house of Israel after those days', declares the Lord, 'I will put My law within them, and on their heart I will write it; and I will be their God, and they shall be My people. "And they shall not teach again, each man his neighbor and each man his brother, saying: Know the Lord, for they shall all know Me, from the least of them to the greatest of them' declares the Lord, 'For I will forgive their iniquity and their sin I will remember no more." Jeremiah 31:31-34.

Jeremiah lived when his country was split in two parts: the houses of Israel and Judah. In the days of this new covenant it will be made only with the house of Israel, for the two parts would be whole again; one nation under the Son of God. All the sins of those who remain, the remnant left at Christ's coming, will be forgiven. It will be easy to forgive them, for this remnant will have been cleansed of those who were impure through the action of the Assyrian's army. Then it will be impossible for them to sin anymore, because they will be the only nation on earth with a perfect ruler. And the rest of these words of Isaiah will be fulfilled. "O people in Zion, inhabitant in Jerusalem, you will weep no longer. He will surely be gracious to you at the sound of your cry; when He hears it He will answer you. Although the Lord has given you bread of privation and water of oppression, He, your Teacher, will no longer hide Himself, but your eyes will behold your Teacher. And your ears will hear a word behind you, "This is the way, walk in it: whenever you turn to the right or to the left. And you will defile your graven images, overlaid with silver, and your molten images overlaid with gold. You will scatter them as an impure thing; and say to them, 'Be gone!' Then He will give you rain for the seed which you will sew in the ground, and bread from the yield of the ground, and it will be rich and plenteous, on that day your live stock will graze in a roomy pasture. Also the oxen and donkeys which work the ground will eat salted fodder, which has been winnowed with shovel and fork." Isaiah 30:19-24.

Whenever you were tempted, were you in doubt about what you should do? Jews living in Israel will not have this problem when Christ returns and removes their iniquity, for they will hear a voice whenever doubts arise, saying, "This is the way."

The Disputed Boundaries

Christ removed the sins of Israel over which He rules, but He does not rule over the world. His first duties are toward His promises to Israel. Two of them now assume major importance. The first is the completion of the re-gathering. Jeremiah, Chapter thirty-one, deals extensively with the subject. Here are some excerpts: "at that time,' declares the Lord, 'I will be the God of all the families of Israel, and they shall be my people: 'Behold I am bringing them from the north country, and I will gather them from the remote parts of the earth.' 'He who scatters Israel will gather him.'" Right now the earth is full of Jews. When Christ comes they will all return to Israel. Where shall they live? This is the second major promise—they shall possess the land from the Euphrates River to the river of Egypt, the Nile River.

Here is the ultimate boundary of Israel. "On that day the Lord made a covenant with Abraham, saying, 'To your seed I have given this land, from the river of Egypt as far as the great river, the River Euphrates.'" Genesis 15:18

The Ten Nations

— — — → The Route of the Assyrian
*The Three to be 'Plucked out'

1. Syria
2. Israel*
3. Jordan
4. Iraq
5. Kuwait

6. Saudi Arabia
7. Yemen
8. Egypt*
9. Sudan *
10. Ethiopia

In a later passage, referring to the land boundaries which the people led by Joshua were to possess, the wording was changed. "And I will fix your boundary from the Reed Sea to the Sea of the Philistines and from the wilderness to the River Euphrates; for I will deliver the inhabitants of the land into your hand, and you will drive them out before you." Exodus23:31. Egypt was cut off because God wanted to remove completely any hopes the people of the Exodus had of ever returning there.

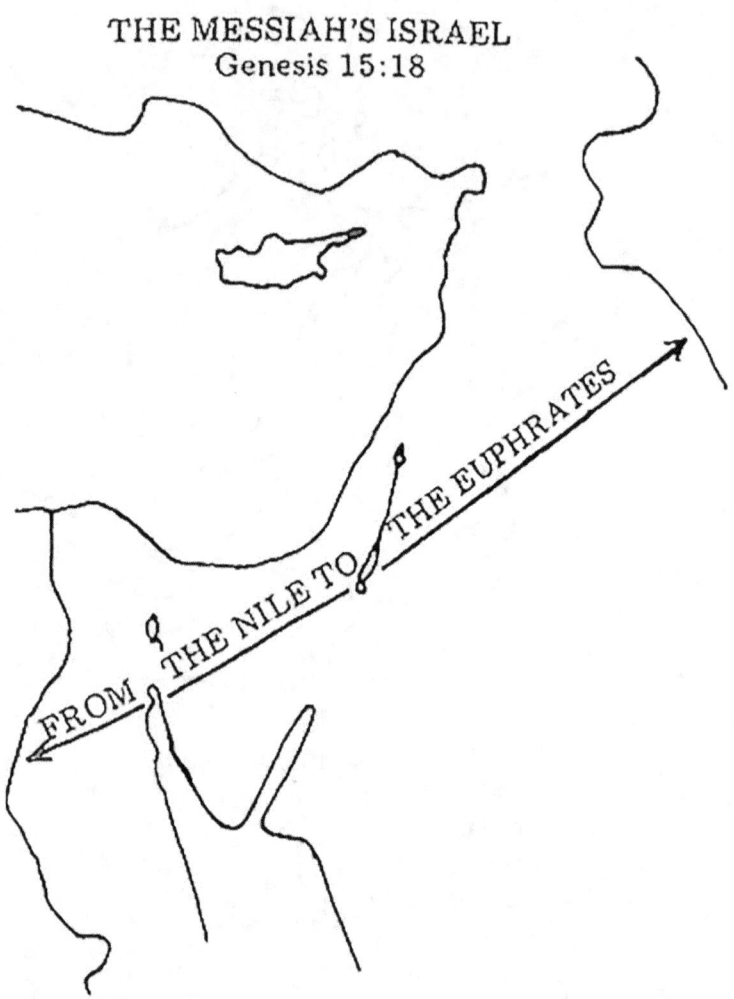

THE MESSIAH'S ISRAEL
Genesis 15:18

FROM THE NILE TO THE EUPHRATES

As the nation of Israel sins and rejects the Lord, the boundaries shrink even more. Numbers 34:2-21 Now, the boundary no longer reaches to either the river of Egypt or Euphrates. The rebellions and the dissatisfactions of the children of Israel had caused their promised territory to be less than what was originally promised to Abraham. This was because the original promise to Abraham did not pertain to them! Paul sets us straight. "Now the promises were spoken to Abraham and to his seed." He does not say, "and to seeds," referring to many, but rather to one, "and to your seed", that is, Christ." Galations 3:16

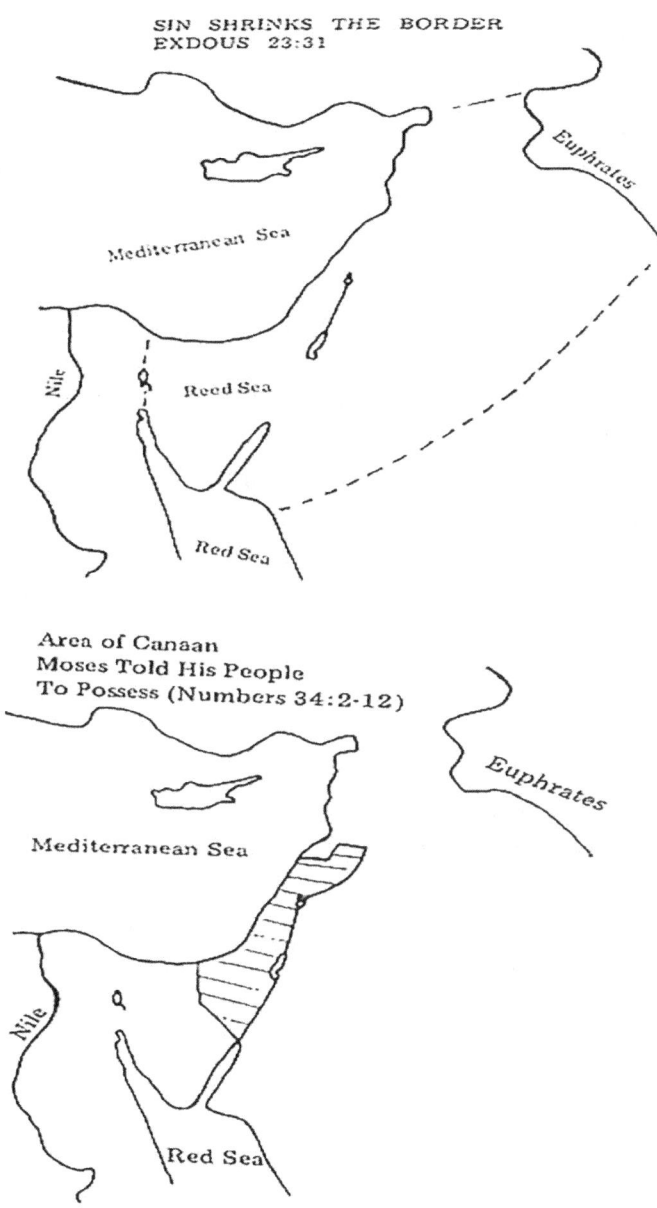

SIN SHRINKS THE BORDER
EXDOUS 23:31

Mediterranean Sea

Euphrates

Nile

Reed Sea

Red Sea

Area of Canaan
Moses Told His People
To Possess (Numbers 34:2-12)

Mediterranean Sea

Euphrates

Nile

Red Sea

The fullness of the promise was that to Christ alone would go the territory extending from the river of Egypt to the great river, the River Euphrates. It was not promised to the people of Israel, and they never possessed this range of territory. They were limited, first from the Reed Sea to the Euphrates, and then, because of their sins, their border was drawn short of the Euphrates itself. Christ alone was to see to the fullness of the original promise!

The nations that currently possess this land are the ten nations that Christ shall smite, cited by Daniel through the vision of Nebuchadnezzar. Which ten nations are these? The possibility exists that when Christ returns the world shall be composed only of ten nations. This possibility, though, would not go along with the explanation of Daniel's vision that the ten nations would come out of the boundary of the fourth kingdom, which was represented by the ram which stood for the Median and Persian Empire. Therefore, the ten nations would come from the boundaries of this Empire. Does the Bible name them? Can we locate the specific territory they would inhabit? Yes, God's Word pinpoints their location.

These peoples lived between the Nile and the Euphrates. Genesis 15:18-21. It is from this area that ten nations shall arise and be destroyed by Christ in the reestablishment and expansion of Israel. In Abraham's time this is the listing of the ten peoples who lived between the Nile and the Euphrates rivers. 1. Amorite, 2. Canaanite; 3. Girgashite; 4. Hittite; 5. Jebusite; 6. Kadmonite; 7. Kenite; 8. Kenizzite; 9. Perizzite; 10. Rephaim.

What are the modern names of these countries? At the time of Christ's return there shall be: (1) Syria, (2) Israel, (3) Jordan, (4) Iraq, (5) Kuwait, (6) Saudi Arabia, (7) Yemen, (8) Egypt, (9) Sudan, and (10) Ethiopia. Major portions, if not all of these countries, will come within the boundaries of Israel under the Power of the returned Christ, who will establish the kingdom. That which was promised to Abraham will come to the ruler of Israel!

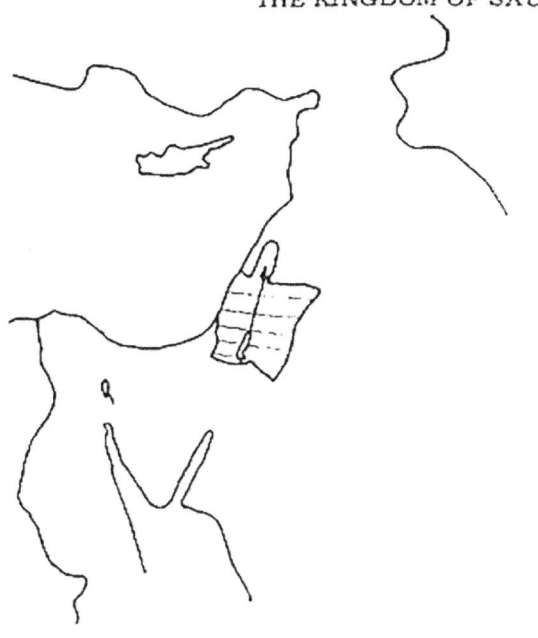

THE KINGDOM OF SAUL

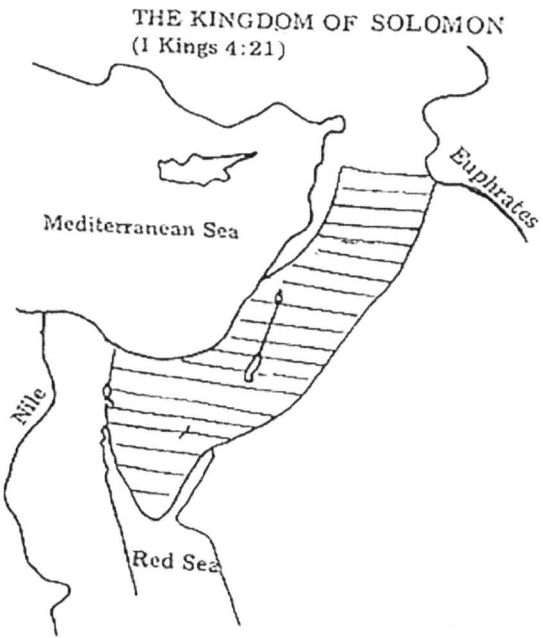

THE KINGDOM OF SOLOMON
(1 Kings 4:21)

Mediterranean Sea

Euphrates

Nile

Red Sea

119

The language of the land of Canaan will be Hebrew when Christ returns. Other nations will speak it too. And, "In that day, five cities in the land of Egypt will be speaking the language of the land of Canaan and swearing allegiance to the Lord of Hosts. One will be called the City of Destruction. In that day there will be an altar to the Lord in the midst of Egypt and a pillar to the Lord near its border. And it will become a sign and a witness to the Lord of Hosts in the land of Egypt; for they will cry to the Lord because of oppressors, and He will send them a Savior and a Champion, and He will deliver them. Thus, the Lord shall make Himself known to Egypt, and the Egyptians will know the Lord in that day." Isaiah 19:18-21. The nation of Israel will expand and stretch from the Euphrates to the Nile under the power of the returned Christ.

Four of these ten nations were specifically named by Daniel, represented by the fierce horn and the three other horns which it plucked out by the roots. We have seen that the nation of the fierce horn will be Assyria, that is the union of Iraq and Syria. We have also seen that the three nations the Assyrian will overrun will be Israel, Egypt, and the Sudan.

Pity poor Egypt and the Sudan! They will cease to exist as inhabited nations. The troubles they felt under the cruel master, the Assyrian, are not severe enough in the sight of God for their past haughtiness. We have seen that Christ will possess the land to the east of the Nile. The land to the west of the Nile will be so severely damaged that every human and animal will be driven from it, and they will not return for forty years.

"Therefore, thus saith the Lord God, 'Behold, I will bring a sword upon thee, and cut off man and beast out of thee. And the land of Egypt shall be desolate and waste; and they shall know that I am the Lord; because He said: The river is mine and I have made it. Behold, therefore I am against thee, and against the rivers, and I will make the land of Egypt utterly waste and desolate, from the tower of Syene even unto the border of Ethiopia. No foot of man shall pass through it, nor foot of beast shall pass through it, neither shall it be in inhabited forty years. And I will make the land of Egypt desolate in the midst of the countries that are desolate, and her cities among the cities that are laid waste shall be desolate forty years; and I will scatter the Egyptians among the nations, and will disperse them through the countries.'

"Yet thus saith the Lord God, 'At the end of forty years will I gather the Egyptians from the people whither they were scattered; and I will bring again the captivity of Egypt, and will cause them to return into the land of Pathros, into the land of the habitation and they shall be their base kingdom. It shall be the basest of the kingdoms; neither shall it exalt itself any more above the nations; for I will diminish them, that they shall no more rule over the nations. And it shall be no more the confidence of the house of Israel, which brings their iniquity to remembrance, when they shall look after them; but they shall know that I am the Lord God." Ezekiel 29:8-16.

Once more the cursed weapons of mankind, or a power very similar to that which was used upon the holy people, will now be used to devastate the rest of Egypt and the Sudan. In memory of this, one city they will possess east of the Nile will be renamed the City of Destruction.

The destruction will really be complete in the area from the tower of Syene to the border of Ethiopia. Gibbon's map, "The Extent of The Roman Empire at the Death of Trajan." locates Syene in southern Egypt. Comparing this to a modern map positions Syene just to the south of Aswan. Now we can see that there will be a complete destruction from Aswan through the whole of the Nile river basin. No one will live or walk there.

Cairo, the city that will be renamed the City of Destruction should then be north of this area.

When Christ returns he shall not return alone. Zechariah stated, "Then the Lord, O my God, will come, and all the holy ones with him." Zechariah 14:5. These holy ones are not the saved of the earth, for the Rapture has not yet taken place. Who then are they? John knows and stated it like this, "And I looked, and behold, the Lamb was standing on Mount Zion, and with him one hundred and forty-four thousand, having His name and the name of His father written on their foreheads." Revelation 14:1. The words of Zechariah are clarified, "All the saints" referred to the number John saw. These are the one hundred and forty-four thousand John mentioned. They were the souls under the altar asking the question, "How long?" But they were told to rest awhile longer until their full number would be attained. Revelation 6:9-11. It will be attained in the coming Assyrian-Israeli war, when the total number of Israelites who have served only the Lord from their birth on, are killed for the testimony of the witness of Christ which they had maintained. These are they who come to life and reign with Christ forever. John wrote, "And I saw the souls of those who had been beheaded because of the testimony of Jesus and because of the word of God, and those who had not worshipped the beast or his image, and had not received the mark upon their forehead and upon their hand; and they came to life and reigned with Christ for a thousand years. The rest of the dead did not come to life until the thousand years were completed. This is the first resurrection. Blessed and holy is the one who has a part in the first resurrection; over these the second death has no power, but they will be priests of God and of Christ and will reign with him for a thousand years." Revelation 20:4-6.

These one hundred and forty-four thousand are the first to receive life and return to reign with Christ, forever. There will be a period of time after He begins to rule with these beloved ones that His rule will have peace. This peace will begin with the death of the Assyrian and the capture of Satan and end with the battle of Armageddon. However long this takes, John felt that the privilege of ruling with Christ would make it seem like a thousand years.

During this period, Israel will be truly blessed. The land expansion will be followed by a population explosion. From all over the world, the Jews will return. "'For behold the days are coming,' declares the Lord, 'when I shall raise up for David a righteous branch; and he will reign as king and act wisely and do justice and righteousness in the land. In his days Judah will be saved, and Israel will dwell securely; and this is his name by which he will be called, The Lord our righteousness. Therefore, behold the days are coming when they shall no longer say: as the Lord lives, who brought up the sons of Israel from the land of Egypt; but: As the Lord lives, who brought up and led back the descendants of the household of Israel from the north land and from all the countries where I had driven them. Then they will live on their own soil.'" Jeremiah 23:5-8.

Hosea proclaimed, "Afterward, the sons of Israel will return and seek the Lord their God and David their king; and they will come trembling to the Lord and to His goodness in the last days." Hosea 3:5 Even Ezekiel prophesied over 350 years after King David was dead and buried, "'Then I will set over them one shepherd, My servant David, and he will feed them; he will feed them himself and be their shepherd. And I, the Lord, will be their God, and My servant David will be prince among them; I, the Lord have spoken." Ezekiel 34:23,24.

Zechariah testified to the same. "Thus says the Lord of Hosts; 'It will yet be that people will come, even the inhabitants of many cities; and the inhabitants of one will go to another saying: Let us go at once to entreat the favor of the Lord, and to seek the Lord of hosts; I will go also.'" So many peoples and mighty nations will come to seek the Lord of Hosts in Jerusalem and to entreat the favor of the Lord. In those days, ten men from the nations of every language will grasp the garment of a Jew saying, "Let us go with you, for we have heard that God is with you." Zechariah 8:20-23. Yes, He is ruling over the nation of Israel. For if we believe that He will return, how can we fail to believe that He will perform the rest of the works written about Him? Praise the God of Israel, for He brought His people home.

The nation now has land and people, but the bounty of God does not stop there. A fertility unknown since the Garden of Eden shall double the produce yielded by the earth. The Psalmist sang, "Thou dost visit the earth and cause it to overflow; Thou dost greatly enrich it; the stream of God is full of water; Thou dost prepare their grain, for thus, Thou doest prepare the earth. Thou dost water its furrows abundantly; Thou dost settle its ridges; Thou dost soften it with showers; Thou dost bless its growth. Thou halt crowned the year with Thy bounty, and Thy paths drip with fatness. The pastures of the wilderness drip and the hills gird themselves with rejoicing. The meadows are clothed with flocks, and the valleys are covered covered with grain; they shout for joy, yes, they sing." Psalms 65:9-13.

Isaiah wrote, "Then they will rebuild the ancient ruins they will raise up the former devastations, and they will repair the ruined cities, the desolations of many generations. And strangers will stand and pasture your flocks, and foreigners will be your farmers and your vinedressers. But you will be called the priests of the Lord; you will be spoken of as ministers of our God. You will eat the wealth of nations, and in their riches you will boast. Instead of your shame you will have a double portion, and instead of humiliation they will shout for joy over their portion. Therefore, they will possess a double portion in their land, everlasting joy will be theirs." Isaiah 61:4-7.

Israel shall be blessed and fabulously wealthy. "Instead of bronze I will bring gold; and instead of iron I will bring silver; and instead of wood, bronze; and instead of stones, iron. And I will make peace your administrators and righteousness your overseers." Isaiah 6:17. Isaiah also said, "The wealth of the nations will come to you." Isaiah 60:5 Haggai recorded, "For thus says the Lord of Hosts, 'Once more in a little while, I am going to shake the heavens and the earth, the sea also and the dry land. And I will shake all the nations; and they will come with the wealth of all nations; and I will fill this house with glory.'" Haggai 2:6,7.

Praise the God of Israel. Not only will He provide land, people, fertility, and wealth from all the nations, He will provide Peace! "And the wolf will dwell with the lamb, and leopard with the kid, and the calf and the young lion and the fatling together; and the little boy will lead them. Also the cow and bear will graze, their young will lie down together; and the lion will eat straw like the ox. And the nursing child will play by the hole of the cobra, and the weaned child will put his hand in the viper's den. They will not hurt or destroy in all My holy mountain, for the earth will be full of the knowledge of the Lord as the waters cover the sea." Isaiah 11:6-9.

Ezekiel likewise testifies, "Thus says the Lord, , 'When I gather the house of Israel from the peoples among whom they are scattered, and shall manifest My holiness among their land which I gave to my servant Jacob. And they will live in it securely, and they will build houses, plant vineyards, and live securely, when I execute judgments upon all who scorn them round about them. Then they will know that I am the Lord their God." Ezekiel 28:25,26.

Praise His holy name!

The Messiah was promised to Israel alone. Yet, when He rules on the throne of David He will not ignore the needs of other nations. They will come to Him for counseling and blessing. "In the last days, the mountain of the house of the Lord will be established as the chief of the mountains, and will be raised above the hills, and all the nations will stream to it. And many peoples will come and say, 'Come, let us go up to the mountain of the Lord, to the house of the God of Jacob, that He may teach us concerning His ways, and that we may walk in His paths, for the Law will go forth from Zion, and the word of the Lord from Jerusalem. And He will judge between the nations, and will render decisions for many peoples; and they will hammer their swords into plowshares, and their spears into pruning hooks. Nation will not lift up sword against nation, and never again will they learn war." Isaiah 2:2-4.

And the men of war will crawl out of their holes in the ground, ashamed of their great strength, crawling on their hands and knees, licking the dust before His feet, seeking forgiveness. Micah 7:16,17

Trouble in Eden

As it was in the Garden of Eden the first time, when sin entered in while God walked there, even so shall problems remain.

The presence of Christ is primarily to remove iniquity, re-gather, expand, bless and rule Israel. He will counsel other nations and bless those that accept and heed His words. Nevertheless, there will still be in the world those who do not fully believe and accept Christ but only pretend obedience. The Psalmist sings of them twice, "Shout joyfully to God, all the earth; sing the glory of His works! Because of the greatness of Thy power Thine enemies will give feigned obedience to Thee. All the earth will worship Thee, and will sing praises to Thee; they will sing praises to Thy name." Psalms 66:1-4 Then again He said, "Oh, that My people would listen to Me, that Israel would walk in My ways! I would quickly subdue their enemies, and turn My hand against their adversaries. Those who hate the Lord would pretend obedience to Him; and their time of punishment would be forever. But I would feed you with the finest of the wheat; and with honey from the rock I would satisfy you." Psalms 81:13-16.

Praise the God of Israel, for He will send them their Savior!

When Christ sets foot upon the earth in front of the Assyrian and slays him, one of His angels standing by will seize the Devil as he attempts to flee from the body. Then he will imprison Satan for a time. Why? God is going to show man, one more time, how depraved he really is. Man sinned the first time in the presence of God through the lie of the Devil. With God again present upon the earth, and with the Devil removed, all men will still not change their minds, turn from their carnal ways, and worship God.

Alongside of bliss, there will be gall at what this Man has done. He will have done what these other prideful men could not do. He will have established peace! When the devil is released, it is to these people that he will go; and he will deceive them. Satan "will come out to deceive the nations which are in the four corners of the earth, Gog and Magog, to gather them together for the war; the number of them is like the sand of the seashore. And they came up on the broad plain of the earth and surrounded the camp of the saints and the beloved city, and fire came down from heaven and devoured them. And the devil who deceived them was thrown into the lake of fire and brimstone, where the beast and the false prophet are also; and they will be tormented day and night forever and ever." Revelation 20:8-10.

Many prophets have foreseen and recorded the events of this battle. Ezekiel names where the participants would come from in his thirty-eighth and thirty-ninth chapters. Here is the essence of the story of these two chapters, with other informative passages inserted.

"II am against you; O Gog, Prince of Rosh, Meshech, and Tubal, Persia, Ethiopia, Put, Gomer, and Beth-togarmah from the remote parts of the north with all its troops—many peoples with. I will turn you about, put hooks into your jaws, and bring you out with all your army. Prepare yourself and be on guard for all your companies assembled about you. In the latter years you will be summoned into the land that is restored from the sword, whose inhabitants have been gathered from many nations to the mountains of Israel and they are all living securely. You will come like a storm; like a cloud covering the land, you and all your troops and many peoples with you." (The number of the armies of the horsemen was two hundred million.) Rev.9:16.

"'It will come about on that day that thoughts will come into your mind, and you will devise an evil plan. You will say: 'I will go up against the land of unwalled villages, against those who are at rest; living securely, without walls, and having no bars or gates; to capture spoil and to seize plunder. On that day when My people Israel are living securely, will you not know it? (And the sixth angel poured out his bowl upon the great river, the Euphrates; and its water was dried up, that the way might be prepared for the kings from the east. (It is highly likely that the earthquake which splits the Mount of Olives in half, so that one half the mountain moves to the north, causes the entire mountain range to move and shuts off the flow of water in the Euphrates River.) They gathered them together to the place which in Hebrew is called Har-Magedon.) Rev.16:12,16. And you will come from your place out of the remote parts of the north, you and many people with you. You will come up against My people Israel like a cloud to cover the land. It will come about in the last days that I shall bring you against My land, in order that the nations may know Me when I shall be sanctified through you before their eyes, O Gog, I shall strike your bow from

127

your left hand, and dash down your arrows from your right hand. You shall fall on the mountains of Israel. I shall give you as food to every kind of predatory bird and beast of the field. You will fall on the open field. (Now this will be the plague with which the Lord will strike all the people who have gone against Jerusalem; their flesh will rot while they stand on their feet, and their eyes will rot in their sockets, and their tongues will rot in their mouths. It will come about in that day that a great panic from the Lord will fall on them; and they will seize one another's hands, and the hand of one will be lifted against the hand of another. So also like this plague will be the plague on the horse, the mule, the camel, the donkey, and all the cattle that will be in those camps.) Zech.14:12-15. Then those who inhabit the cities of Israel will go out and make fires with the weapons and burn them, both shields and bucklers, bows and arrows, war clubs and spears; for seven years they will make fires of them. It will come about on that day that I shall give Gog a burial ground there in Israel, the valley of those who pass by east of the sea, and it will block the passerby. So they will bury Gog there with all his multitude, and they will call it The Valley of Hamon-Gog. For seven months the house of Israel will be burying them in order to cleanse the land.'" ("Multitude-multitudes in the valley of decision! For the day of the Lord is near in the valley of decision." Joel 3:14. And bring them down to the valley of Jehoshaphat." Joel 3:2. These verses describe the valley to be formed when the feet of Christ touch the Mount of Olives which is just east of Jerusalem.) "'And as those who pass through the land pass through and anyone sees a man's bone, then he will set up a marker by it until the buriers have buried it in the valley of Hamon-Gog. Even the name of the city (Jerusalem) will be Hamonnah. So they will cleanse the land. Son of Man, speak to every kind of a bird and to every beast of the field; "Assemble and come, gather from every side to My sacrifice which I am going to sacrifice for you, as a great sacrifice on the mountains of Israel, that you may eat flesh and drink blood. You will be glutted at My table with horses, charioteers, mighty men, and all the men of war. I will set my glory among the nations; and all nations will see My judgment which I have executed, and My hand which I have laid on them. And the house of Israel will know that I am the Lord their God from that day onward. I will not hide My face from them any longer, FOR I SHALL HAVE POURED OUT MY SPIRIT ON THE HOUSE OF ISRAEL,' declares the Lord" (emphasis mine).

Consider the participants of the attacking army. According to Ezekiel 38:1-6, they are: Gog of the land of Magog, who is the Prince of Rosh, Mesheck, and Tubal. Walvoord says this about Gog: "It seems clear according to this that the army will come from the north. If the terms such as 'Rosh' are traced, which is close to the word Russia, and 'Meshech,' which many say refers to the city of Moscow, a clear identification can be made in this portion of scripture of a great army coming down from Russia upon the land of Palestine.'" Walvoord, THE RETURN OF THE LORD. And why shouldn't it be? Russia was one of the major suppliers of weapons to the Assyrian. One of the lies the Devil will use to deceive the rulers of Russia will be similar to the following: "How foolish have we been? When the earthquake killed the Assyrian, why didn't we stop this new upstart Jew from taking over and reestablishing his country? But now they will be easy prey for us. They are rich. They do not have an army. They have no protection. Let us go there and once and for all erase these Jews from the face of the earth."

The allied forces will be: Persia, Cush, Put, Gomer and Beth-togarmah. Who are their modern counterparts? Persia, was the last of the four great Asiatic empires which was bounded on the west by Turkey, on the north by Transcaucasia and the Caspian Sea, on the east by Afghanistan and Beluchistan, and on the south by the Persian Gulf and the Arabian Sea. Much of this area Christ will then be ruling, within the expanded boundary of Israel we have already discussed. Two countries, though, will still remain to be allies, as they are east of the Euphrates. They are half of Iraq and all of Iran.

Cush will come from Ethiopia. Put from Libya west of Egypt.

Gomer settled on the north of the Black Sea and then spread southward and westward to the extremities of Europe. Three modern countries in this area are: Rumania, Bulgaria and Yugoslavia.

Tomgarmah was a son of Gomer, who was a son of Japeth. His descendants settled in the north part of Armenia. Armenia is now divided between Iran, Turkey, and the USSR.

We now have a picture of this army composed of much of the Communist block in Europe, along with Iraq and Iran, as kings of the east who resent the expansion of Israel, and the Communist sympathizers Libya and Ethiopia.

The time for the horrors of Armageddon will come. It will be at the Last Passover. Every Jew will live while two hundred million men die as they attempt to fulfill their intention, once and for all, to wipe every Jew and the nation of Israel off the face of the earth. When they invade Israel, energy from a powerful source of radiation will wither their flesh away. Their eyes will rot in their sockets, and their tongues will rot in their mouths, in the same way in which a microwave oven cooks its food—the radiation energy stirs the molecules of flesh to such great activity that the moisture is heated up and instantly evaporates from the body.

Muscles will no longer respond to nerve impulses; nerves themselves will no longer operate. The cartilage and ligaments will not be able to prevent the bones from falling to the ground. Soon, the stench of death will reach the birds of prey and they will come to feed on what is left. Every man and beast of the invading army will die in this fashion, while the Jews are passed over once again!

The last major burial detail will then form. Their work will be easy, because the mass grave for the army will have been opened when Christ's feet touched the Mount of Olives and it split in half. The valley in between therefore will have two purposes: first, it will identify Christ; then it is going to receive and hide the remains of the bodies that litter the earth. The whole army of Gog will be interred there.

After seven months of this detail, another search will be made. Every last bone of this mass of humanity will be cast into the valley. Then it will receive a new name: the Valley of Hammon-gog. Even Jerusalem will be renamed Hammonah because of the army buried there.

Praise the God of Israel for His judgments upon the earth!

They will come.

At this time, we need to reexamine some Scriptures about Armageddon, the sequence of events of Christ's rule, Armageddon, and the Rapture. In Revelation 20:7-9, John records that the period of Christ's rule, which he called the one thousand years, would be terminated by the Battle of Armageddon. This battle would also be prompted by the angel who will pour out the sixth vial of God's wrath—Revelation 16:12-11. It will be heralded by the sixth trumpet of Revelation 9:13-21. Therefore, the Rapture, which accompanies the seventh trumpet, will occur after the battle of Armageddon is fought.

In the beginning the Lord walked upon the earth with Adam, yet the serpent caused sin to enter into the Garden of Eden. Later, Cain talked with God about his offering, and when Cain went from the Lord's presence he killed his brother Abel. Even so, sin will remain in all parts of the world, except the nation of Israel, in spite of the power and presence of Christ, in spite of the outcome of the battle of Armageddon. The things of mammon will still remain, and so "the rest of mankind, who were not killed by these plagues, did not repent of the works of their hands, so as not to worship demons, and the idols of gold and of silver and of brass and of stone and of wood, which can neither see nor hear nor walk; and they did not repent of their murders nor their sorceries nor of their immorality nor of their thefts." Rev.9:20,21.

Because of this, the Lord will seek to bring retribution. At the end of His reign on the throne of David He will fulfill the words of Daniel. "I kept looking in the night visions, and behold, with the clouds of heaven One like a Son of Man was coming, and He came up to the Ancient of Days and was presented before Him. And to Him was given dominion, glory and a kingdom, that all the peoples, nations and men of every language, might serve Him. His

131

dominion is an everlasting dominion which will not pass away; and His kingdom is one which shall not be destroyed." Dan.7:13,14.

When Christ finishes fulfilling the prophecies to the nation of Israel He will go back to His Father to give a report and receive His coronation as king of all the earth. Then the last day for this earth, the day of His wrath, will come suddenly upon man.

The Day with Rapture and Wrath

The last day will begin with the resurrection and the Rapture. Christ stated, "This is the will of Him who sent Me, that of all that He has given Me I lose nothing, but raise it up on the last day." John 6:39. The last heavenly day is then when the Rapture occurs. Therefore, the Rapture is not only post-millennial, it is also pre-wrath!

This return will be with power and glory. "For just as the lightning comes from the east, and flashes even to the west, so shall the coming of the Son of Man be. And He will send forth His angels with a great trumpet and they will gather together His elect from the four winds, from one end of the sky to the other." Matthew 24:27,31.

Another description of this event goes, "Behold, I tell you a mystery; we shall not all sleep, but we shall all be changed, in a moment, in the twinkling of an eye, at the last trumpet; for the trumpet will sound, and the dead will be raised imperishable, and we shall be changed." 1 Corinthians 15:51,52.

Most enlightening of all the scriptures on the subject is, "For if we believe that Jesus died and rose again, even so God will bring with Him those who have fallen asleep in Jesus. For this we say to you, by the word of the Lord, that we who are alive and remain until the coming of the Lord shall not precede those who have fallen asleep. For the Lord Himself will descend from heaven with a shout, with the voice of the archangel, with the trumpet of God; and the dead in Christ shall rise first. Then we who are alive and remain shall be caught up together with them in the clouds to meet the Lord in the air, and thus we shall always be with the Lord." 1 Thess.4:14-17.

Thus the seventh trumpet will be blown at the start of the last day, ushering in the Resurrection and Rapture, causing the believers to rise and meet Christ in the air.

The seventh trumpet heralds these events, even as John recorded, "But in the days of the voice of the seventh angel, when he is about to sound, then the mystery of God is finished, as He preached to His servants the prophets." Rev. 10:7. And the seventh angel sounded; and there arose loud voices in heaven, saying, 'The kingdom of the world has become the kingdom of Our Lord, and of His Christ; and He will reign forever and ever' And the twenty-four elders who sit on their thrones before God, fell on their faces and worshipped God saying, thanks, 'We give Thee thanks, O Lord God, the Almighty, who art and wast, because Thou has taken Thy great power and hast begun to reign. And the nations were enraged, and Thy wrath came, and the time came for the dead to be judged, and to give their reward to Thy bondservants the prophets and to the saints and to those who destroy the earth. And the temple of God which is in heaven was opened; and the ark of His covenant appeared in the temple, and there were flashes of lightning and sounds and peals of thunder and an earthquake and a great hailstorm.'" Rev.11:15-19. Christ will return at last in power and great glory as king of all the earth. "And I looked and behold, a white cloud, and sitting on the cloud was one like a Son of Man, having a golden crown on His head and a sharp sickle in His hand. And another angel came out of the temple, crying out with a loud voice to Him who sat on the cloud, 'Put in your sickle and reap, because the hour to reap was come, because the harvest of the earth is ripe.' And He who sat on the cloud swung His sickle over the earth; and the earth was reaped." Rev.14:14-16.

The harvest will then have taken place. The first sickle will be put in and the wheat will be gathered into the barn. The saved will be removed from the earth and will meet their returning king and Lord in the air. Then they will watch as Christ begins to judge those evil people who remain. The last day, the "Day of Wrath," will have finally dawned, a day of horrors such as have never been;

Isaiah's "Day of Vengeance, the Year of Recompense will have begun. Isaiah 34:8.

"Because of this will not the land quake and everyone who dwells in it mourn? Indeed, all of it will rise up like the Nile and it will be tossed about, and subside like the Nile of Egypt. 'And it will come about in that day,' declared the Lord God, 'that I shall make the sun go down at noon and make the earth dark in broad daylight. Then I shall turn your festivals into mourning and all your songs into lamentation; and I will bring sackcloth on everyone's loins and baldness on every head. And I will make it like a time of mourning for an only son, and the end of it will be like a bitter day!" Amos 8:8-10.

The Lord will roam from one end of the earth to the other, seeking out all His prey. His prey will help Him bring about part of their own destruction. Imagine one thousand ICBM's belonging to Russia, China, and the United States with no righteous man left in their midst. Individual missile men from each country undoubtedly will have been raptured; and then no righteous man will remain. Will any of those immoral men remaining wait for an excuse? Consider the confusion of these men. If their president is caught up, they will say, "The enemy kidnapped him or developed a new weapon. Let's retaliate" The buttons will then be pushed. The rockets will fire and the missiles will rise and perform the act they were created for. Nations will fall. The earth will shake. The sky will become dark with pollution. The words of the prophet Isaiah filly expound the events of this day.

"Enter the rock and hide in the dust." Isaiah 2:10.

"The mountains quaked; their corpses lay like refuse in the middle of the street. Isaiah 5:25.

"They will pass through the land, hard pressed and famished, when they hunger they will be enraged and curse their King and their God as they face upwards. Then they will look to the earth, and behold, distress and darkness, the gloom of anguish; and they will be driven away into darkness." Isaiah 8:21,22.

134

"The sun will be dark when it rises, and the moon will not shed light. I will make mortal man scarcer than gold." Isaiah 13:10-12.

"The multitude of your enemies shall become like fine dust." Isaiah 29:12.

"All the nations are as nothing before Him." Isaiah 40:17.

"I will lay waste all the mountains and hills, and wither all their vegetation; I will make the rivers into coastlands, and dry up the ponds." Isaiah 42:15.

"Who is this who comes from Edom, with garments of glowing colors from Bozrah, this one who is majestic in apparel, marching in the greatness of His strength? It is I who speak in righteousness, mighty to save. Why is Your apparel red, and Your garments like the one who treads in the winepress? I have trodden the wine trough alone, and from the peoples there was no man with Me. I also trod them in anger and trampled them in My wrath; and their blood is sprinkled on My garments, and I stained all my raiment. For the Day of Vengeance was in My heart and My year of redemption has come. And I looked, and there was no one to help, and I was astonished and there was no one to uphold; so My own arm brought salvation to Me, and My wrath upheld Me. And I trod down the people in My anger and made them drunk in My wrath, and I poured out their life blood on the earth." Isaiah 63:1-6. This is the second part of the harvest; this is the reason for the second sickle. The tares must be burned.

"And another angel came out of the temple which is in heaven, and he also had a sharp sickle. And another angel, who had power over fire, came out from the altar; and he called with a loud voice to him who had the sickle, saying, 'Put in your sharp sickle, and gather the clusters from the vine of the earth because her grapes are ripe! And the angel swung his sickle to the earth, and gathered the clusters from the vine of the earth, and threw them into the great winepress of the wrath of God, and the winepress was trodden outside the city, and blood came out from the winepress, up to the horse's bridles, for a distance of two hundred miles." Rev.14:17-20

After the wheat is gathered into the barn the tares will be gathered and burned. The tares are the evil men upon whom Christ will vent His wrath. The river of their blood will flow six feet deep for two hundred miles. One thing is lacking in this description of the river. How wide is it? Let's assume a small river of one hundred feet of width.

Now we are talking about a volume of blood that measures 6' x 100 x 5,280' x 200 = 633,600,000 cubic feet of blood. One man possesses eight pints or one gallon of blood. One cubic foot will hold seven and one-half gallons or the blood of seven and one-half men. 633,600,000 x 7.5 = 4,752,000,000 deaths to make a river just one hundred feet wide. Five billion is about the world population now, but it is expected to reach thirty billion before 2070. All the billions that remain unraptured will die on this Day of Wrath. The winepress of my God is awesome!

"Those slain by the Lord on that day shall be from one end of the earth to the other. They shall not be lamented, gathered or buried; they shall be like dung on the face of the earth." Jeremiah 25:33. There will be no one interested or able to bury them. All will die. The work of their hands will also perish.

"I will cut off your horses from among you and destroy your chariots. I will also cut off the cities of your land and tear down all your fortifications!' Micah 5.10,11. Will you be one still walking the earth and looking for a city; even though none remains? How long will you last with no food, water, or companionship? Curse God and die, for your opportunity for salvation has passed.

"The Lord will punish the host of heaven on high, and the kings of the earth on earth. They will be gathered together like prisoners in the dungeon, and will be confined in prison; and after many days they shall be punished." Isaiah 24:21,22.

"There is to be one law and one ordinance for you and for the alien who sojourns with you!" Numbers15:16. Why? Because the Law is the promise of God, His commandment for us to live by He must obey it as we must; for it is His Law, and it is impossible for God to have a double standard. And the standard is this: "When you reap your harvest in your field and have forgotten a sheaf in the field, you shall not go back to get it." Deut.24:19. So when God reaps His harvest there will be no changing of positions between the wheat and the tares. God will take all who are His in the Resurrection and Rapture which signals the beginning of the Day of Wrath. Then Christ Himself shall burn the tares. "Therefore, just as the tares are gathered up and burned with fire, so shall it be at the end of the days." Matthew 13:40. When all are resurrected, raptured or dead, what then?

"Lift up your eyes to the sky, then look to the earth beneath; for the sky will vanish like smoke, and the earth will wear out like a garment, and its inhabitants will die in like manner, but My, salvation shall be forever, and My righteousness shall not wane. Isaiah 51:6.

When the saved have been raptured and the tares burnt up and imprisoned, then God will change this heaven and earth like a garment, and they will be changed. Psalms 102:26.

So the harvest is finished, "And I saw a great white throne and Him who sat upon it, from whose presence earth and heaven fled away, and no place was found for them. And I saw the dead, the great and the small, standing before the throne, and the books opened; and another book was opened, which is the Book of Life; and the dead were judged from the things which were written in the books according to their deeds. And the sea gave up the dead which were in it, and death and Hades gave up the dead which were in them; and they were judged, every one of them according to their deeds. And death and Hades were thrown into the lake of fire. This is the second death, the lake of fire. If anyone's name was not found written in the Book of Life, he was thrown into the lake of fire. And I saw a new heaven and a new earth; for the first heaven and the first earth passed away, and there is no longer any sea. And I saw the holy city, New Jerusalem, coming down out of heaven from God, made ready as a bride adorned for her husband. And I heard a loud voice from the throne, saying, 'Behold, the tabernacle of God is among men, and He shall dwell among them, and they shall be His peoples, and God Himself shall be among them, and He shall wipe away every tear from their eyes; and there shall no longer be any death; there shall no longer be any mourning, or crying, or pain; the first things have passed away." Revelation 20:11-21:4.

God does not desire the death of any person, but everyone will receive the sure reward of his labor, be it good or bad. Those who look forward to the return of Christ will rise to meet Him. Those who do not believe will perish and meet Him a little later. Every person who ever lived will acknowledge that God is, and there is no other.

Then mankind will have the opportunity to spend eternity either with God or without God. Each man must make his own choice. It is urgent that it be done now, for after the Rapture no one will be able to change his chosen way.

Choose ye this day.

CHAPTER VIII

Establishing Perspectives

Moreover, Jehoshaphat said to the King of Israel, please inquire first for the word of the Lord 2 Chronicles 18:4.

Have you ever heard a statement such as this? "Israel is not the church, and the church is not Israel. When Israel cast aside the claims of Christ, God set Israel aside and started another program. Today, neither one has any part in the purpose or blessings of the other."

"God is not a man, that he should lie." Numbers 23:19.

How foolish we are today to make our thoughts more important than His words. The promises which God made to Israel cannot be set aside. Nor can the promises which he made to the church be ignored or discounted. If there are two programs, we must be operating simultaneously, for nothing of either program can be found to limit the other.

Therefore, this chapter seeks to uncover the perspective of the word in three areas: the resurrection, the tribulation, and the kingdom rule. Let's concentrate upon the words of the prophets of old, for they observed the last days in their visions and recorded them under the Spirit's guidance. Let us seek answers to specific questions prompted by the word to establish the difference between truth and tradition.

THE RESURRECTION

Let me ask you, "What do you know that you know, is going to happen to you when Jesus returns?" He is going to take me off the planet. Are you going to go by yourself or are you going to have company? Other believers will go with me.

What is the nationality of the first group of people to rise in this event, and what is the size of their country when it occurs? I don't know. A good knowledge of the Old Testament is required to answer this question, so maybe I should stay in the new testament with you.

When is it possible for this event to occur? At any time!

Why do you expect to depart soon and suddenly, when the only thing Paul taught you about the rapture is that something else happened first? What happened first? I don't know!

You do get your primary concept of the rapture from 1 Thessalonians 4:13-18? Yes. This passage states that something else happened first. What event is the rapture bonded to by the unbreakable bond of the word of the living God? I don't know. Let's look at verses 16 and 17 of the passage.

"The Lord himself will descend from heaven with a shout, with the voice of the Archangel, and with the trumpet of God; and the dead in Christ shall rise first. Then we who are alive and remain shall be caught up together with them in the clouds to meet them in the air, and thus we shall always be with the Lord."

What two words of this passage are commonly taken as the definition of the term rapture? The two words "caught up". Now the only thing this passage taught you about the catching up was that something else happened first. What happened first? The dead in Christ rose first. If, "caught up" is the definition of the word rapture, what event is the dead in Christ rising known as; by what name is this event called? It's called the resurrection!

So the answer to the question, when does the rapture occur? Has always been easy. It has always been after the resurrection. Therefore the rapture has no relationship to the tribulation or the kingdom. So we should never have asked the question, "When does the rapture occur?" We should have been asking the question, 'When does the resurrection take place?' Are we ever taught when the resurrection occurs?

Here's the situation in John chapter 11 verses 22 and 23; Lazarus has died. Jesus has finally met Martha and said to her, "your brother will rise again." To which Martha replied, "Yes Lord, I know he will rise again in the resurrection, on the last day."

Where did Martha get her answer? She did not say 'Lord you taught us' The Lord did not rebuke her and say that was wrong. Since they only had the Old Testament then, what Scripture put the resurrection on the last day, and if they knew that 2000 years ago, why don't we know this today? Let's get at the heart of the matter. Did Jesus ever say anything that wasn't absolutely perfectly true? Everything he said was true. So look at what he said.

"For I have come down from heaven, not to do my own will, but the will of him who sent me. And this is the will of him who sent me, that of all that he has given me I lose nothing, but raise it up on the last day. For this is the will of my father, that everyone who believes in him, may have eternal life; and I myself will raise him up on the last day." John 6:38-40.

Paul taught the resurrection preceded the rapture. Jesus said the resurrection occurred on the last day. He did not say, "The last day for the church age!" Jesus was explicit. His meaning was clear. You just don't know what the "last day" means.

God made this promise to Noah after the flood. "While the Earth remains, seed time and harvest, and cold and heat, and summer and winter, and day and night shall not cease." Genesis 8:22. The last day is referring to that specific point, in which this Earth and its heavenly system will be destroyed. 'While the Earth remains' means that there is coming a time when it will no longer exist. Therefore, the last day clearly refers to the putting aside of everything of the old creation. The resurrection is the first part of the last day. So as the last day begins the resurrection of the righteous dead occurs, followed by the rapture which will remove

141

all the remaining living believers from the planet. Then the time of worldwide trouble, called the day of wrath comes upon all the rest of mankind. Then all the wicked who remain on the planet will be killed without exception.

Martha's answer to the Lord, came from the ending of the book of Daniel. "But as for you, go your way to the end; then you will enter into rest and rise again for your allotted portion at the end of the age." Daniel 12:13. The end of the age is just another way of saying the last day.

Martha's conduct and statements show that she believed Jesus had the power to heal any disease of an ill person, even the power to keep him alive. She bemoaned the fact that Jesus did not arrive soon enough to heal Lazarus. She had no intuition concerning what the Lord was about to do. Nor did she hope to see Lazarus again on this earth, although she did expect to meet him in the resurrection on the last day.

We can see that Martha had an understanding of the Scriptures, but she could not see how the Lord could use them in any way which would help her brother on that day. She was sure that the normal process of decay had set in upon the body of Lazarus. She did not expect the Lord to simply stand and call Lazarus forth from the tomb, which is exactly what he did.

Luke records Paul's defense before Agrippa. "Why is it considered incredible among you people if God does raise the dead?" Acts 26:8

If, as you have shown, the resurrection occurs on the last day and others teach that it happens at the beginning of Daniel's 70th week, how many resurrections are there?

The Scriptures teach that there'll be three resurrections. Paul spoke about two of them, "but this I admit to you, that according to the way which they call a sect I do serve the Lord serve the God of our fathers, believing everything that is in accordance with the law, and that is written in the prophets; having a hope in God, which these men cherish themselves, that there shall certainly be a resurrection of both the righteous and the wicked." Acts 24:14,15.

142

Resurrections for both the righteous and the wicked are obviously two of the resurrections mentioned in the Bible. You have already read about the resurrection of the righteous. But have you ever heard of the resurrection of the wicked?

There is a passage in the Old Testament which treats both of them in the context of the events of the last day. In this particular chapter, there are two groups of people mentioned who witness and partake of the events associated with the destruction of this Earth.

One group is happy, they are singing, rejoicing, and praising the Lord. "They raise their voices, they shout for joy. They cry out from the West concerning the Majesty of the Lord. Therefore glorify the Lord in the East, the name of the Lord, the God of Israel in the coastlands of the sea. From the ends of the Earth we hear songs, glory to the righteous one:" Isaiah 24:14-16. Paul may have wondered where is this happy group of people located? Then he realized they are no longer upon the Earth, for they do not partake of the destruction which comes upon everyone who was left behind.

The other group is unhappy. They hear the shouting and the singing and know full well what their end is to be. Suddenly, all of them are believers in God, but since they never responded to a salvation call, not one of them was saved. They never felt the need for a personal relationship with God through his son Jesus Christ. Now it is too late for any of them. To all who remain, citizens, priests, servants, masters, maids, mistresses, buyers, sellers, lenders, borrowers, creditors, and debtors; it will be the same. They are scattered and burnt up. Then all the wicked dead are removed from the Earth.

"So it will happen in that day, that the Lord will punish the host of heaven, on high, and the Kings of the Earth, on Earth. And they will be gathered together like prisoners in the dungeon, and they will be confined in prison; and after many days they will be punished." Isaiah 24:21,22.

Then on this last day on the heavenly calendar, the Earth itself will be destroyed.

"For the Windows above are open, and the foundations of the earth shake. The earth is broken asunder, the Earth is split through, the Earth is shaken violently. The Earth reels to and fro like a drunkard, and it totters like a shack, for its transgression is heavy upon it, and it will fall, never to rise again." Isaiah 24:18-20.

After his conversion on the road to Damascus, Paul reevaluated all that he had been taught from the Old Testament. He could then present clearly the Old Testament doctrines in a new light. I feel he used Isaiah chapter 24 as the basis what he taught in First Thessalonians chapter 4.

The New Testament doctrine of the harvest balances the scales with this passage from Isaiah. Explaining the parable of the wheat and the tares, Jesus said, "the one who sows the good seed is the Son of Man, and the field is the world; and as for the good seeds, these are the sons of the kingdom; and the tares are the sons of the evil one; and the enemy who sowed them is the devil, and the harvest is the end of the age; and the reapers are the Angels. Therefore just as the tares are gathered up and burned with fire, so shall it be at the end of the age. The Son of Man will send forth his angels, and they will gather out of his kingdom all stumbling blocks, and those who commit lawlessness, and will cast them into the furnace of fire; in that place there shall be weeping and gnashing of teeth. Then the righteous will shine forth as the sun in the kingdom of their father. He who has ears, let him hear. Matthew 13:37-43.

The word is plain. What Isaiah said, Jesus verified. That is because Isaiah spoke the word of the Lord; who is Jesus. Jesus knew what he told Isaiah to say. So the harvest is the combination of the removal of all mankind from the Earth through the resurrections of the righteous and of the wicked, and then the destruction of this Earth.

Jesus personally spoke of the two resurrections. He said, "Do not marvel at this; for an hour is coming, in which all who are in the tombs shall hear his voice, and shall come forth; those who did the good deeds, to a resurrection of life, those who committed the evil deeds to a resurrection of judgment." John 5:28, 29.

The third resurrection is a very limited one; but it too was spoken of in both the Old and the New Testaments. Remember Ezekiel's Valley of the dry bones. "And they came to life, and stood on their feet, at exceedingly great Army. Then he said to me, "Son of Man, these bones are the whole house of Israel; behold, they say, our bones are dried up, and our hope has perished. We are completely cut off. Therefore prophesy, and say to them, thus says the Lord God, behold I will open your graves and cause you to come up out of your graves, my people; and I will bring you into the land of Israel. Then you will know that I am the Lord, when I have opened your graves and caused you to come out of your graves, my people. And I will put my Spirit within you and you will come to life, and I will place you on your own land. Then you will know that I, the Lord, have spoken and done it." Ezekiel 37:10-14

This fallen Army that rises to stand again is the same Army which perished in the New Testament under the beast's power. "And after the 3 1/2 days the breath of life from God came into them, and they stood on their feet; and great fear fell upon those who were beholding them. And they heard a loud voice from heaven saying to them, "Come up here". And they went up into heaven in the cloud, and their enemies beheld them." Revelation 11:11,12.

The Lord taught that he would die and be buried, and would rise again. So, when he was placed in the tomb, his enemies requested and obtained guards for the tomb in order to ensure that no one would be able to steal the body away and falsely proclaim that he had risen. All of these unbelieving guards were awake on the morning of the third day, when Angels came to roll the stone away and to display the empty tomb. The guards did not waste any time getting back to the rulers to give witness of what they had seen.

In like manner, when Israel's army perishes, it too will have guards. The primary mission of the guards will be to see that no one does anything with the highly contaminated, radioactive bones. These guards will also witness the reality of the vision of the Valley of Dry Bones. They will be startled as they observe bone bump into bone, heads rolling to join necks, spines form, arms shoulders and ribs snap into place, waists, legs ankles and feet align themselves into proper order.

The guards will watch with awe as they see cartilage, muscles, and skin cover the skeletal frames. Then the wind will stir, and those who were dead will begin to breathe again. They will stand on their feet and once more begin to move. Suddenly, they will be clothed and, from the sky, a clear and loving command will echo; come up here!

The guards who had watched them will quake with fear as they see these bodies rise without using any antigravity machinery.

"And when he broke the fifth seal, I saw underneath the altar the souls of those who had been slain because of the word of God, and because of the testimony which they had maintained; and they cried out with a loud voice, saying, "How long, O Lord, holy and true, will you refrain from judging and avenging our blood on those who dwell on the earth?" And there was given to each of them a white robe; and they were told that they should rest for a little while longer, until the number of their fellow servants and their brethren who were to be killed even as they had been, should be completed also. Revelation 6:9-11.

And I heard the number of those who were sealed, 144,000 sealed from every tribe of the sons of Israel:" Revelation 7:4

"And I looked, and behold, the Lamb was standing on Mount Zion, and with him 144,000, having His name and the name of His father written on their foreheads." Revelation 14:1

"And they came to life and reigned with Christ for 1000 years." Revelation 20:4

The 144,000 is the total sum of all the prophets of Israel. The prophets are the ones who arise and return with Jesus to establish his kingdom. They are the first fruits resurrection which is the next one to occur. They all return with Jesus. They establish and rule in the kingdom. The resurrections of the righteous and the wicked take place at the end of the Messiah's kingdom. The sons of Israel rise first. If they do not rise first you never will rise.

"And it will come about in that day, that the Lord will start his threshing from the flowing stream of the Euphrates to the Brook of Egypt; and you will be gathered up one by one, O sons of Israel. It will come about also in that day that a great trumpet will be blown;" Isaiah 27:12

In order to differentiate this from current theological doctrine, let me present two diagrams: the first is based upon information in the book, The Return Of The Lord, by John F Walvoord; and the second from information taught in this book.

CHART I

WALVOORD'S SEQUENCE

Resurrection and rapture
(general interval)
Ezekiel 38 and 39 battle
World dictator signs treaty
Antichrist attacks
Great tribulation
Jesus returns with the saved
Gentiles judged
Israel re-gathered
Kingdom rule
Great white throne judgment
New heaven and Earth

CHART 2

MY SEQUENCE

Peace treaty over Ezekiel's Israel	+	
Antichrist attacks (day 1290)	:	70TH WEEK
(middle of the 70th week)	:	
	:	
Jesus returns with 144,000	:	
(at the end of the 70th week)	+	KINGDOM RULE
	:	
Armageddon	:	
	:	
Resurrection and rapture	+	
	:	
Living wicked destroyed	:	
	:	THE LAST DAY
Heaven and Earth destroyed	+	
Judgment		
New heaven and new earth		

Why is there such a great difference? In my opinion, it is the result of not understanding the three types of tribulation and grouping them all together.

TRIBULATIONISM

What is tribulation? It is nothing more than a time of trouble. What are the three types of tribulation and how do they differ? When I look at the tribulation Scriptures I find they fall into three different categories: 1. Personal trouble; 2. Israel's great tribulation; 3. Worldwide trouble called the day of wrath.

When you go through the tribulation references in a concordance and place them into one of these three categories, you will find about two thirds refer to personal troubles, about one third refers to Israel's time of great tribulation, and only a few refer to the time of worldwide trouble.

Is it possible for all the references that you look at to occur at the same time? Can we continue to group them all together arbitrarily; with Ezekiel chapters 38 and 39 and the passages in Revelation; and pretend that we don't need to study them because we are going to be lifted out of them before they occur? We have seen that the rapture is bonded to and follows the resurrection. So what relationship could it possibly have to personal trouble or Israel's great tribulation?

Trouble should not upset a believer; it has another purpose. Trouble teaches us how to obtain peace. Jesus said, "These things I have spoken to you, that you may have peace, in the world you have tribulation, but take courage; I have overcome the world." John 16:33

If you look to the world to solve your problems, you will not find peace. Peace can only be found when you place all which is yours into the Lord's control. Putting him in charge means that you must treat the thing as if it were his; and you must use it according to his laws, precepts, rules, and regulations. If you do not know what these laws are this is a good time for you to get a concordance or a Bible study guide. Then study to find these precepts, except them, and apply them to what you are doing.

This is how you enter the kingdom of God and attain its peace while you're still on this earth: you see, the laws which we obey proclaim to all the status of our citizenship towards the government that has established those laws. Earthly obedience frees us from the threat of retaliation by those charged with the responsibility to administer the law and mete out its punishment. The decision to obey or to disregard the law is up to each individual. Earthly governments may not catch every infraction of the law; but God is perfect, and he will! You cannot be choosy. No one can pretend with him. If you want his peace which passes all human understanding, and if you desire his help, you must do it his way.

Troubles become a teacher through which we learn how to obtain the security, sustenance, and support; for each and every situation or problem we approach God with. God's willingness to help us through every need develops in us the sureness of his loving response, which becomes the basis for peace. It is also our encouragement to call upon him for help in all of life's confrontations.

Each of us should take time to consider that God could strike us with the whip every time our thoughts or deeds go astray from his desires. Wisdom and love restrains him from that course of action, because it would only breed resentment and hatred in those to whom he would teach perfect love. So he watch-fully permits us to go our way and sets reminders in our paths. This provision for help is ready, but it is not used until his help is desired and asked for.

We need to learn to seek his help quickly and without complaint. We should feel free to present our petition, to acknowledge our problem if we don't know the cause or see the solution. Then we need to ask for his help and guidance in order to obtain a response.

Does the word protect us from trouble? No, it seems to be a magnet, drawing troubles to us. In the parable of the sower, Jesus taught how the word comes to us where we are and told of the one who follows the sower to keep the word from growing in his garden. Matthew 13:19-23.

Every place the sower went, he sowed the word; everyone in that place heard the word; all who heard, received the word.

Individual receptivity was the measure of the fertility which would support the seed as it sprouted and sought to grow. Every seed tried to grow, but some did not get covered with soil, all Satan had to do was come like a bird and pick up them and eat them from the life of the one who understood nothing of them. Another received it with joy as the word got a little deeper. It was more than beak deep; pecking could not reach it, so Satan persecuted the message the word pertained to. If the seed was of healing, he brought sickness. If it were of law, for example the law against committing adultery, he offered sexual temptation. If it pertained to mercy, he brought anger. So the person who heard the word but followed after his own heart and perception, having no firm root in himself, could not use the word for his own benefit; and it perished from his life.

In another individual, the word remained, sprouted, and grew; but it did not flower. The ground in which it was planted was not cultivated. It had been mulched, but the only things growing there were thorns, and they were lush, thick, and strong. These thorns (the cares of the world) are so well established that the new word cannot receive any light to grow. So it cannot absorb any additional nutrients.

A Bible teaching church simply does not seem to be of value to such an individual. Besides he may reason, if I went to such a church the people there would expect me to give something; and my money is too tight already. Gas and oil now cost me as much as my car payment. I don't know how much I could afford to give in donations or charity. Inflation is eating my savings away. I may lose my job shortly if the company lays off some employees or closes down the plant for a while. Things are bad and I just don't see how God could possibly help me. Excuses choke the word of God.

Every sprout which is not moistened withers and dies. The moisture becomes the life force when the sun shines upon it. The heat differential from the root to the leaf causes the intake of the nutrients and minerals which the plant needs for growth and reproduction. Yet even then, most plants will not reproduce unless pollen is transmitted by the wind or by insects such as the bee. Fertile ground therefore is not enough. One day of rain will not provide enough water for healthy growth. One day of sunshine is not enough. Thorough cultivation is not enough. All this may be provided, yet the crop will still come to naught if there is no wind or bee to carry the pollen.

A good farmer makes every preparation then takes every precaution he can plan for in advance. Soil temperature, acidity, fertility, weeding, and water drainage are but some of the necessary ingredients to produce healthy plants. When everything has been done that can be done, the farmer does not simply plant one seed and quit. His livelihood depends upon the abundance of the harvest, so he plants all the seeds which the field will support. Then he waits for God's blessings upon his efforts.

It rains. Then it stops and there is no rain for a period of time. It may get hot or cold. The wind blows and then dies down. The farmer returns to the field to check the progress of the growth of his crop. He cultivates it to remove the weeds and to make the soil more receptive to the next rain. He examines the insect population for type and number to determine whether an insecticide is called for and how much might be needed. He must tend to every need which is in his power to meet.

The son of God, as the sower of the seed, sows the word everywhere; to every individual. No one will be able to claim ignorance of God's will on the Day of Judgment.

God blesses the efforts of those who speak the word in their daily lives. Those who speak of God's power and blessing help to cultivate and prepare the ground to encourage the word to grow. This preparation is the key which will open the heavenly resources to the one who hears, receives, and understands the word of God. The word grows strong; it flowers and produces more seed like itself for the sower to sow. Thus, the word provides strength to overcome the difficulties and obstacles set in our way, and this makes us strong in the knowledge and practice of obtaining God's help to get us through our personal problems.

Luke records how Paul and Barnabas preached the word, "strengthening the souls of the disciples, encouraging them to continue in the faith, and saying, 'Through many tribulations we must enter the kingdom of God.' Acts14:22.

152

The purpose of going through the tribulation is to strengthen God's children. The planted word provides the assurance that God does, indeed, care. This encourages hope that God will provide for our needs in times of trouble. Hope enables us to ask for help without doubting. It is the father's responsibility to raise the children and to provide for all their needs. God is the perfect father. It is impossible for him to shirk his responsibilities. God will take care of his children!

He is watching over everything that happens to you. He knows when a sparrow dies and how many hairs you have upon your head. You should rejoice and not be afraid. The glory of the father is seen through his abundant provision for the obedient child. Obedience and abundance go hand-in-hand. Disobedience reduces God's provision to the mere level of survival. Existence is not abundant living. Hear the father, and you will find His presence strong enough to conquer every situation.

"Who shall separate us from the love of Christ? Shall tribulation, or distress, or persecution, or famine, or nakedness, or peril, or Sword? Just as it is written, for thy sake we are being put to death all day long; we were considered as sheep to be slaughtered. But in all these things we overwhelmingly conquer through Him who loved us. For I am convinced that neither death, nor life, nor angels, nor principalities, nor things present, nor things to come, nor powers, nor height, nor depth, nor any other created thing will be able to separate us from the love of God, which is in Christ Jesus our Lord." Romans 8:35-39.

Live in obedience and every situation will work to glorify God, His support will be immediately apparent.

"Great is my confidence in you, great is my boasting on your behalf; I am filled with comfort. I am overflowing with joy in all our affliction." 2 Corinthians 7:4. Then Paul said to the Ephesians, "I ask you not to lose heart at my tribulations on your behalf, for they are your glory." Ephesians 3:13.

It seems then, that tribulation is of benefit to Christian growth, and the rapture is not related to personal troubles. Is this true?

That's true. If the rapture is meant to protect us from something, it cannot be the personal troubles of our lives. If it were, people would have been disappearing and not dying, down through the ages.

So, let's look at the next category of scriptures relating to tribulation.

ISRAEL'S GREAT TRIBULATION.

Lets reflect upon the events that Israel is about to go through. Daniel's 70th week begins with a peace treaty. This peace treaty ends the fighting over Ezekiel's Israel. The 70th week is divided in half. The first 3 1/2 days are supposed to be peaceful and joyous. Then the Antichrist attacks, overruns Israel and kills two thirds of its people. Then he rules over Israel until Jesus returns. This desecration of the holy land and its people is the time of Israel's great trouble.

A common tradition in Christianity today holds the church is going to be raptured off the earth to take them out of this horrible time. Is this a good doctrine?

No its not. It is based upon two concepts which confuse what the word has fixed. First it does not differentiate the geographical limitations of the scriptures which refer to Israel alone, as opposed to those which include the entire world.

The rapture is not meant to spare Christians from the ordeal Israel is about to endure. It does not have that purpose because Israel has specific borders. Only the people in the borders will bear the burden of the boastful, arrogant, irreverent Antichrist.

Second: if the rapture were to happen before the time of Israel's great tribulation, a scripturally impossible work would have to spontaneously blossom and prosper. If the Christians were removed, unbelievers would have to be converted without the benefit of preaching; and in the three and a half days of the first half of the 70th week, they would evangelize the world. "A great

154

multitude which no one could count ... who come out of the great tribulation." Revelation 7:9-14.

If these words indicate a partial rapture, followed by Israel's tribulation scenario; then God, who does not change, must change His way of doing business. Can anyone be saved after the rapture? After every believing and commissioned preacher is removed?

Ah ha! You say. Not every preacher will be removed: two will be left behind. Well if all the preachers have not been removed, the church has not left either. The church will still be here during Israel's trouble.

Many teachers say this because they cannot find the church present in the Revelation between chapters four and nineteen. Yet, when one looks there it is easy to find. Remember a lampstand stood for a church. The two witnesses were called, "the two olive trees and the two lampstands." By definition two churches are present in Revelation chapter 11. If these two churches were not removed by the rapture; the rapture has not taken place. The promise is the dual events of the resurrection-rapture, will remove all believers at the same time.

Recall Zechariah's vision of the golden bowl. Seven golden pipes connected the bowl to seven golden lampstands. The golden bowl was the house of the Lord in Jerusalem. The seven lampstands, that is the seven churches, were connected to the golden bowl. No church has the strength to sever its pipe lifeline. No church can rise alone! Even Romans chapter 11 teaches gentiles were grafted into the rich root of the olive tree. The branches that are then cut off are thrown into the fire because of unfruitfulness.

Why would you want to leave just as all Israel is about to be saved?

Israel is the olive tree, you were grafted into. If the saved of Israel do not depart, you won't either! All scripture is given to the Jew first, and also to the Greek.

I've asked this important question before, and I'm asking it again! When Christ returns to this planet, how do you know it is He and not some imposter? When He returns to the planet, He comes back to the Mount of Olives and an earthquake splits it in half from the east to the west, from the Mediterranean Sea to the Dead Sea. This earthquake identifies the Messiah. He is the one standing there with nail scarred hands, and a pierced side. The earthquake opened valley, is also the burial site for the men of the army of the battle of Armageddon. About two hundred million dead bodies will be thrown into it.

The kingdom rule, which John called 1000 years in Revelation chapter 20, begins when Jesus returns to the top of the Mount of Olives and ends at the beginning of the battle of Armageddon. However long this takes it will not actually be 1000 years.

Nor can the Ezekiel chapter 38 battle take place during Israel's tribulation. This is like saying that after the Antichrist has destroyed two thirds of the population of Israel, then Israel is victorious over Armageddon's Army; despite the fact the Antichrist is their ruler. Why wasn't the Antichrist credited with the victory? If he was the Victor; why is Christ credited with the victory? See how foolishly we can think when we don't know the Scriptures.

THE DAY OF WRATH

So far you have taught the rapture is not related to personal troubles, Israel's tribulation period, or Armageddon. That means the rapture is related to the worldwide trouble which you mentioned earlier. Is that so?

That's right. Personal troubles are a growth process to enable people to apply the commandments of the Lord to their lives, for their blessing. Israel's trouble is likewise to prepare them for the coming of the kingdom of Israel's Messiah. The limited nature of this type of testing does not present a need to remove all the believers from the face of the earth. But this need does exist when we consider the third tribulation category: the worldwide period of trouble called the day of wrath.

Confusing the scriptures which refer to the day of wrath with those associated with Israel's great tribulation, is the cause for all the difficulties encountered while trying to relate the rapture with the various tribulation passages. This has given rise to the debates which argue that the rapture is either, pre-tribulational, mid-tribulational, or post-tribulational. It is even called pre-millennial and post-millennial.

Our previous discussion of the rapture showed that it followed the resurrection. This is the only event to which the rapture is linked. The study of the resurrection positioned this event on the last day, according to the words of Jesus himself, according to Jewish tradition, and according to the closing words of the book of Daniel. My conclusion was then made that every event which had a time period associated with it must occur before the believers take off and leave this earth forever.

Is there a time period associated with Israel's tribulation? Yes, it's seven years split into 2-3 1/2 half year periods. Is there a time period associated with the kingdom rule? Yes, it's 1000 years. Is there a time period linked to the cleanup of the Army of Gog and Magog? Yes, it takes seven months to bury the dead.

Since the resurrection occurs on the last day, all these events that had time periods associated with them have to happen before the last day arrives. Nowhere in the Bible will you ever find a word that a believer is saved from the tribulation. You can survive and live through tribulation. But wrath kills you!

"Much more than, having now been justified by his blood, we shall be saved from the wrath of God through him." Romans 5:9. God's wrath is what you're going to be saved from.

Isaiah chapter 24 clearly depicts the events of the last day. It is explicit. There's nothing hidden about its meaning. In it there are two groups of people. The happy group is shouting "glory to the righteous one." This shout is so loud it can be heard from one end of the Earth to the other. Then the second group, the ones who are left behind, are killed without exception until everyone is dead. This is what happens on the day of wrath. After all the wicked are killed, all the wicked who ever were are removed from the planet. Then the planet itself is destroyed.

Even the wicked who are left after the resurrection and rapture remove God's people from the Earth; know this day by its right name, "fall on us and hide us from the presence of him who sits on the throne, and from the wrath of the Lamb; for the great day of their wrath has come; and who is able to stand?" Revelation 16:16, 17.

Understand that the harvest is in three parts. First, all the believers, both alive and formerly dead, will be removed from the Earth into God's presence. Second, all the wicked that remain will be killed and then all the wicked who ever were will be removed from the Earth. Third, when no man is left upon the surface of the earth it will be just as Jesus said, "heaven and earth will pass away, but my words shall not pass away. But of that day and hour no one knows, not even the angels of heaven, nor the son, but the father alone." Matthew 24:35, 36. After everyone is removed from the planet, heaven goes silent, and waits for God to say, "Put that place away!"

The believers departure arrangements were made to escape the wrath of God! The wrath of God will fall upon everything and everyone left behind when all the believers are carried into the father's presence.

If you possess this hope, your future will be uplifting. If you do not have this hope, then there is no future for you.

CHAPTER IX

Revelations Sevens

Who has given heed to his word and listened? Jeremiah 23:18

John's Revelation is the hardest book to understand that was ever written! It's simply a paradox that it's included in the most popular best-seller of all time: the Bible. But it is the least read portion. Most people if they read it at all, stop after only one reading. That's what I did when I was 10 years old and read the Bible for the first time. When I finished Revelation I said what kind of a book is this? It's not like any of the other books of the Bible. So I stopped reading it. Even though I read the Bible once or twice a year back then, when I finished Jude, I'd go back to Genesis. At the age of 16, I read it again and found something I could understand. John's locusts jumped right out at me and I understood what he was looking at when he said what he said. Revelation chapter 9 was the key to opening up the rest of the book.

Unfortunately when it is read and a question comes to mind, there is no one who can provide a satisfactory answer. Trying to understand John's Revelation becomes frustrating. God still encourages the desire to know in the people who continue to read it. So we must take care not to divorce the book of the Revelation from the rest of the Scriptures. Yet it has been divorced. The doctrine responsible for the divorce is tribulationism.

The tribulation has become a theological escape clause. The claim is, "I won't be here then. It doesn't apply to me, so I don t have to know it. Therefore, since I don't have to know it, how can I be expected to teach it to you?" This is the attitude of many Bible teachers.

159

If the teacher does not understand, how can the student? If as I have already taught, the locusts are mans modern means of land transportation; then 5 trumpets have already blown.

John's Revelation could already be unfolding around us and we are completely oblivious to it. The desire to know is increasing among God's people. God has promised that in the last days we will clearly understand. Jeremiah 23:20. So in the hope of enabling you to understand, let me present my contribution of an approach to the book of the Revelation.

SEVEN SEALS

John's unfolding of his vision begins with the book held in God's hand. It has writing from cover to cover and is sealed with seven seals. A diligent search is conducted to find someone worthy enough to open this book. No one is found who is worthy enough to open or to look into the book; no one, until the Lamb of God, freshly slain, appears and approaches God to receive the book.

This is the starting point for the events which occur. The starter's pistol was fired when the book changed hands. The lamb which was slain and shed its blood did not perish. The risen Christ came into his father's presence. He received the book and began to break it seals. Therefore these events started in the time period of 32 to 70 A.D. and will go until they are finished.

Seal one. "And I saw when the Lamb broke one of the seven seals, and I heard one of the four living creatures saying as with the voice of thunder, "come." And I looked, and behold, a white horse, and he who sat on it had a bow; and a crown was given to him; and he went out conquering, and to conquer." Revelation 6:1,2.

Don't get bogged down in speculation over a meaning for a phrase which is not defined anywhere else in the Bible. This writer possessed a bow, about which some commentaries remarked that it had no arrows. Yet the rider was crowned with governmental authority, and permission to go out and to conquer whoever he was directed to face. No archer ever won a battle with the bow unless he used arrows with it. They must be implied in this case because of the fighting which ensued, as the nations were stirred up to face him.

Seal two. "And when he broke the second seal, I heard the second living creature saying, "Come." And another, a red horse, went out; and to him who sat on it, it was granted to take peace from the earth, and that men should slay one another; and a great sword was given to him. Revelation 6:3,4. The fighting was stirred up by the first rider and it blossomed into warfare, which took peace from the earth. From the arrows shot at a distance the fighting became sword to sword combat where the advantage lay with the bearer of the greater sword.

Seal three. "And when he broke the third seal, I heard the third living creature saying, "Come." And I looked, and behold, a black horse; and he who sat on it had a pair of scales in his hand. And I heard as it were a voice in the center of the four living creatures saying, "a quart of wheat for a denarius, and 3 quarts of barley for a denarius; and do not harm the oil and the wine." Revelation 6:5,6.

Whenever fighting becomes widespread the food supplies and sources are intentionally destroyed. An unprepared people are quickly brought to their knees by the loss of their food and medicine. The war's effects do not end when the battle is over. Tillers of the soil grow fewer as they die or are maimed in their role as a soldier. God did not want his people to fight this way. "When you besiege a city a long time, to make war against it in order to capture it, you shall not destroy its trees by swinging an ax against them; for you may eat from them, and you shall not cut them down. For is the tree of the field a man, that it should be besieged by you? Only the trees which you know are not fruit trees you shall destroy and cut them down, that you may construct siege works against the city that is making war with you until it falls." Deuteronomy 20:19, 20.

Seal four "And when he broke the fourth seal, I heard the voice of the fourth living creature saying, "Come." And I looked, and behold, an ashen horse; and he who sat on it had the name death;

and Hades was following with him. And authority was given to them over a fourth of the Earth, to kill with the sword and with famine and with pestilence and by the wild beasts of the earth." Revelation 6:7,8. Fighting, war, famine, and disease spread to cover one fourth of the Earth.

One fourth of the Earth was given to these four Horsemen. On this basis alone, one might acknowledge that these four have long since gone forth, for this century has already seen two world wars and man now has the capability to completely destroy the whole Earth. The bow and the sword have had their day, fire and brimstone now hold sway.

Seal five. "And when he broke the fifth seal, I saw underneath the altar the souls of those who had been slain because of the word of God, and because of the testimony which they had maintained; and they cried out with a loud voice, saying, "How long, O Lord, holy and true, will you refrain from judging and avenging our blood on those who dwell on the earth?" And there was given to each of them a white robe; and they were told that they should rest for a little while longer, until the number of their fellow servants and their brethren who were to be killed even as they had been, should be completed also." Revelation 6:9-11.

Who do these souls belong to? They belong to the prophets of Israel. 144,000 is the total number of them. But all of them are not yet dead. Since they are in God's presence, they know how short the time is getting and they are wondering how much more time is it going to take.

Seal six. "And I looked when he broke the six seal, and there was a great earthquake; and the sun became black as sackcloth made of hair, and the whole moon became like blood; and the stars of the sky fell to the Earth, as a fig tree casts its unripe figs when shaken by a great wind. And the sky was split apart like a scroll when it is rolled up; and every mountain and island were moved out of their places. And the Kings of the Earth and the great men and the commanders and the strong and every slave and free man, hid themselves in the caves and among the rocks of the mountains;

and they said to the mountains and to the rocks, "fall on us and hide us from the presence of him who sits on the throne, and from the wrath of the Lamb; for the great day of their wrath has come; and who is able to stand?" Revelation 6:12-17

When do the resurrection and the rapture occur? Before seal six is broken, for at its breaking all the unregenerate people, who remain on the Earth, know this day for what it is and call it by its proper name, the day of wrath. They have witnessed resurrection of the dead and the catching up of the living, and they know what is in store for them. These were not justified by Christ's blood, and now they are the objects of the wrath of God.

This destructive sequence is ample proof that the book of Revelation does not record the events in chronological order. If anything, it must consist of sequential flashbacks, for after all the mountains are destroyed, it will be impossible to find them to identify any of them. Yet a mountain is named in a later passage. "And I looked, and behold, the lamb was standing on mount Zion, and with him 144,000." Revelation 14:1. If all the mountains are destroyed at seal six, mount Zion must also be destroyed at that time. So the lamb and the 144,000 would have to have been upon it sometime before it was destroyed. John is bringing one storyline to the end, and then another, and then another, until he gloriously ends it.

We also read that when the seventh bowl of wrath is poured out, "every island fled away, and the mountains were not found." Revelation 16:20. You must either have a re-creation of the Earth or an agreement that seal six and the seventh bowl refer to one and the same event; the worldwide outpouring of God's wrath. God's wrath is so forceful that no person, place, or thing is left standing. This Earth, the solar system, and the entire universe will be annihilated. But they're going to be replaced by an entirely new heaven and Earth.

Seal seven. "And when he broke the seventh seal, there was silence in heaven for about half an hour." Revelation 8:1.

Look again at the events of this last day; the day of wrath. The resurrection and the rapture will remove all of the believers from the Earth. The unbelieving wicked who are left behind will all be killed. Then the resurrection of the wicked will remove all the wicked from the planet. Then this heaven and earth will be destroyed never to be found again. The resurrection of the wicked brings all these unbelievers into God's presence. They came in the resurrection to the judgment. John 5:29.

You see, in the beginning God wrote a book before he created anything. This book contains the names of every person who would ever be born on this planet. You have until you die to say Lord forgive me, or when you die your name disappears from this book. When its seventh seal is opened, heavens roll call is read; and the names of everyone who came to heaven in the resurrection and the rapture are announced.

"And I saw a great white throne and him who sat upon it, from whose presence Earth and heaven fled away, and no place was found for them. And I saw the dead, the great and the small, standing before the throne, and books were opened; and another book was opened, which is the book of life; and the dead were judged from the things which were written in the books, according to their deeds. And the sea gave up the dead which were in it, and death and Hades gave up the dead which were in them; and they were judged, every one of them according to their deeds. And death and Hades were thrown into the Lake of fire. And if anyone's name was not found written in the book of life, he was thrown into the Lake of fire." Revelation 20:11-15.

The resurrection to the judgment, means that it is not a trial. There will not be any witnesses on your behalf if you stand before the throne. The book in heaven's library with your name on it will be opened, and you will be judged according to your own words and your own deeds. Your own words and your own deeds will condemn you to hell. All God does is pass the judgment, "Depart from me you worker of iniquity, into that Lake of fire. Go!" Know that if you are angry with God today, God will be angry with you on judgment day. His word is, yours are not, so you can't win. You will burn for eternity.

Now that John has taken the seal trumpets from their beginning to their end, he announces the trumpet judgments.

Seven trumpets

Trumpet one. "And the first sounded and there came hail and fire, mixed with blood, and they were thrown to the earth; and a third of the Earth was burned up, and a third of the trees were burned up, and all the green grass was burned up." Revelation 8:7.

What an awful sight this is to the casual reader. Storm and fire are going to burn one third of the Earth. History does not record such a catastrophe; so this event must still remain in the future. Will there come a time when one third of the trees and all the green grass will be burned up? Trees and grass to not possess blood. Blood is possessed by that which moves and breathes. Was it because of the plants that the flood came? Most definitely not! The waters of the flood rose because the sins of man kept increasing. Sin was the reason God decided to kill every living breathing creature except for Noah, his family, and those who were on the ark. Then God made a promise.

"And the Lord smelled the soothing aroma; and the Lord said to himself, I will never again curse the ground on account of man, for the intent of man's heart is evil from his youth; and I will never again destroy every living thing, as I have done. While the Earth remains, seed time and harvest, and cold and heat, and summer and winter, and day and night shall not cease." Genesis 8:21, 22.

This seems to be a contradiction. At the first trumpet God destroyed the vegetation of the Earth and not its people. Did God lie? If this passage is interpreted literally, apparently he did. But if one takes this passage in a figurative sense, one must seek the meaning and not demean him.

Jeremiah used the tree in a symbolic sense when he wrote that the Lord called the houses of Israel and Judah, "A green olive tree."

165

Jeremiah 11:16,17. So here is an example of the tree being used to represent a nation. Using the national sense for tree gives the words of Jesus a clear meaning. "Behold the fig tree and all the trees; as soon as they put forth leaves, you see it and know for yourselves that summer is now near." Luke 21:29, 30. When you see Israel and all the nations blossom you know the end is near.

God promised not to hurt the natural tree anymore (until the Earth is destroyed) because of the deeds of men. So the natural tree cannot be what is affected by the sound of the first trumpet. But since the tree stood for a nation, we are looking at one third of the nations being destroyed. So what does the grass refer to? "You allow also that your descendants will be many, and your offspring as the grass of the earth." Job 5:25. The grass represents offspring. It also represents flesh. Isaiah 40:6

So trees represent nations and grass represents national offspring. When this group of one third of the nations was destroyed, their ethnic base as also destroyed so that their nation could never be reformed.

What happened to the world after the lamb was slain? Where is Caesar? Has Rome survived? Does anything of the Roman Empire remain? No it perished in 428 A.D. One could almost say it covered one third of the known Earth. Romes fall could be the fulfillment of biblical prophecy.

Trumpet two. "And the second angel sounded, and something like a great mountain burning with fire was thrown into the sea; and a third of the sea became blood; and the third of the creatures, which were in the sea and had life, died; and a third of the ships were destroyed." Revelation 8:8,9.

The use of the word "like" in this passage indicates an imitation. Something resembling a great mountain is being described by John. Daniel spoke of the stone that became a great mountain. The stone is the returning Jesus, and the great mountain is the kingdom he establishes. Daniel 2:35. So "like a great mountain" is the devil's imitation kingdom. The devil was allowed to have this imitation kingdom in heaven, until Jesus rose victorious from the grave. Then his kingdom was banished from heaven. The false kingdom fell in flames down to the nations of the earth. The sea it fell into is identified as all of mankind. Revelation 17:15. Mankind was struck by the burning anger of those who had been ejected from heaven.

While Satan had his imitation kingdom in heaven, he was using an earthly kingdom from Nebuchadnezzar to the Roman Empire, to establish his own plans and to thwart God's plan for the Earth. He occupied his earthly kingdom when he was driven from heaven.

Trumpet three. "And the third angel sounded, and a great star fell from heaven, burning like a torch, and it fell on the third of the rivers and on the springs of waters; and the name of the star is called wormwood; and a third of the waters became wormwood; and many men died from the waters, because they were made bitter." Revelation 8:10, 11

John heard a star represented an Angel. Revelation 1:20. A great star represents the devil himself. He was kicked out of heaven only to spread the bitterness of his removal among the men of earth.

Jesus said, "I was watching Satan fall from heaven like lightning." Luke 10:18 Satan learned that his power was only what God permitted, and he had no power or authority of his own. "And there was war in heaven, Michael and his Angels waging war with the Dragon. And the Dragon and his Angels waged war, and they were not strong enough and there was no longer a place found for them in heaven." Revelation 12:7-9.

Trumpet four. "And the fourth angel sounded, and the third of the sun and a third of the moon and a third of the stars were smitten, so that a third of them might be darkened and the day might not shine for a third of it, and the night in the same way. Revelation 8:12

This does not mean that the rotation of the Earth was speeded up so that the time of day was reduced by one third. Instead, the power of light used to penetrate the atmosphere was limited. Somehow, the air is made dirty; it is full of dirt particles and pollution. This reduces the power of light to penetrate and illuminate the Earth.

During the day, the eye can now see only two thirds as far as John remembered that he could see. The objects in the distance which he knew to be there, he could not see. At night, the moonlight was also weaker, and fewer stars could be observed. The power of light was being hindered. The current level of Earth's atmospheric pollution already meets or exceeds this observation. As a navigator in the United States Air Force, flying in a C-130E over the Belgian Congo, I could see Lake Victoria crystally clear, from 150 miles away. As we were returning to the southeast coast of the United States, on a clear day, the pollution was so bad the coast could not be seen until we were within 16 miles of it; all because of smog, smoke, and dust pollution.

Trumpet five. "And I looked, and I heard an eagle flying in mid-heaven, saying with a loud voice, woe, woe, woe, to those who dwell on the earth, because of the remaining blasts of the trumpet of the three angels who are about to sound! And the fifth trumpet sounded . . . And out of the smoke came forth locusts upon the Earth." Revelation 8:13-9:1. The locusts are coming! The locusts are coming! The locusts are here! Woe is me, woe are you, for our eyes have beheld them! I have already revealed the Locusts to be man's modern means of land transportation: the car, truck, bus, train, and airplane. If you accepted that teaching, you must acknowledge that five trumpets have already blown!

We can no longer say that we are waiting for the events of Revelation to occur. The locusts are already upon us. We are right in the middle of all that Revelation is saying. We are surrounded by the unfolding prophecies, but we do not see or hear them.

Trumpet six. "The first woe is past, behold, two woes are still coming after these things. And the sixth Angel sounded, and I heard a voice from the four horns of the golden altar which is before God, one saying to the sixth Angel who had the trumpet, 'release the four angels who are bound at the great River Euphrates.' And the four Angels were released, so that they might kill a third of mankind." Revelation 9:12-15.

168

The sound of this trumpet is the clarion call that gathers the Army of 200 million men for the battle of Armageddon. One third of mankind, means about 2 billion people are going to be killed. This will happen at the end of the period of the kingdom rule, that John called 1000 years. This is what happens after the stone becomes a great mountain, and just before it expands until it fills the whole Earth. The war does not kill everyone.

"And the rest of mankind, who were not killed by these Plagues, did not repent of the works of their hands, so as not to worship demons, and the idols of gold and of silver and of brass and of stone and of wood, which can neither see nor hear nor walk; and they did not repent of their murders nor their sorceries nor of their immorality nor of their thefts." Revelation 9:20,21.

The war did not kill everyone. Two thirds of mankind was left. But they did not deviate from charging after the cares of their lives. Even with the Lord God of creation, present in the land of Israel, they still do not repent and become saved. The lamentation that they could have repented shows the spirit of God is still operating for salvation at this time. They do not realize the small amount of time they have left to repent. "But in the days of the voice of the seventh Angel, when he is about to sound, then the mystery of God is finished, as he preached to his servants the prophets." Revelation 10:7.

Trumpet seven. "And the seventh Angel sounded; and there arose loud voices in heaven, saying, "The kingdom of the world has become the kingdom of our Lord, and of his Christ; and he will reign forever and ever." And the 24 elders, who sit on the thrones before God, fell on their faces and worshiped God, saying, "We give thee thanks, O Lord God, the Almighty, who art and who wast, because thou has taken thy great power and hast begun to reign. And the nations were enraged, and thy wrath came, and the time came for the dead to be judged, and the time to give their reward to thy bondservants the prophets and to the Saints and to those who fear thy name, the small and the great, and to destroy those who destroy the earth." Revelation 11:15-18.

The mystery of God is finished when you see God! You will see him after the seventh trumpet sounds. The seventh trumpet sounds at the beginning of the last day. The resurrection and rapture remove God's chosen from the Earth and the day of wrath kills all those who are left behind. And the resurrection of the wicked brings them to the judgment.

Seven bowls of wrath

Bowl one. "And I heard a loud voice from the Temple, saying to the seven angels, 'go and pour out the seven bowls of. the wrath of God into the Earth.' And the first angel went and poured out his bowl into the Earth; and it became a loathsome and malignant sore upon the men who had the Mark of the beast and who worshiped his image." Revelation 16:1,2.

This is the second passage to refer to the Mark of the beast. The first one said, "And he provides that no one should be able to buy or sell, except the one who has the Mark, either the name of the beast or the number of his name. here is wisdom. Let him who has understanding calculate the number of the beast, for the number is that of a man; and his number is 666." Revelation 13:16-18. Here three groups are identified by those who have the following: one. The Mark; two. The name of the beast; or three. The number of his name. So the two who were punished by God's wrath were those who have the Mark or the name of the beast. The third group was not punished even though it was within the devil's economic system.

The economic system prevents you from being able to buy or sell unless you have the number. The devil chose a number for himself: 666. Then he required everyone in his economic system to have a number of their own, without which they could not buy or sell. Without the number assigned to your name you cannot get a job, so you won't earn any money to be able to buy or sell.

Bowl two. "And the second Angel poured out his bowl into the sea, and it became blood like that of a dead man; and every living thing in the sea died." Revelation 16:3. A sea stands for a nation.

This nation ceased to exist. I say this nation was Israel in 70 A.D. because of the next bowl.

Bowl three. "And the third angel poured out his bowl into the rivers and the springs of waters; and they became blood. And I heard the Angel of the waters saying 'righteous art thou, who art and who wast, O holy one, because thou didst judge these things; for they poured out the blood of saints and prophets, and thou hast given them blood to drink, they deserve it.' And I heard the altar saying, 'yes, O Lord God, the Almighty, true and righteous are thy judgments.' "Revelation 16:4-7. What nation poured out the blood of the Saints and the prophets?

Israel did! So not only was Israel destroyed as a nation, but the Jewish practice, 'see you next year in Jerusalem' was put to a stop. There was no Israel. There was no Jerusalem. There were no Jews in Israel. They have all been driven from the land. So the rivers that fed the sea were dried up. No Jews came to visit. The Temple was not there. The Lord was not there. No sacrifice could be offered there. Israel was no more.

Bowl four. "And the fourth angel poured out his bowl upon the Sun; and it was given to it to scorch men with fire. And men were scorched with fierce heat; and they blasphemed the name of God who has the power over these plagues; and they did not repent, so as to give him glory." Revelation 16:8,9. I say this is an atomic bomb going off. And the next bowl follows in a heartbeat. Day 1290 has arrived.

Bowl five. "And the fifth Angel poured out his bowl upon the throne of the beast, and his kingdom became darkened, and they gnawed their tongues because of pain, and they blasphemed the God of heaven because of their pains and their sores; and they did not repent of their deeds" Revelation 16:10,11. Atomic bombs put prodigious amounts of pollution into the air. When it settles out of the atmosphere it is radioactive. Even without a wound, this dust will cause pain to penetrate the body. Look up, curse God and die, along with two thirds of Israel.

Bowl six. "And the sixth Angel poured out his bowl upon the great River, the Euphrates; and its water was dried up, that the way might be prepared for the Kings from the East.

And I saw coming out of the mouth of the Dragon and out of the mouth of the beast and out of the mouth of the false prophet, three unclean spirits like frogs; for they are spirits of demons, performing signs, which go out to the Kings of the whole Earth, to gather them together for the war of the great day of God, the Almighty. ("Behold I am coming like a thief. Blessed is the one who stays awake and keeps his garments, lest he walk about naked and men see his shame.") And they gathered them together to the place which in Hebrew is called Har-Magedon. Revelation 16:12-16.

Jesus said, he will come as a thief. He will come unexpectedly back to Israel. When he returns to the top of the Mount of Olives, an earthquake is going to split it in half. The movement to the north of the earthquake fault, will push the entire anti-Lebanon mountain range to the north. I feel this motion will shut off the flow of the Euphrates River, preparing the stage for the battle of Armageddon.

Bowl seven. "And the seventh angel poured out his bowl upon the air; and a loud voice came out of the Temple from the throne, saying, "It is done." And there were flashes of lightning and sounds and peals of thunder; and there was a great earthquake, such as there had not been since man came to be upon the Earth, so great an earthquake was it, and so mighty. And the great city was split into three parts, and the cities of the nations fell. And Babylon the great was remembered before God, to give her the cup of the wine of his fierce wrath. And every island fled away, and the mountains were not found. And huge hailstones, about 100 pounds each, came down from heaven upon men; and men blasphemed God because of the plague of hail, because its plague was extremely severe. Revelation 16:17-21.

This outpouring of wrath is what the Lord's people are spared. How long will you live after a 100 pound hailstone hits you on the head? Do you think you will be the only one who gets hit?

No building can survive this kind of attack. Anyone in it is dead. Everyone is dead from one end of the Earth to the other. The earthquake completely destroys the planet. To help you see the parallel descriptions of the same event in a different series of judgments I have prepared a chart to teach you.

CHART 3

The Seven lists

SEALS	TRUMPETS	BOWLS
1. To conquer	war	malignant sore
2. To take peace	1/3 of nations die	Israel destroyed
3. famine	bitterness	Jews persecuted
4. pestilence	smoke/pollution	fierce heat
5. "how long?"	locusts	great pollution
6. day of wrath	armageddon	armageddon
7. judgment	resurrection/rapture	day of wrath

CHART 4

The sevens interwoven

Bowls 1, 2, 3	Israel destroyed
seals 1, 2	
trumpets 1, 2	
seals 3, 4	
trumpets 3, 4	roman empire falls
trumpet 5	locusts
seal 5	"how long?"
bowls, 4, 5	abomination of desolation
trumpet 6, bowl 6	armageddon
trumpet 7	resurrection/rapture

seal 6. bowl 7	day of wrath
	heaven and earth destroyed
seal 7	judgment

Look at the sequence. Study the relationships of the judgments. Know that if we are in the last days is it time to understand. These are the last days. So let me present my last argument for sequential coherency: the biblical timeline.

CHAPTER X

Days of Heaven

"My loving-kindness I will keep for him forever, and my covenant shall be confirmed to him. So I will establish his seed forever, and his throne as the days of heaven" Psalms 89:28, 29.

"If no one knows what will happen, who can tell him when it will happen?" Ecclesiastes 8:7 NASB

On July 20, 1969, two men: Neil Armstrong and Edwin Aldrin; set foot upon the moon. Many of us remember taking part in their epic journey through the miracle of radio and television. The extensive news coverage made many of us feel like we were there, and for a brief period of time, let us suppose that this is so. Imagine you are the man on the moon.

As a lunar inhabitant, you see a feather of light descend from the sky and take on a different shape. The fire is bright, and you do not take your eyes off it until it is swallowed by the dust and disappears. When the dust settles you see an odd shaped metallic egg nesting there. Out of the egg come two living, moving, talking beings. Their awkward movements are humorous, so you feel no fear and move closer. You stalk them from rock to rock until you are close enough to hear what they are saying. You realize that they are talking to another being beside themselves, so you do not reveal your presence. The plan for their departure the next day registers in your mind and you decide to leave for the moment, but with the intention of returning to watch them take off. Do you see them when you return one day later? Most assuredly not! They

175

have already gone. You wonder "How is it that they are already gone?" And you leave the spot bewildered and somewhat sad.

Your knowledge of the universe, it turns out was simply too small. You were not aware that one day upon the Earth was 24 hours long while one day on the moon was 28 Earth days long. You did not know that they were discussing Earth days, not moon days.

It has been exactly this way with man and God's calendar. Man's knowledge is extremely limited; he habitually seeks his own pleasure, and seldom contemplates that God has a calendar and that it does have a fixed relationship to the Earth's calendar. Space traveling men know that there is a relationship of time between worlds. The spiritually moving man realizes that God's time is related to the events which happened according to his clock. Just what does this relationship consist of? How can we discover it? The special time periods of Christ's second coming relate it to us.

Daniel overheard the conversation of two angelic travelers who are speaking of these events according to the calendar in use at the place they had just left. They were relating that calendar to certain specific things which have happened or which were going to happen, on the earth.

"Then I heard a holy one speaking, and another holy one said to that particular one who was speaking, "How long will the vision about the regular sacrifice apply, while the transgression causes horror, so as to allow both the holy place and the host to be trampled?" And he said to me, "for 2300 evenings and mornings; then the holy place will be properly restored." Daniel 8:13, 14.

This conversation begins a unique study of the time periods and the second coming message. Consider how God has worked previously. Whenever he sent word about an event which had a specific time period included within it, that time period was exact and in accordance with the Jewish calendar Some examples of this method follow. God told Abram his offspring would be enslaved and be slaves for 400 years in a land which was not theirs. Genesis 15:13.

God said to the Hebrew children, "according to the number of days which you spied out the land, 40 days, for every day you shall bear your guilt a year, even 40 years, and you shall know my opposition." Numbers 14:34

Isaiah told Hezekiah that God was going to heal him and add 15 years to his life. 2 Kings 20:5,6.

Jeremiah said that they would serve the king of Babylon for 70 years. Jeremiah 25:11.

Each of these prophecies received its own exact fulfillment according to the Jewish calendar. Yet from the point of the 2300 days, it is very difficult to find this clear relationship.

Why did God hide the time promises of the second coming story from his own people? 2500 years have elapsed since the time of Daniel. Still every generation of believers has awaited the Messiah's coming. This hope has been one of the reasons which helped them hold fast to their faith in his appearing. What would their faith have been like if they knew that he would not come for 2500 years? They would have been like servants who knew their master was not going to return for a very long time. They would eat, drink, and be merry, and they would lord it over the other servants. But when the master returns unexpectedly and sees what is taking place, he will cut those servants in pieces. Luke 12:35-48 Men did not know for 2500 years, perhaps because God felt that man did not need to know. It was not a necessary part of his religion. God does not seek to discourage his own. The faith of believers is to be an encouragement to themselves and to others around them. Positive aspects were given. Yet not every generation was required to understand them. Understanding is required for the generation that's going to see it happen. There is a widespread feeling that this generation is ushering in the period of the last days. If this is so, we are going to be held accountable for what we understand. If this is that generation, and if we search out the truth, we will recognize all of God's words as they approach and unfold to great expectations.

In times past, God spoke to man in terms of exact Earth time; reckoned to the Jews at a year to a day rate. Since God does not change, he must still be working in this manner. He still foretells events with an exact time period, but now he is using the heavenly calendar for it. This is where the two space travelers that Daniel overheard had come from. They were using the time system at their own launching pad. God's clock, God's calendar, the heavenly days. The Jewish rate was confirmed through the story of Daniel's period of 70 weeks.

A prior researcher, Sir Robert Anderson, in his book The Coming Prince, verified the events of the first 69 weeks historically. So Robert Anderson claims they were fulfilled to the exact Earth day.

His work provided the following outline: 69 weeks of seven days each equals 483 days. The day to year rate meant that this was 483 years of 360 days each for a total of 173,880 days.

The commandment to restore and rebuild Jerusalem was issued on the first of Nissan in the 20th year of Artaxerxes reign. Nehemiah 2:1. He began to rule in 465 BC, so 20 years later is 445 BC.

That year Nissan one occurred on March 14. This period of 69 weeks terminated when the king came riding on a colt the foal of a donkey. Zechariah 9:9. John 12:15. John baptized Jesus in the 15th year of the reign of Tiberius Caesar. Luke 3:1. His rule began in A.D. 14 and 15 years later is A.D. 29. Jesus ministered for three years which brings it to A.D. 32. This was the year Jesus visited Lazarus at Bethany, six days before the Passover. John 12:1. That year, Passover came on Nissan 14 which was April 10 on the calendar we use today. Palm Sunday was on April 6, when Christ was hailed as the Messiah.

Now here's the math. 445 BC plus A.D. 32 is 477 years minus one year for calendar crossover equals 476 years. 476 years times 365 days equals 173,740 days. To this we add the 24 days from March 14 to April 6. 173,740+24 equals 173,764. Add 119 days for the leap years. 173,764+119 equals 173,883. Subtract a day for each 128 year period. 173,883-3 equals 173,880 days. This is the total number that he started with so he concluded the 69 week period was fulfilled to the exact day! Therefore it should follow that the 70th week will be a period of time that is seven years long.

Since this principle of substituting a year for a day was so accurate, it should be applicable to the other prophetic times. Unfortunately, when it was used for the 2300 days nothing seemed to work out right. The principal was right, but the application was not. The critical scripture for the starting point had not yet been found. The sacrifice was taken away more than once, and it is due to be stopped again. Here are some interruptions to the sacrifice.

Shishak, the King of Egypt, took away the treasures of the house of the Lord. 1 Kings 14:25, 26. In the reign of Jehoash the people sacrificed on high places and let the Temple fall into a state of disrepair. 2 Kings 12:1-5. Nebuchadnezzar plundered the Temple of the Lord, carrying his booty and the vanquished Jews to Babylon. 2 Chronicles 36:6,7. Titus also interrupted it when he destroyed the Temple and scattered the Jews to the far ends of the earth. As one can see, there were many interruptions to the regular sacrifice, and none of these is the particular one which we are seeking.

The right passage only implies its importance. It occurred when the ark entered the Temple of King Solomon and God removed the sacrifice himself. "The priests could not stand to minister because of the cloud." 1 Kings 8:10, 11. God marks time by what he does. His calendar is his plan for mankind. In his plan, the glory cloud prevented the priests from ministering and performing the daily sacrifice.

The time this occurred historically is not recorded with accuracy. Yet it can be discovered through a roundabout approach. Reconsider the question which prompted the 2300 day answer.

Note the wording, "to allow both the holy place and the host to be trampled." This wording is very close to another time period. "How long will it be until the end of these wonders?"

And I heard the man dressed in linen, who was above the waters of the river, as he raised his right hand and his left toward heaven, and swore by him who lives forever that it would be for a time, times, and half-a-time; and as soon as they finish shattering the power of the holy people, all these events will be completed." Daniel 12:6,7.

God's chosen people the Jews, were trampled when their power was shattered. If they still had power, they would not have permitted themselves to be trampled. Since both periods concluding description is the same, it would seem to indicate that the period of time, times, and half-a-time, was part of the 2300 day period. "Time" is generally interpreted to mean one year, "times" is two years, and "half-a-time" is one half a year. This is a total period of 3 1/2 years of 360 days each for a total of 1260 days. Since both periods end by mentioning the restoration, the 1260 days must be the last part of the 2300 day period. Then the ark entered the Temple 1040 days before the 1260 days began. 1040 days ended when Israel was overrun and all power was removed from the holy people and they were trampled underfoot. This event also marked the beginning of the 1260 days of mistreatment. If this crossover occurred in A.D. 70 when Titus attacked, we should be able to apply the principle of substituting "day" for "year" to obtain acceptable results. First, let us go backwards to when the ark entered the Temple.

Again, here's the math. 1040x360 equals 374,400 days. 374,400 days divided by 365.25 equals 1025 Earth years. 1025 years before 70 A.D. is 956 BC if the historical record is good, we should be able to obtain a result close to this. Different dates are given by historians for the start of Solomon's rule. Marks and Margolis, in The History Of The Jewish People, starts it in 973 BC.

Mac Milian in Adam To Daniel, starts it in 963 BC. This averages to 968 BC. The Temple was completed in the 11th year of Solomon's reign. 1 Kings 6:38. Solomon finished his own house in the 13th year of his reign. 1 Kings 7:1. The ark was then brought up at the feast of the seventh month that year. 1 Kings 8:1,2. In the 13th year means 12 full years have passed. 968 BC-12 equals 956 BC. The principal works.

Unfortunately when we go the other direction it does not work as well. 1260x360 equals 453,600 divided by 365.25 equals 1242 years. A.D. 70+1242 equals 1312. This should have been when the principal would indicate that the trampling of the Jewish people was at an end. However, since the Jews were not in power, God could use a different rate for the 1260 days. If he doesn't it would seem impossible to place credence in our exchange of day for year. You remember the word "trampled" in the reference to the 2300 days. It is virtually the same terminology used by John. "And there was given me a measuring rod like a staff; and someone said, "rise and measure the Temple of God, and the altar, and those who worship in it. And leave off the court which is outside the Temple, and do not measure it, for it has been given to the nations; and they will tread under foot the holy city for 42 months." Revelation 11:1,2.

The phrase "tread underfoot" means the same as the word "trampled." This 42 month period, when converted to days, is 1260 days. 42x30 equals 1260. This is the same length as Daniel's time, when the power of the holy people was shattered. So the period John described has to be the same one Daniel saw, but from a slightly different viewpoint. Both Daniel and John obtained their visions from the same Angel. They are not individual events, but dual witness to the same incident. When did this period begin and when did it or will it end? How long were the Jews trodden underfoot? How long was their power shattered? When was their power and their position restored? Hear the words of Jesus.

"But when you see Jerusalem surrounded by armies, then recognize that her desolation is at hand. Then let those who are in Judea flee to the mountains, and let those who are in the midst of the city depart, and let not those who are in the country enter the city; because these are days of vengeance, in order that all things which are written may be fulfilled. Woe to those who are with child and to those who nurse babes in those days; for there will be great distress upon the land, and wrath to this people, and they will fall by the edge of the sword, and will be led captive into all the nations; and Jerusalem will be trampled underfoot by the Gentiles until the times of the Gentiles be fulfilled. Luke 21:20-24.

This prophecy by Jesus was first a warning to his generation that Jerusalem was shortly to be overrun and the Jewish people would be driven to foreign nations. Titus accomplished this in 70 A.D. The period called "the times of the Gentiles" would last until the holy people obtained Jerusalem once more. Their repossession of Jerusalem ended the time. That is why the principle of substituting day for year did not work for this time period. It was not the Jewish rate. It ran until Jerusalem was re-inhabited by its people. God provided the ending with his Six-Day War in 1967. The rate was concealed because it depended upon the ending. That is why Daniel was told, "Go Your Way, Daniel, for these words are concealed and sealed up until the end time." Daniel 12:9.

This concealment was effective because the rate could not be determined until Jerusalem was restored. The 1260 days then, ran from 70 A.D. until 1967. This is a total of 1897 years. This provided a rate to the Gentiles of the day for about 1 1/2 years. It was more gracious than the day-year rate to the Jew. Mankind could not know this difference until the times of the Gentiles had ended.

The Jews are not being trampled anymore. Their power has been returned. They live in Jerusalem again. So the 2300 days which included the 1260 days is over. We are in the end time! All of the remaining events are about to be completed. To acknowledge their imminence, let us look more closely at the interwoven relationships of the 1260 days.

After John was told the Gentiles would tread underfoot the holy city for 42 months, Gabriel said, "and I will grant authority to my two witnesses, and they will prophesy for 1260 days, clothed in sackcloth." Revelation 11:3. When the Gentiles were up, the Jews were down. Their power was shattered; they were trampled underfoot. The Jews prophesied clothed in sackcloth.

The similarity of the terminology suggests that the expressions: time, times, and half-a-time; 42 months; and 1260 days are all one and the same. In fact John uses all of these terms in the intermediate passages of Revelation; between the trumpet and the bowl judgments.

"And a great sign appeared in heaven: a woman clothed with the sun, and the moon under her feet, and on her head a crown of 12 stars; and she was with child, and she cried out, being in labor and in pain to give birth. And another sign appeared in heaven: and behold, a great red Dragon having seven heads and 10 horns, and on his heads were seven diadems. And his tail swept away a third of the stars of heaven, and threw them to the Earth. And the dragon stood before the woman who was about to give birth, so that when she gave birth he might devour her child. And she gave birth to a son, a male child, who is to rule all the nations with a rod of iron; and her child was caught up to God and to his throne. And the woman fled into the wilderness where she had a place prepared by God, so that there she might be nursed for 1260 days. Revelation 12:1-6.

This woman stood for the holy city of Jerusalem, and ruled the 12 tribes of Israel. When the Christ was about to be born, Satan had made preparations to kill him before he could set up his kingdom.

When the child, the Christ was born, Satan rejoiced that he was able to crucify him; only to know despondency when the body rose from the grave into the presence of God. Then Satan set about to destroy the people of the kingdom, lest it should be quickly set up and Satan's time be diminished. He sought an entire end to God's plan which he knew was to be completed shortly. Yet by his actions he fulfilled the scriptural events prophesied for the holy people.

Once more he removed the sacrifice. His servant Titus destroyed Jerusalem and the Temple and every glorious thing in the land. The population was decimated. One third died in the siege, one third was slain by the sword, and one third was scattered before the wind with the sword chasing them. Ezekiel 5:1-4. The remnant of them was spared and set apart to be tried by fire at a later time. Not all of Israel perished. The woman had a place prepared for her in the wilderness where she would be nourished until those who were bound up could return to the nation of Israel.

This began the 1260 days which would end when the Jews returned to repossess Jerusalem. They would return for the woman did give birth to the child.

Back in heaven however, the devil was not faring so well. All out war had been declared. God had had enough, so he ordered Michael the Archangel, and the holy angels, to drive Satan from heaven.

Satan discovered he was not as strong as God. Michael wounded him and he fell from heaven, smitten and bitter. "For this reason, rejoice, O heavens and you who dwell in them. Woe to the Earth and the sea, because the devil has come down to you, having great wrath, knowing that he has only a short time And when the dragon saw that he was thrown down to the Earth, he persecuted the woman who gave birth to the male child. And the two wings of the great eagle were given to the woman, in order that she might fly into the wilderness to her place, where she was nourished for a time and times and half a time, from the presence of the serpent." Revelation 12:12-14.

The Scriptures verify each other. The woman was nursed for 1260 days, and for time, times, and half a time; from the nearness of the serpent. Therefore these two periods 1260 days and the time, times, and half-a-time are, at least in the instance of Israel in the wilderness, one and the same. During this time, the great Dragon, the serpent of old the devil, the one called Satan sought to devour the male child, persecute the woman, and then made war with the rest of her offspring. "And the serpent poured water like a River out of his mouth after the woman, so that he might cause her to be swept away with a flood. And the Earth helped the woman, and the Earth opened its mouth and drank up the river which the Dragon poured out of his mouth. And the Dragon was enraged with the woman, and went off to make war with the rest of her offspring, who keep the commandments of God and hold to the testimony of Jesus. Revelation 12:15-17.

"And there was given to him a mouth speaking arrogant words and blasphemies; and authority to act for 42 months was given to him." Revelation 13:5. So the Dragon the devil sought to devour the male child, persecute the woman and her offspring, and to blaspheme God. He did all this during the period of 1260 days: time, times, and half-a-time; and the 42 months. All of these are one and the same. The expressions are different ways to say the same thing. What better way to conceal the truth, until a generation could see the events even as they were completed. The phrases, "shattering the power," "trod underfoot;' "clothed in sackcloth," "nursed in the wilderness," and "speaking arrogant words and blasphemies" describe the events of this time.

The 10 nations in the Scarlet beast resist the lamb when he comes. They join forces and unite in their purpose to prevent him from establishing his kingdom. Their opposition lasts for just one hour on the heavenly calendar. Revelation 17:12. One hour represents one 24th of the heavenly day or 1/24 of an earthly year which is half a month or 15 days. That is as long as the fighting to establish the kingdom lasts. 15 days is how long the beast and the 10 nations survive after the Lord returns. In these 15 days the kingdom expands from the Nile River to the Euphrates River. These 10 nations all become kingdom Israel. Daniel's stone cut out without hands, has finally dropped upon the toes of the image and crushed them. The glory of the 10 nations was blown away and lost as chaff before the wind. Daniel 2:35.

How long must we wait then, for the kingdom of God to come? The 2300 days, which included the 1260 days, is over Does this mean that God's calendar has run out of time? No there are still a few more events to be completed. "And from the time that the regular sacrifice is abolished, and the abomination of desolation is set up, there will be 1290 days. "How blessed is he who keeps waiting and attains to the 1335 days! But as for you, go your way to the end; then you will enter into rest and rise again for your allotted portion at the end of the age." Daniel 12:11-13.

The last chapter of the book of Daniel links the periods of 1260 days, 1290 days, and 1335 days. These are not three separate periods of time, but three marks on the same measure; that which measures right to the end of the age. The time measured from the point when the power of the holy people was shattered unto day 1260 when it was restored, promised the rest of the events would be completed quickly. This viewpoint concludes that day 1290 occurs just 30 days after day 1260. Day 1260 ended in June, 1967. 30 days later the Abomination of Desolation arrives. We are also told the Abomination of Desolation is set up in the middle of the 70th week. Daniel 9:27. Since the Abomination of Desolation occurs specifically on day 1290, day 1290 must occur in the middle of the 70th week. So the 70th week sits on day 1290 like goalpost! There are 3 1/2 days before day 1290 and 3 1/2 days after it. There are two references to this last half of the 70th week.

"And he will speak out against the most high and wear down the Saints of the highest one, and he will intend to make alterations in times and in law; and they will be given into his hand for a time, times, and half-a-time." Daniel 7:25

This time period Is the last literal one to occur, as it immediately precedes the 2300 day time which changed future references to the heavenly calendar. It cannot refer to the last 1260 days of the 2300 days, during which the power of the holy people was shattered. When they fled into the wilderness of the world the Earth helped them and swallowed up the curses the Dragon sent after them.

Even though the Dragon went off to make war with the rest of their offspring, they were not given into his hand; at least not like they will be during the last half of the 70th week. "And when they have finished their testimony, the beast that comes up out of the abyss will make war with them, and overcome them and kill them. And their dead bodies will lie in the street of the great city which mystically is called Sodom and Egypt, where also their Lord was crucified. And those from the peoples and tribes and tongues and nations will look at their dead bodies for 3 1/2 days, and will not permit their dead bodies to be laid in the tomb. And those who dwell on the Earth will rejoice over them and make merry, and they will send gifts to one another, because these two prophets tormented those who dwell on the Earth. And after the 3 1/2 days the breath of life from God came into them, and they stood on their feet; and great fear fell upon those who were beholding them. And they heard a loud voice from heaven saying to them, "Come up here." And they went up into heaven in the cloud, and their enemies beheld them. Revelation 11:7-12.

The one who signed the treaty with them at the beginning of the 70th week breaks the treaty in the middle of the week and kills them. He does not permit their dead bodies to be buried, so they continue to lie in the streets of Jerusalem "where the Lord was crucified" The dead bodies are not disturbed until the end of the week when they again receive life and respond to the command, "come up here" When these bodies rise the last troubling week for Israel is finished. Her everlasting glory arrives. The lamb, the Jesus Christ himself, is back upon the Earth to set up his kingdom meant to rule as long as David did. This supposition is made because, if I am reading the calendar correctly, there are only 40 1/2 days left day from day 12 93 1/2 to the last day, day 1335. Day 1335 is the day on which this earthly age ends. King David ruled for 40 1/2 years. 2 Samuel 5:5. Adding 1290+3.5+40.5 brings us to the end of day 1334 and the start of day 1335.

Some astute reader may object strongly to this, one can hear him bellowing, "Stop! What you mean by saying that there are only 40 1/2 days left? Isn't Christ supposed to rule for 1000 years?"

Actually he is supposed to rule for a lot longer than that. David said, "Thy kingdom is an everlasting kingdom." Psalms 145:13.

Then my reader may ask what is the purpose of the 1000 years? This is the period during which the devil is to be chained so that he cannot have any effect upon the events of this Earth. From the disclosing of the 2300 day period, we have seen that there are no more literal time periods in the second coming story. Therefore the thousand years mentioned in the book of Revelation is not literal either "But do not let this one fact escape your notice, beloved, that with the Lord one day is as 1000 years, and 1000 years as one day." 2 Peter 3:8. This is but a turn of King David's phrase, "for a day in thy courts is better than 1000 outside." Psalms 84:10. If this is the source for the thousand years, then it is only necessary for this period to be one day long.

The pure joy of being in the kingdom in the courts of the Lord, with the Lord present, makes this sufficient if it is simply one day long. The devil is imprisoned at the beginning of the thousand years when Jesus establishes His kingdom, and he is not released until it is time for the battle of Armageddon. When the devil is released he secures the release of his four Angels, who had been bound at the great River Euphrates. "And the four Angels, who had been prepared for the hour and day and month and year, were released, so that they might kill a third of mankind." Revelation 9:15. It was the preparation of the Angels which took 391 days +1 hour. When they were ready they were bound so that the fighting would not occur prematurely. When where they bound? Precisely when Satan was.

They were ready to fight when the kingdom was established on day 1293 1/2. Their preparation began 391 days earlier. 1293-391 equals 902. 902x1.5 equals 1353. 1353+70 equals 1423 as the year their preparation began.

Another unique time period is left for us to scrutinize. It is the reference to the locusts and how "they have tails like scorpions, and stings; and in their tails is their power to hurt men for five months." Revelation 9:10. Five months is 150 days. If you have accepted the concept of the locusts described earlier, you will agree that it is logical to assume they will endure until the last day; day 1335. 1335-150 equals 1185. From day 1185 there are 75 days to day 1260. From day 1260 there are 75 days until day 1335. Day 1260 was the year 1967. 75x1.5 equals 112. 1967-112 is the year 1855. This was the year the locust's power to hurt began. This was the year when the use of the steam locomotive was really promoted.

The 1335th day was the basis for the Jewish doctrine of the last day. This was where Martha got her answer from when she met

Jesus after Lazarus had died. As the last day, it is the day Jesus pinpointed as the day in which the resurrection will take place.

Now we can construct a basic chart relating all of these times into a coherent well related chart. Some caution should be used for the days of the future events, as we cannot know what part of the day, whether morning, noon, or night, when God will decree the event should be accomplished. This uncertainty could result in as much as a year and a half of Earth time.

We will not know the day or the hour until it occurs. Also with regards to the 70th week Matthew 24:22 is in operation. "And unless those days had been cut short there would no flesh have been saved." So I expect both the beginning and the end of the 70th week to be cut short.

The chart also includes Ezekiel's 430 day period computed at the Jewish rate. Ezekiel 4:1-17. This yields 430x360 divided by 365.25 equals 427 years. This was when no word would come from God to Israel, and no prayer would go from Israel to God. Malachi the last Old Testament prophet, died in 433 BC. 433-427 equals 6 BC. This was the year that John the Baptist was born.

Here is my presentation of the heavenly calendar. Since I'm presenting the timeline, I will also include my genealogical step charts which have crossover points that lead from chart to chart.

They are the alpha to the Omega biblical Earth time. From these genealogical step charts we can learn some very interesting facts not otherwise known. The first chart shows how the lives of two men span the period from creation to the flood. Adam lived for 930 years. Methuselah lived for 969 years. Since the flood occurred in 1656 their lives overlapped for 243 years. Enoch was translated just 57 years after Adam died. From the second chart when Noah died Abraham was 58 years old. Noah's son Shem, who was also lifted up by the ark, outlived Abraham by 35 years.

Do not demean the word of God by saying that Abraham was called out of a godless land to journey to the land God was going to show him. If anything, he was called to travel to a godless land. Surely there was a knowledge of God in the land of Ur, for years later, Abraham required a wife for Isaac to come from the relatives he had left.

Finally, the genealogy gives no year of birth for any son of Jacob. All that it gives us is the year of life when Jacob appeared before Pharaoh at 130 years of age. Jacob lived an additional 17 years in Egypt and died at the age of 147.

Galatians 3:17 states the law was given 430 years after the promise. Jews count the time as Abram +15 to Isaac, +60 to Jacob, +130 to Jacob meeting the Pharaoh, for 205 years of that time. The book of Jasher said Israel was in Egypt for 210 years, for a total time of 415 years. Joseph arrived 22 years before his father came. The 4 generations were Levi, Kohath, Amran, and Moses

ALPHA TO OMEGA TIME CHART REFERENCES

Adam to the ark. Genesis 5:1-32.

From ark to ark. Genesis 9:28, 29; Genesis 11:10-32; Genesis 15:13; Genesis 21:5; Genesis 25:7; Genesis 25:26; Genesis 35:28; Genesis 47:9, 28; first Kings 6:1; Exodus 12:40, 41.

The heavenly days. Nehemiah 2:1; first Kings 8:9-11; Ezekiel 4:1-6; Daniel 8:13, 14; Daniel 9:24-27; Daniel 12:7, 11, 12; Luke 1:5-20; John 12:1; revelation 9:5, 10, 15; revelation 11:2,3,9; revelation 12:6, 14; revelation 17:12.

CHART 5

PREDILUVIAN GENEOLOGICAL STEPCHART

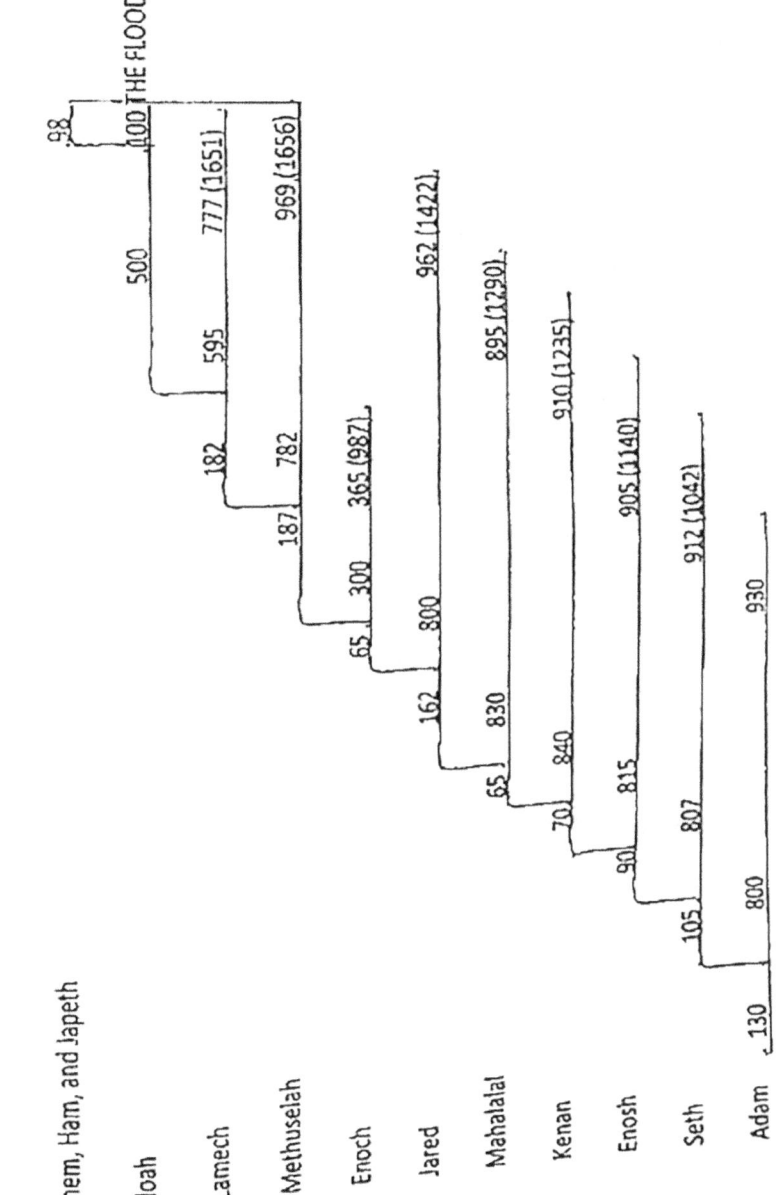

PREDILUVIAN GENEOLOGICAL STEPCHART

(From Adam to the ark)

CHART 6

ANTEDILUVIAN GENEOLOGICAL STEPCHART

scriptures

GENESIS 9:28,29; 11:10-32; 15:13; 15:18-21; GALATIONS 3:16,17
GENESIS 21:5; 25:7,26;35:28; 47:9,28; EXODUS 12:40;
1 KINGS 6:1,38; 7:1; 8:2,10,11; 2 CHRONICLES 3:2; 7:1,2

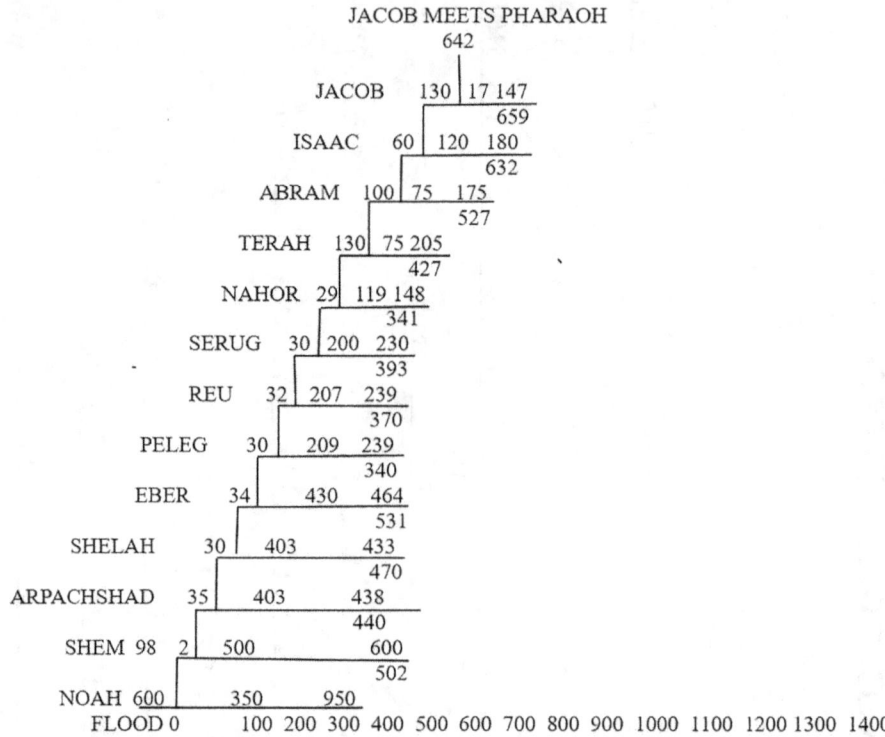

ABRAM was 85 at the promise. The law was given 430 years later. 437+430=867-642=225 years in Egypt. The Jewish timeline goes from the promise, +15 to Isaac, +60 to Jacob, +130 to meeting Pharaoh, for 205 years, leaving Israel in Egypt for 225 years. The book of Jasher has Israel in Egypt for 210 years. Joseph was in Egypt for 22 years before Jacob arrived.

1343 SOLOMON CROWNED.
867+480=1347 start of TEMPLE CONSTRUCTION.
1356 THE ARK ENTERS THE TEMPLE.

192

CHART 7

THE HEAVENLY CALENDAR

Descriptive event

Start of 2300 days+1040 days
   Glory cloud stops the daily sacrifice as the ARK
   enters the temple
	956 BC

Start of the 69 weeks Commandment to rebuild Jerusalem	445 BC
Malchi's death 430 year interbiblical silence	433 BC
John the Baptist born	6 BC
o Calendar	

End of the 69 weeks
   Christ enters Jerusalem as Messiah the Prince
   and is killed
	32 AD

Start of 1260 days, end of 1040 days
   Temple destroyed, sacrifice ended, Israel
   scattered
   Times of gentiles begins
	70 AD

Roman Empire falls	428
Four angel start to prepare	1423
Locusts power to hurt begins (1335-150=1185)	1855

End of 1260 and 2300 day periods
   Jews repossess Jerusalem
   Times of gentiles ends
	1967

Israel occupies Lebanon Syria and Iraq unite, war with Israel	
Start of the 70th week Israel and Assyria sign peace treat	

Day 1290. The middle of the 70th week
  Abomination of Desolation
  Assyria overruns Israel Egypt, and Sudan

End of 70th week
  Christ returns to Mt. of Olives, earthquake
  splits it.
  144000 prophets return as well. Jews called
  back home
  Kingdom rule begins.

Armageddon
  Dead are buried in earthquake valley

Day 1335, The Last Day
  Resurrection and Rapture
  Day of Wrath
  Wicked ressurected
  Heaven and earth destroyed

Judgment

New heaven and earth created. New Jerusalem comes

WITH GOD FOR ETERNITY, OR WITHOUT

CHART 8

TIMES OF BIRTH FOR JOHN AND JESUS

I Chronicles 24	NEW	FULL	7BC	6BC

1. JEHOIARIB ○NISAN   MONTH 9 ⁄ 4. JOHN BORN

2. JEDAIAH   ○ 14 PASSOVER

3. HARIM ○IYAR   17 FIRSTFRUIT

4. SEORIM   ○

5. MALCAIJAH○SIVAN   6 PENTECOST

6. MIJAMIN   ○

7. HAKKOZ ○TAMUZ

8. ABIJAH   ○ 1. ZECHARIAS SEES GABRIEL

9. JESHUA ○AV

10. SHECANIAH ○ 2.JOHN CONCEIVED

11. ELIASHIB ○ELUL

12. JAKIM   ○ MONTH 1

13. HUPPAH ○TISHREI 10 ATONEMENT 5. JESUS BORN

14. JESHEBEAB ○ MONTH 2

15. BILGAH ○CHESVAN

16. IMMER   ○ MONTH 3

17. HEZIR ○KISLEV

18. HAPPIZZEZ ○MONTH 4

19. PETHAHIAH ○TEVET

20. JEHEZKEL ○ MONTH 5

21. JACHIN ○SHVAT 3. MARY MEETS GABRIEL

22. GAMUL   ○ MONTH 6

23. DELAIAH ○ADAR

24. MAAZIAH ○ MONTH 7

1. JEHOIARIB ○ADAR 2

2. JEDAIAH   ○ MONTH 8

If Jesus died on a feast day of Israel, He was born on one because all the feasts are about Him!

1. Zecharias meets Gabriel.

2. John The Baptist conceived.

3. Elizabeth meets Mary in her sixth month

4. John The Baptist born in first month, Nisan

5. Jesus is born in the seventh month, possibly on the tenth day, the Day of Atonement, for He would atone for all sin, even yours, ask him.

14 Nisan, PASSOVER: Lord Crucified

17 Nisan, FIRSTFRUITS: Lord Resurrected

6 Sivan, PENTECOST: Baptized in Jordan

10 Tishrei, ATONEMENT: Jesus Born

CHART 9

RUNNING PROPHECY EVENT CHART

	Day	seal	trumpet	bowl
CRUCIFIXION/32 AD				
BURIAL				
RESURRECTION				
ASCENSION (LAMB FRESHLY SLAIN RECEIVES SEVEN SEALED BOOK)				
ISRAEL DESTROYED /70 AD	0			1, ,2, 3
		1	1	
		2	2	
		3	3	
ROME FALLS /428		4	4	
LOCUSTS /1855	1185		5	
HOW LONG?		5		
JERUSALEM RESTORED /1967	1260			
EZEKIEL'S ISRAEL TREATY				
ABOMINATION OF				
DESOLATION /1290	1290			4, 5
JESUS RETURNS	1293.5			
ARMAGEDDON	1301		6	6
RESURRECTION/RAPTURE	1335		7	
DAY OF WRATH		6		7
WICKED RESURRECTION				
HEAVEN AND EARTH DESTROYED				
JUDGMENT		7		
NEW HEAVEN AND EARTH				
WITH GOD FOR ETERNITY OR WITHOUT				

CHAPTER XI

Over the flood and out of the fire

"But because of your stubbornness and unrepentant heart you are storing up wrath for yourself in the day of wrath and revelation of the righteous judgment of God." Romans 2:5.

If you were living the life you live now in the days of Noah, would it have placed you on the Ark or in the water of God's wrath? Likewise, if you lived in Sodom and Gomorrah, would these cities have been spared because of your righteous testimony? Is your life a witness to your neighbors, that they too, might not be involved in the final fire?

In the Garden of Eden, God planted two trees: the tree of life and the tree of death. (That is, the tree of knowledge of good and evil.) It was clearly communicated of this latter tree, "in the day that you eat from it you shall surely die." Genesis 2:17.

God named these two trees, but he gave Adam the task to name everything else. Life was an option for Adam. Had he ever eaten from the tree of life he would never have eaten from the other. So Satan sought to destroy Adam before he could choose life.

Adams temptation came through Eve. Because he loved her, he took and ate of the fruit which she offered to him. If he refused to eat that fruit which Eve had already eaten; if he had thought about Eve's situation; would have thought the fruit of the tree of life could erase the damage done by eating the fruit of this other tree? I don't believe it could, but it would have permitted the one who knew the difference between good and evil to live forever. The possibility that a sinner might now reach out, take and eat the fruit of the tree of life, and live to sin forever with no fit judgment;

caused God to place Adam and Eve out of the garden of Eden. God then transplanted the tree of life into heaven and destroyed Eden. Then God placed a curse upon the ground and caused man to labor over it by the sweat of his brow.

As time progressed, Adam and Eve began to have children. They taught their children everything which took place in the Garden of Eden. They must have done so, for when Cain matured he became a farmer. I feel Cain wanted to show God that he could and would obey him. Cain thought his obedience and work would prove to God that he was worthy to have the curse lifted. So he gathered seed, tilled the ground to plant it, plucked weeds and thorns away, watched the grain ripened, and then brought a portion of it as an offering to the Lord. Cain felt good as he anticipated final approval of all his labor. But he did not check to see if God would approve of his goals or work, nor would he know the outcome until he presented the results of his labor to the Lord.

Since God's approval was necessary for his efforts to have any lasting effects, Cain should have sought God's approval before he ever started. God's approval of the project would also require God's participation in it. Day by day, Cain would have rejoiced over the sun and dew which caused his food to grow. When it was harvested and a portion was offered to the Lord, Cain's offering would have been accepted just like Abel's was; for Abel was returning unto the Lord a portion of what was the Lord's already. When they both brought their offerings, Abel's offering was accepted while Cain's offering was put on hold. Both were involved in the good work of providing food for survival. When each man brought his offering, it was important to see both men were accepted into the presence of the Lord.

The essence of any offering must be an acknowledgment that it is but a partial return of that which is already God's. Cain's offering failed to do this. Cain became extremely depressed.

Since the offering had been rejected, he couldn't even explain his reasons for becoming a farmer. All his hopes and plans were suddenly worthless. He was so upset that he could not speak or even be sociable. His secret project would never be described. He had not sought anyone's advice or counsel, so he was not obliged to offer an explanation. This was his own project, but it had an outcome he did not expect. Since he was human, he could not make his disappointment go away. Then he found out that God can reject or delay accepting an offering, for God looks on the heart and understands its motive. It was because of this issue with Cain that Jesus said, "If therefore you are presenting your offering at the altar, and there remember that your brother has something against you, leave your offering there before the altar, and go your way; first be reconciled to your brother, and then come and present your offering." Matthew 5:23, 24. I feel Jesus gave this first instruction because of the first offering which was rejected.

The Lord knew what was wrong when he met with the brothers. He told Cain, "If you do well, will not your countenance be lifted up? And if you do not well sin is crouching at the door; and its desire is for you, but you must master it." Genesis 4:7. The Lord told Cain he needed to correct his family relationship. Cain understood what was required of him. When he did get together with Able to talk with him and show Able the work of his own field, he was still angry and his pride was in control. Cain's offering was not rejected because of what it was, but because of Cain's attitude.

Was the rift between Cain and Abel so great that Abel had never before seen Cain's work? Did it come about that after Cain spoke to the Lord he took his brother to his garden to show him all the work? Was Cain still thinking to impress Abel? Was that why Cain became so upset? Did Abel's lack of concern for his brother's work cause him to slight Cain's efforts to bring recognition for his harvest? Did Cain misinterpret Abel's seeming unconcern for his work as an open rejection of him? Was that why Cain became so angry that he struck and killed his brother?

Surely the Lord knew what was happening: and that is why he went to Cain to show him what the secrecy and lies had made of him. "Where is your brother?" The Lord asked Cain. And Cain replied, "Am I my brother's keeper?" Then why is his blood crying out to me from the ground? What have you done? When Cain admitted his actions he realized that in years to come, others would hear what Cain had done and they would seek to kill him! The Lord in his judgment of Cain, did not permit the object of this fear to become manifested in reality. His judgment is tempered with mercy. So he placed a mark upon Cain, to prevent anyone from killing him. Other men learned the lesson of Cain, "then men began to call upon the name of the Lord." Genesis 4:26

The waters of Noah

Noah and his family were the first people to survive a flood. His account is interesting reading. Genesis 6:1-8:22. To this day the story causes people to say that the earth was completely buried under 15 cubits of water (22 feet). Then they began reminisce and speculate over what happened to all that water. Some said God had the power to create and then remove all the water of the flood. God must have done so for Noah seems to say it. These words seem to glorify the Lord by implying a new act of creation. However they do not survive when closer attention is devoted to the details of the event.

This view implies that our forefathers were men of great intelligence, knowledge, and foresight. It argues that Noah knew all the geographical features of the Earth without ever having traveled around it. It belittles the fact that God commanded Noah to build the ark out of concern for Noah's safety and well-being during this great catastrophe. Noah could not steer the ark, for it had no rudder or sail. Noah could not make the ark go where he wanted it to go. The view also implies that Noah had enough foresight to fashion a depth gauge to measure how high the water was going to rise. Most striking of all, it required Noah to have known the location of Mount Everest, which is the highest real estate of the Earth. Noah was even able to recognize the top of this mountain when God caused the ark to float over it, allowing Noah to see under all that water just so he could measure water which covered it.

This really sounds foolish doesn't it? Is it any wonder that the world does not want these religious fables taught in their schools, when those who believe the Bible is the word of God, treat it so lightly?

This speculation creates a quandary about the flood because the details of Noah's testimony have not been understood, or related to, the creation account of Moses. Pay attention to the recorded details! Noah's own statement was that he did not see the mountain peaks until 73 days after the ark came to rest. So he could not have seen a mountaintop when they were under the water.

Atmospheric dew watered the Earth from creation on. Genesis 2:6. Noah had never seen a cloud before the days of the flood. So his words begin to make more sense when you look at them through his knowledge and viewpoint. When the door of the ark was closed and sealed shut by God, it was too late for Noah's neighbors to escape the effects of the new forms of water. In the sky, they saw the first aspect of God's new work: a form of water which was new to man, the cloud, was appearing and growing thick and dark. The cloud blotted out the sun, and increased the wonder and fear in the lives of the people. You could not discern whether it was near or far. And it was so high one would naturally think, "If it is way up there it can't be a threat to us. This cannot be what Noah was warning us about. From what we understand Noah to mean the water has to rise. That's already so high we have nothing to fear from it."

How pleased they must have felt reflecting upon the "fool" who was hiding in his ark. What an insignificant thing to worry about.

Clouds are a device which atmospherically cycles water from one location to another. They are created to grow to provide the second new form of water. They fill with moisture until they can't hold anymore and then they release the water that they have in them. Suddenly, someone walking along outdoors may have felt the drop of water and thought, "Rain, it's raining. There is water falling out of that thing in the sky! However it is still coming from the wrong direction. We still have nothing to fear. Hey! Look at what's happening to the ground. Notice how it feels like a soft cushion? What is this spot of water? Look at how it's pooling! Where did it come from? Is this how Noah meant that the water was going to rise? Maybe we better talk to him.

Noah! Noah! Didn't you tell us that the water was going to rise?"

"Yes!" Noah may have responded. I told you all that my God told me. He instructed me to build this ark, to enter it, bring in the animals, and the flood would come. I marvel at the fact he put the water over our heads and dropped it at our feet. I can surely see the water is beginning to rise. Truly the flood is upon us!

"Noah? Please open the door and let us in!" Their voices becoming more conciliatory.

"I'm afraid I can't. God closed the door and sealed it shut!" Noah said. "Then throw us a rope!", desperation evident in the voices. This is the point at which the simple view of the flood falters.

It must clearly and effectively answer the question, "Did Noah have a rope upon the ark?" By a "rope" should be meant anything that Noah could lower over the side of the ark to measure the depth of the water and would also enable Noah's neighbors to climb on board. If Noah had such a rope and did not use it, then by gross negligence he became mankind's first mass murderer. The Scriptures do not place this blame upon Noah, so he could not have had such a thing on board.

"Sorry," Noah calls to the anxiety laden people outside of the ark as the waters are rising. "God did not tell me to make one. I don't have one on board."

"God. God! You can't do this to us!" The crowds began to murmur looking heavenward and addressing a deity they have never come to know on a personal basis. They never learned about him and his commandments through their high priest or religious leaders.

If Noah did have a rope to throw over the side of the ark to measure the depth of the water with, he would have used it to save those whom he could have saved. He had no rope nor did he see any mountain peak until after the waters began to recede and the ark came to rest. What did he measure then, and how did he measure it? The rain that fell was not the primary source of the floods water.

This is not meant to belittle the capability of rain occurring for 40 consecutive days and nights, to cause a flood of waters to rise. The greatest amount of rain ever recorded was 8 inches during 15 min. of a tropical rainstorm. If this rate could be sustained for 40 days, it would result in a staggering 2560 feet of rainfall. This is a truly prodigious amount but there still would not be enough to completely inundate the Earth. Besides the rain was not the primary source of the floods water.

Humor me for a moment, I want you to teach me how the worldwide biblical flood occurred. All you have to do is give me simple answers to easy questions.

Q. Where did the water for the flood come from?

A. It rained.

When you say that it rained there is at least one being jumping up and down, clapping his hands, stamping his feet, yelling to the high or low what ever he yells at, saying I got another one who uses half the truth, just like I do. But then this raver comes back at you with a slap in the face, a stab in the back with a twist, saying, "Well you know it's the natural law of God, it's a scientific fact; the water which falls as rain here, had to rise from someplace else. Rain is a cycle. You cannot have a worldwide flood from rain alone; so if that's all the book can teach you it's filled with nothing but myths and fables. Why don't you throw it away and be done with it?" You gave the devil this opportunity because you did not believe what the book says.

So it has come to pass in this nation that the Bible no longer can be found in the majority of its classrooms. Even prayer to the God of this Bible has been banished. Why has this taken place?

Because only half the truth has been used!

You see Noah gave two sources for the water of the flood. He said, "The fountains of the great deep were opened, and the floodgates of the sky." Genesis 7:11. The floodgates of the sky produced the rain which was the secondary source of the water. The primary source came from the fountains of the deep. Consider for a moment what would be required to place a fountain of water right at your feet. You have to dig or drill a hole. That gets you down to the water, but you don't want to lower a bucket. So in this generation you install a pump in the well. The pump pressurizes the water and pushes it up and out of the well.

Q. What is there available at the ocean floor that can pressurize water worldwide?

A. I don't know. Let's approach this problem from the other side of the flood, looking again at some facets that help clarify this event.

Q. When this planet was first created, what kind of a surface did it have?

A. It was similar to the way it is now. There is another view of this planet you should be aware of. Let me quote two verses while leaving off the last word for you to say.

"In the beginning, God created the heavens and the earth. And the earth was without form and void. And darkness covered the face of the deep, and the spirit of the Lord moved upon the surface of the ____." Genesis 1:1,2. The word is water.

Q. If the surface of this planet was all water, where was the land?

A. Under the water? That's correct and that brings us to the essence of Genesis 1:9. Essentially God said, "Let the dry land appear." Now this is the question holding the key to our solution.

Pay attention to what this question asks. Direct your answer only to what the question asks.

Q. What had to happen to the land for the land to get to where it could dry out?

A. It had to rise above the water. So the planet we have now is a result of the land which is above the water having risen up out of the water. But is land elastic?

Q. When the land was made to expand in size, does it stretch like a balloon or does it crack?

A. It cracks. So if the land was entirely under the water before it started to move, all of the cracks which are the proof that the land moved, should still be under the water.

Now, here you are at the bottom of the ocean floor as the land starts to move. There is a crack forming at your feet and it is getting longer and wider and deeper. What happens to the water as the land begins to rise and the crack grows? As the crack widens the water goes down into the crack. So not only did the land rise, but the water also went down into the crack. In order to put things into perspective, let's get back to our problem of the fountains of the great deep.

Q. If God brought the land out of the water to make this planet livable, what is the only thing he needs to do to create a worldwide flood?

A. He'd make the land go back down under the water to where it was when he first created it.

Q. What happens to the water in the cracks as the land recedes?

A. As the crack closes it pushes the water up out of the crack.

Now you know how the fountains of the great deep work. But do you actually know whether or not these cracks really exist? Up until the 1850s no man knew about the cracks in the bottom of the ocean floor. When the transatlantic telephone cable was laid on the ocean floor, from Lisbon Portugal to New York City, and they crossed the great trench off the Azores; all of a sudden they were using one, two, three, four, five, six more miles of cable then the distance they just covered. Engineers were pulling their hair. All they knew for certain was the cable was going to the bottom of the ocean floor and it did not break because they still had continuity. The engineers just did not know what the ocean floor looked like. Neither did you unless you remembered reading in the 38th chapter of the book of Job, two of the interesting questions God asked Job. One was, "Have you walked in the recesses of the deep?" Job could have replied God you know I have never even been swimming, how could I possibly know what is down there? The second question was, "Where were you on the day that I created a channel for the flood?" Job had no answer.

So God, showing he was God revealed the existence of the cracks to mankind for thousands of years before any man ever found one. This is one aspect of the proof that God is God.

When the ark came to rest in the mountains of Ararat, it did not get there on its own. The ark had no motor, rudder, anchor, or sail. The only way the ark could get into the high ground was for the land to recede. As the land sank below the water, the onrushing water would carry the ark to the location where the higher land was descending, and this is where the ark would be when the land emerged once more.

Two other scientific facts about this planet were discovered within the last 150 years. The first is that the diameter of this planet is 26 miles greater at the equator than it is at the poles.

(C=pi x d) It only takes a total of 82 miles of crack width along the equator's 25,000 mile circumference, to account for this 26 mile difference in diameter. Contrary to popular belief, the swelling of the planetary beltline was not caused by centrifugal force generated by spin rate. The equator got fatter as the land rose up and out of the water.

Then scientists found that all the continents are surrounded by cracks and crevices under the water on the ocean floor. When these cracks were examined, the scientists swore that the land or rock on that side of the canyon is a perfect fingerprint match to the rock on the other side of the canyon. They concluded these rocks used to be touching each other. But they never asked the question, what would this planet look like if all those sides were touching once more? It would be as it was before God rearranged the land, when the world was created in the condition of a worldwide flood.

Q. Scientists are fairly certain the Ice Age ended 10,000 to 20,000 years ago. What caused the Ice Age to end?

A. I don't know. Of course you do! What did this planet look like before the land rose out of the water? Wasn't it a gigantic swimming pool with large ice cubes at each end? And then when the land rose out of the water, what happened to the temperature of the planet? It rose because the sun can get land hotter than it can get water. Land absorbs the sun's heat while water reflects it.

So not only did the land rise and the water go down, but the temperature also increased, reducing the size of the ice caps to what the new geography of the planet could sustain.

Scientist further contend dinosaurs lived 1 million years ago. If a dinosaur was alive 1 million years ago was it a land or water animal? It would have to be a water animal.

And where did it lay its eggs? It would have had to lay them under the water, on the ocean floor. What happened to those eggs when the nest they were in was lifted up out of the water as the land rose, allowing the sun to shine upon them? The eggs would have spoiled because their incubation temperature was not maintained, and not another single dinosaur could be born.

The living dinosaurs could have adapted to the land so they could have lived as long as it was possible for them to live, but when the last one died they were forever extinct. On the other hand, if they were created at the time of all the other animals; there were no dinosaurs on the ark. If they could not swim continuously for more than 150 days, they drowned.

In the Paluxy River southwest of Fort Worth Texas, dinosaur footprints have been found in the shale rock of the river's bed. We know that no dinosaur ever left a footprint on a rock.

When the dinosaur came there to drink, the River's bed was clay, silt, or loam. The question scientists have not asked or answered yet is what turned the soft material of the rivers bed into rock virtually overnight, preserving the footprints. There is no glazing of the rock so heat could not have been the preserving factor. The answer is found by applying two of the facts we have already mentioned. The equatorial diameter of the planet is 26 miles greater than the polar diameter. Somehow this planet has gotten fatter in its middle. All the land at the equator used to be 13 miles below its current position. The land at 30° north latitude was 6 1/2 miles lower than it is now. And surrounding the continents there are cracks in the ocean's floor. As the land sinks the cracks close.

In water every 34 feet of depth increases the atmospheric pressure by one g. So at 340 feet we have 10 atmospheres of pressure. At 3400 feet there is 100 atmospheres of pressure. At 34,000 feet there is 1000 times atmospheric pressure. (15 PSI x 1000= 15,000 pounds per square inch.) This much pressure turns mud into rock overnight, or at least during the 150 day period, that the rivers bed was going down under the water, and rising back above it again. The rivers bed was mud when it went down; but it was rock when it came back out from under the water. Scientists want to date this footprint in the rock to 113 million years ago. But since the flood only took place about 4440 some odd years ago, the rock is dated to the flood. Scientists missed it by 113,000,000 years.

If Noah did not have a depth gauge he could not measure the waters rise, so he must have measured the water which fell. If Noah had a water jar one cubit deep on the roof of the ark, which could be filled by the rain water; and he emptied it 15 times during the 40 days of rain, he could conclude that 15 cubits of water fell on or covered everything. This rainfall rate would average out to one quarter of an inch per hour. This rate is capable of being sustained for a long period of time by an extensive cloud cover. Every meteorologist now follows Noah's example and measures the amount of rain which falls. Clouds brought the rain. What happened to the clouds when the rain stopped? Did the clouds immediately disappear? If not, how long did they remain? Did the clouds surround the ark with fog so that Noah could not see anything?

This seems to be what Noah recorded. Noah said the ark came to rest upon (or among) the mountains of Ararat, after 150 days. On the mountains of Ararat is not necessarily on Mount Ararat.

The ark did not come to rest on the mountain peak or in any precarious position. Its cargo was too precious to chance a slip or tilt down the mountainside as the land rose. It came to rest on a flat surface below the mountain peaks. The wind was caused to blow as the water subsided, but it still took 73 more days to carry the rest of the clouds away so that the mountain peaks could be seen again.

What direction did this wind come from? Consider the geography of the Middle East. A North wind brings a chill and increases the drying out time. A West wind brings more moisture and clouds, adding to the problem. A South wind would be warmer but would keep the clouds and moisture pushed against the mountain range. An east wind deposits is moisture over Korea, Manchuria, and China. Then its temperature increases over the 5000 foot plains so that the wind arrives in the Middle East both hot and dry. The hot and dry East wind clears the clouds out of the mountain range.

40 days after the clouds have been blown away, Noah sent out a raven which did not return. Seven days past and he sent out a dove which returned. The next week he sent it out again and it returned with an olive leaf in its beak. Olive trees grow between sea level and 4000 feet of elevation, so this meant the Earth had started to reproduce again. The week after this he let the dove

out again and it did not return. Now it was 313 days after the rain had begun, and Noah removed the covering of the ark. Even with the arks covering removed, the only way onto or off the ark was through its door.

God washed the Earth clean by the flood waters. Then he promised that there would never again be a worldwide flood and everything of creation would continue as it was until the day reserved for its total obliteration. When he cleansed the earth without destroying it, He used the ark to carry eight people who pleased him over the destructive effects of the flood. How will he preserve his people when he finally destroys this Earth, the solar system, and everything that is in the heavens?

It wasn't the water that caused the flood. The land moved, it rose out of the first worldwide flood of creation to make this planet livable; then at the time of the flood it sank below the water and rose back out of the water again. If you were not on the ark and lifted above the waters of the flood, waters of the flood killed you.

It's time to stand up and be counted.

There are two records of the Bible for the census that King David accomplished. The first one in 2Samuel chapter 24 begins by saying the anger of the Lord against Israel incited David to number Israel. The second passage in 1 Chronicles chapter 21 said that Satan stood up against Israel and moved David to number Israel.

You should be able to conclude from this, that the devil knows when the Lord is angry. When he sees the Lord's anger he recognizes an opportunity to get involved and ensure that the Lord stays angry. The devil causes bad counsel to be given to the person who is responsible to do what the Lord said. Suddenly, King David was faced with a real problem. Anger was in front of him, and anger was behind him. So what does he do? How does he get the job done?

In Numbers chapters 21 and 26, you can read the accounts of the first two censuses which Moses conducted. When Moses was asked to conduct the first census, God gave Moses the names of

12 men who were the heads of the 12 tribes of Israel. At that time, Israel was in camp laid out by tribes and families. So the census was quickly finished. The first census counted 603,550 men, who are able to go to war. Everyone of these men, except Caleb and Joshua the son of Nun, died in the wilderness during the 40 years of wandering. The census taken just before Israel entered the land of Canaan counted 601,730 men able to go to war. By these two counts God showed that he was able to maintain the size of Israel, even when he punished them.

When David was king, the 12 tribes of Israel occupied the whole land. David did not ask God how he should do this census. David did not even have any priests in his court to advise him.

So David made a personal choice, and commanded Joab the commander of his Army, to conduct the census. This was the point at which the devil could twist the conduct of the census.

Joab despised the thought of doing a national census. But Joab could not change the mind of King David. So Joab reluctantly set out to do the census. But the commander of an Army is not interested in a total count of the people. He only wants to know how many men are fit to go to war. So Joab does a draft registration instead of the census. Joab does not count any Levite or Benjamite. No priest is even aware that a census is going on. So no one is able to insist it be done correctly. When Joab reported 1,570,000 men who could draw the sword, David's heart sank. David knew something had gone wrong. But David did not know what it was.

The census was legal, but God specified how it should be done, in Exodus 30:12-16. This is what God required. "When you take a census of the sons of Israel to number them, then each one of them shall give a ransom for himself to the Lord, when you number them, that there may be no plague among them when you number them. This is what everyone who is numbered shall give: half a shekel according to the shekel of the sanctuary (the shekel is 20 gerahs), half a shekel as a contribution to the Lord. Everyone who is numbered, from 20 years old and over, shall give the contribution the Lord. The rich shall not pay more, and the poor shall not pay less than a half shekel, when you give the contribution to the Lord to make atonement for yourselves. And you shall take the atonement money from the sons of Israel, and shall give it for the service of the tent of meeting, that it may be a memorial for the sons of Israel before the Lord, to make atonement for yourselves."

When you read the census, you see what went wrong. No one paid the atonement price for their soul. Since the atonement price was not paid, the law required the plague to come.

When the plague came, 70,000 men died. Those who died, died unredeemed. None of them had paid the price for the redemption of their soul. God's anger against Israel enabled the devil to collect 70,000 souls.

God's census

The day is fast approaching when God is going to conduct his own census. The atonement price of the census was a memorial to the Lord. Everyone was to pay this price, no one could pay more or less. This feature is a reflection of the way God will conduct the final count of his people. The account will include everyone who ever was, is, or will be.

How will you redeem your soul when God counts it? What is the price God is seeking? Consider your soul; does it own anything? No it does not. Then how shall you make payment?

You shall not. Your soul is God's property. When your sin separates you from God, only God can redeem you. His price is not the lowest, for he is the highest bidder. That's why the money from census was called the Lord's Memorial. The Lord's offering was most beloved, spotless, and perfect. God gave his son as a sacrifice for the sins of the world. You are the one who needs to decide if the sacrifice which could take away the sins of the world, is sufficient to take your sins away. You must either accept it for your life, or reject it.

When you accept the Lord's sacrifice for your sin, your soul's redemption price is considered paid. You are in the group whose names are recorded in the book God kept his hand until he gave it to his resurrected son.

Remember, the book of life was written and sealed, before God created anything. In the beginning it contained the name of everyone would ever be born on this planet. All mankind was created to have fellowship with God; this was our only purpose for existence. If all of mankind does not attain this goal, it will not diminish God's glory. When each unredeemed person dies, their name disappears from this book. Jesus said he would not lose anyone that God had given him, but raise them up on the last day. All of his people will rise at the same time.

All of them will be removed from the Earth before the final fire begins.

If you are one of those that the Lord is angry with, the devil has already stood up against you. The devil is trying to make sure you never get your life straightened out. He wants you to join him in his final misery. You are unhappy now. You will be extremely unhappy then.

When God removes all of his people from the Earth, what need does he have for those who are left behind? What happened to the tares after the wheat was brought into the barn?

They were burned and completely destroyed. The plague comes upon all who did not accept the redemption price. The day of wrath arrives with all its gore. When it arrives any chance for salvation has passed. There is no other hope, no other chance for those who did not rise, and they know it!

The secular humanists of the world would like to think they would rejoice for the opportunity to lead mankind without the influence of Christ or Christianity. They utterly fail when the opportunity arises. The thought of evolutionary beneficence will quickly become survivalist bestiality. Nothing else remains when the hope of God is removed. Greed for what the departed have left behind will prompt mass looting, killing, and ravaging of all that remains. The popular slogan will be, "They didn't take it when they left, so it's mine!"

Unfortunately, when your hands are full of booty you can no longer protect yourself. When the one speaking to you notices this he will pull his weapon and wound you or kill you. Then he will take all that you had taken for himself. And so on, and so on, and so on. No policeman will arrest you. The firemen will not put out any fires. No doctor will treat your wounds.

Factories will close for lack of people to operate them. No more crops will be harvested. All grocery stores will be looted. Those who are alive will be afraid to go to sleep.

Everyone will be doing his own thing. Chaos will reign. No strong man will deliver himself or his nation from the plague that has come upon them. People will fall smitten like flies.

When everyone is dead, God resurrects all the wicked dead to the judgment.

When there is no one left on the planet, these words of Jesus will have real meaning. "Heaven and earth will pass away, but my words shall not pass away. But of that day and hour no one knows, not even the Angels of heaven, nor the son, but the father alone." Matthew 24:35,36. No man knows the day or the hour because there is no man left on the planet to care.

Heaven goes silent and waits for God to say, "Put that place away now."

When this heaven and earth are gone the judgment sits. The seventh seal, the last seal on the book of life is opened. The roll call of the redeemed it is read. Everyone who came by way of the resurrection of the righteous and the rapture, hears their name read.

Then the other books in heaven's library are opened; and one by one every person hears from their own book their own words and deeds which condemn them. The judgment is not a trial.

No accuser will be permitted to stand point a finger and say, "this one did or said thus and so to me!" No other witness will be permitted to stand up and explain away the words and deeds of the one receiving his judgment. When all the wicked have had their turn to stand in front of the throne all God does is pass the judgment. "Depart from me you worker of iniquity into that Lake of fire, right over there, prepared for the devil and his Angels. Go!" Then all the wicked will enter into the final fire, where they shall remain throughout eternity.

Trust me, this is not the place you want to be for all eternity.

Once you die it is too late for you to change your mind. While you live, your name remains in the book of life. So stand up while you can and be cleansed of your spiritual leprosy.

The way for the leper to be cleansed is found in Leviticus 14:12-18. The leper who would be cleansed had to bring a sacrificial lamb and a log of oil to the high priest. The high priest was ministering as God. He took the sacrificial lamb in his arms and lifted it up, settled the weight, swung it to the right and back to center, and swung to the left and came back to center and lowered the lamb to the ground. Then he killed the lamb, took some of its blood, and applied it to the right ear lobe, the right thumb, and the big toe of the right foot. Then he presented the log of oil in the wave offering. Then he poured some of the oil into the palm of his left hand, and seven times he dipped his right finger into that oil, and threw it out into seven different directions. Then he put some of the oil on the blood of the right ear lobe, and on the blood of the right thumb, and on the blood of the right toe; then he put all the rest of the oil in his left hand onto the head of the leper.

A leper was forced to live outside the camp. He had no fellowship with anyone in the camp. When he came to the high priest with the lamb and the log of oil, the high priest put the lamb on the cross and killed it. (The wave motion was the sign of the cross.) Then ministering with the log of oil, he proclaimed the Lamb of God had been slain for the sins of the world, and sent this message to the seven churches of the world.

The blood of the lamb was applied to the ear, the thumb, and the toe; because you sin because of what you hear, what you do, and where you go. When you hear the word in your ear, that the blood of the lamb was shed for your sin, and you believe it; the word of the Lord, the anointing oil, is put on the blood on the ear, on the blood on the thumb, and on the blood of the big toe. Then all the rest of the oil in the priest's hand is put on the top of your head. This is so that you can be directed by your thoughts, guided by the word of the Lord, so that what you hear, what you do, and where you go, can be a blessing to you and everyone around you. Cleansed of your leprosy you are able to enter into the joy of the Lord.

Arise, stand up and sing your new song, "glory to the righteous one!" It is your ticket to get into the right line. The line that is left is heading into the Lake of fire.

The 1040 day period hidden in the 2300 days

When my studies showed me that both time periods of the 2300 days and the 1260 days, had the same ending description a conclusion was drawn that the 2300 day period began 1040 days before the 1260 day period. (2300-1260=1040)

The 1260 day period began with the destruction of Herod's Temple on the 9th of Av in 70AD. The 9th of Av occurred on 4 August, 70 AD. So this was the end of the 1040 days.

Since each year of the Jewish calendar stood for one day on the heavenly calendar; this gives a total period of 1040x360=374400 days. The 4th of August is the 216th day of the year.

Then to the calendar crossover is 69x365.2425=25210.7 days.

Then 955x365.2425=348806.6 days.

When the Ark of God was brought into the Temple King Solomon had just finished building; the Glory cloud filled the Temple and prevented the priests from ministering, and the 2300 day period did begin. This event took place during the 7th month feast. The seventh month is now called Tishrei, but then it was known as Ethanim. 1 Kings 8:2 The 7th month begins with the blowing of trumpets on the first day. The 10th day is the Day of Atonement. The 15th day begins the feast of booths which is an 8 day feast. The Ark was brought up during this feast period.

From John 7:14 we see Jesus coming to the temple in the middle of this feast, in His day. So if one says the Ark came to the Temple in the same way, at the middle of the feast, this would mean it happened on the 19th day of Tishrei 956 BC.

Tishrei 19 was on the 25th of June that year; the 177th day of the year with 188 days to go. So we now have a total number of days for the whole of the 1040 day period.

956 BC, 19 Tishrei to the end of the year:	188
955 to calendar crossover:	348806.6
Crossover to end of 69AD:	25201.7
70AD to 4 August:	216
Total number of days	374412

This is only 12 days difference between the two runs of numbers. The 1040 day period is acceptably accurate!

DANIEL'S TIMELINE
Updated with the God Factor (+7)

$$T+2T+1/2T=$$
$$360+720+180=$$
42 months x30=
1260 days

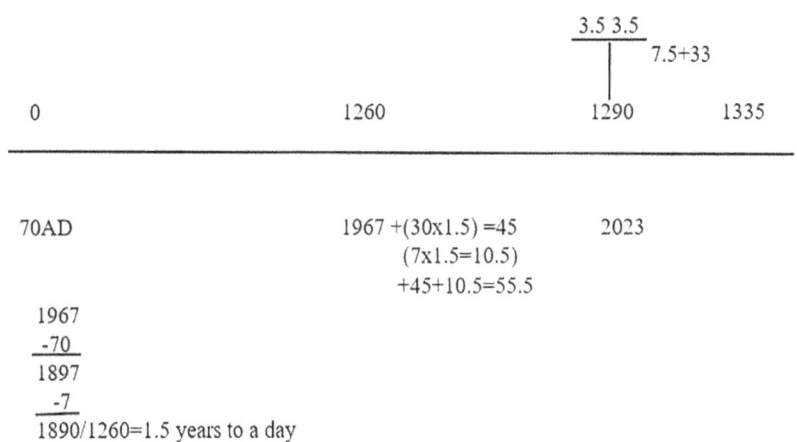

```
                                        3.5 3.5
                                         |   7.5+33
0                     1260              1290      1335
_____

70AD              1967 +(30x1.5) =45    2023
                     (7x1.5=10.5)
                   +45+10.5=55.5
   1967
   -70
   1897
    -7
1890/1260=1.5 years to a day
```

You can see we are past the time period for the seventieth week to have begun. Only God knows how much longer it will be. Just know that we are very close to the next event of Bible Prophecy being fulfilled. When it starts, it will happen quickly. Repent and change your ways while you still have time to do it. Prepare your heart for the Lord's coming to establish His Kingdom.